P9-DGT-549

Be A
Better
Reader

Level A / Seventh Edition

Contents

Copyright © 1997 by Globe Fearon Educational Publisher, a division of Simon & Schuster, One Lake Street, Upper Saddle River, New Jersey 07458. All rights reserved. No part of this book may be reproduced or transmitted in any form or by any means electrical or mechanical, including photocopying, recording, or by any information storage and retrieval system, without permission in writing from the publisher.

Permission is given for individual classroom teachers to reproduce pages AT1-AT14 for classroom use. Reproduction of these materials for an entire school system is strictly forbidden.

Printed in the United States of America

C12

5 6 7 8 9 10   99 00 01

ISBN 0-8359-1918-8

Globe Fearon Educational Publishers
A Division of Simon & Schuster
Upper Saddle River, New Jersey

Be A Better Reader

By Nila Banton Smith

NEW! *The Seventh Edition of Nila Banton Smith's Classic Program*

- Teaches the reading, comprehension, and study skills that students in grades 4-12 need

- Applies these skills to the content areas:
  - Literature
  - Social Studies
  - Science
  - Mathematics

- **Lessons always begin with instruction** so that students learn successfully (and independently) before they apply a skill.

- **Focuses on one important skill in each Lesson** so that students concentrate on a skill and master it—independently.

- **Reading, comprehension, and study skills include:**

  literal comprehension

  interpretive and inferential comprehension

  critical and creative reading

  main idea

  cause and effect

  fact and opinion

  sequencing

  details

  literary concepts (such as plot and theme)

  following directions

  graphic and pictorial aids

  locating information

  reading symbols

  previewing

  outlining

  classifying

  problem solving

  reading rate

  and much more

- **Student independence** Instruction is in the student's book, so that students work and learn *independently*.

- **Each unit follows the same structure** so that students know what to expect and can work independently:

  A Lesson with a literature selection

  A Lesson with a social studies selection

  A Lesson with a science selection

  A Lesson with a mathematics selection

  Several brief "worksheet" Lessons that reinforce important phonics (in levels A–C), comprehension, and study skills

- **Vocabulary Instruction** Students learn vocabulary words *before* they read. Students also learn to use different types of *context clues* to increase vocabulary power: definitions, synonyms, antonyms, appositives, details, comparisons and contrasts, examples, and similes.

- **Easy to manage in your classroom** Use with individual students, small groups, or the entire class. *Be A Better Reader* is used successfully with students working below level, on level, and above level. (Level A— grade 4 reading level, Level B—grade 5, and so on to Level F—grade 9.)

- **Lessons may be used in any order** Correlate Lessons to your curriculum. Use them for reinforcement of specific skills or as a complete program.

- **Each Lesson ends with a Real Life Connection** that applies what students have learned to their own lives, communities, or interests.

- **Each unit ends with a brief Lesson on a practical life or school-to-work skill,** such as how to fill out a job application and order form; how to read a bus schedule, floor plan, map, and help wanted ads; and how to follow directions.

- **Assessment tests are free** in the *Annotated Teacher's Edition* (Level A—F).

First, a sample
Be A Better Reader
Lesson with

Instruction first on one comprehension or study skill, then on vocabulary

A content area reading selection

Written comprehension activities

A written activity on the Lesson skill

(See Level A, Lesson 44)

Sample Lessons ||||➡

Lessons begin with instruction.

Lesson 44

1 Primary Source

Reading a Social Studies Selection

2 ▶ **Background Information**

The Nez Percé lived in the plateau country, an area that is now where the states of Washington, Oregon, and Idaho meet. The Nez Percé originally called themselves Nee Me Poo, which means "the Real People." French-Canadian fur trappers called them Nez Percé and the people adopted the name, pronouncing it *nez purse*.

The most famous chief of the Nez Percé was Chief Joseph, whose Indian name was Thunder Traveling to Loftier Mountain Heights. Joseph was 31 years old when he became chief after the death of his father.

In this lesson, you will read about Chief Joseph. You will also read the stirring speech that he delivered to President Hayes in Washington, D.C.

3 ▶ **Skill Focus**

Using a **primary source** will help you learn about past events. A primary source is a firsthand account. It is usually written by a person who took part in the event being described. Primary sources give facts about events. They also give insight into the thoughts and feelings of the

people in the events. Letters, speeches, and newspaper articles, are primary sources.

Often textbooks, magazines, encyclopedias, and so on, will contain excerpts, or pieces, of primary source materials. These excerpts are usually set apart in some way from the rest of the text.

When reading a primary source, use the following two steps.

1. **Find out all you can about the primary source.** Ask yourself the following questions.
   a. What type of document is it? Is it a letter, a report, an article, or a speech?
   b. Who wrote it? Was the author part of the event?
   c. When was it written?
2. **Study the primary source to learn about a past event.** Try to distinguish facts from opinions. A fact can be proven. An opinion is a judgment that reflects a person's feelings or beliefs.
   a. What facts can I learn from this document?
   b. What was the author's opinion about what was reported?

4 ▶ **Word Clues**

Read the sentences below. Look for context clues that explain the underlined word.

> As the early <u>settlers</u> moved west, they came into conflict with the Indians who lived there. The settlers had left their homes to find new land. They wanted land for farming and for raising cattle.

If you do not know the word *settlers* in the first sentence, read the next two sentences. They give details about the settlers. The details tell more about the word so that you understand it.

Use **detail** context clues to find the meaning of the three underlined words in the selection.

5

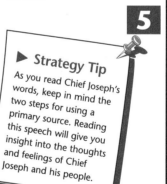

▶ **Strategy Tip**

As you read Chief Joseph's words, keep in mind the two steps for using a primary source. Reading this speech will give you insight into the thoughts and feelings of Chief Joseph and his people.

1

Lessons and skills are easy to find—Lessons are numbered and give the skill in the title.

2

Background Information—provides students with important content, cultural, and historical information and tells students what the selection is about.

3

Skill Focus—Instruction comes first—so that students are successful later.

4

Word Clues—Vocabulary instruction—before students read and need help.

5

Strategy Tip—gives students background and reminds them to use the Lesson skill.

A Great and Honorable Leader

The Gold Rush

The Nez Percé lived peacefully in their country for hundreds of years. They had experienced good relations with the white trappers and explorers. But in 1860, white prospectors illegally entered Nez Percé territory and found gold. During the gold rush, thousands of miners settled on Nez Percé reservation lands, disobeying an earlier treaty. For the first time, friction developed between whites and the Nez Percé.

In 1863, under pressure from the gold miners to remove the Nez Percé from valuable mineral sources, the U.S. government demanded that the Nez Percé cede, or give up, about 6 million acres of reservation land. The majority of Nez Percé refused. A government commissioner bribed several chiefs who sold the land and signed the treaty. The government official reported to the U.S. government that he had secured all lands demanded "at a cost not exceeding 8 cents per acre."

As a result of the land sale, the Nez Percé divided into "treaty" and "nontreaty" bands. Among those who were angry about the selling of Indian land was Tuekakas, also known as Old Joseph. By 1871, thousands of settlers had moved onto reservation land, as was allowed by the new treaty. Near his death, Old Joseph spoke to his son Young Joseph about their homeland:

> *My son, my body is returning to my mother earth, and my spirit is going very soon to see the Great Spirit Chief. When I am gone, think of your country. You are the chief of these people. They look to you to guide them. Always remember that your father never sold his country. You must stop your ears whenever you are asked to sign a treaty selling your home.*
>
> *. . . My son, never forget my dying words. This country holds your father's body. Never sell the bones of your father and your mother.*

6

Chief of Peace

Upon his father's death, Joseph became the civil, or peace, chief of his father's band. Joseph held many councils, or meetings, with civil and military officials. In 1873, Joseph convinced the government that it had not legally secured title to the reservation lands. The government ordered the whites to move out of the territory. However, the government then reversed its decision under pressure from Oregon politicians and settlers.

7

This map shows the retreat of the Nez Percé.

6

Primary Sources—In social studies selections, primary source materials aid comprehension, as well as provide valuable first-hand accounts of events and people.

7

Illustrations, photos, and captions increase interest and aid comprehension.

Understanding the dilemma of the U.S. government, Joseph continued to strive for a peaceful solution to the land problem. In 1877, General Oliver O. Howard concluded that the only solution was to force all the Nez Percé off their land and onto a reservation in Washington.

Many of the "nontreaty" Nez Percé wanted to fight for their land. Chief Joseph didn't want to fight. He knew that fighting would only bring death and sadness to his people. Joseph believed that he had no other choice but to lead his people to the reservation. So in the spring of 1877, Joseph agreed to the demands of the U.S. government. Several other nontreaty bands joined Joseph's for one last gathering on their land. While there, several men decided to seek revenge on white settlers for the death of one's father and for other grievances. They killed four white settlers.

8 Knowing that General Howard would send troops after them, the bands withdrew to Whitebird Canyon. Thus began a remarkable <u>retreat</u>, in which the Nez Percé fought, alluded, and outwitted one military force after another for four months. With about 750 people, including sick and elderly people, women, and children, the Nez Percé circled over a thousand miles trying to reach safety in Canada.

The soldiers who fought Chief Joseph thought that he was a great and honorable man. The soldiers knew that the Nez Percé never killed without reason. They could have burned and destroyed the property of many settlers, but they did not. Joseph and his people fought only to defend themselves and their land. The white soldiers were also impressed with their ability to allude the army for so many months and over so many miles.

"I Will Fight No More, Forever"

But the end finally came. Unaware that the army under Colonel Nelson A. Miles was in close <u>pursuit</u>, the Nez Percé camped less than 40 miles south of the Canadian border. At the end of a five-day siege, Chief Joseph decided to <u>surrender</u> to Miles on October 5, 1877. He rode into the army camp alone and handed his rifle to the soldiers. He said:

> I am tired of fighting. My people ask me for food and I have none to give. It is cold and we have no blankets, no wood. My people are starving. . . . Hear me, my chiefs. I have fought, but from where the sun now stands, Joseph will fight no more, forever.

After Joseph's surrender, the U.S. government ordered them onto a reservation in Kansas, then to a disease-ridden reservation in Oklahoma. Many of the Nez Percé died of malaria and other sicknesses.

Chief Joseph pleaded on behalf of his people to gain permission to return to a reservation in the Northwest. In 1879, Chief Joseph traveled to Washington to plead his case to President Hayes.

Chief Joseph's Speech

If the white man wants to live in peace with the Indian, he can live in peace. There need be no trouble. Treat all men alike. Give them the same laws. Give them all an even chance to live and grow.

All men are made by the same Great Spirit Chief. They are all brothers. The earth is the mother of all people, and all people should have equal rights upon it. You might as well expect all rivers to run backward as that any man born a free man should be contented penned up and denied liberty to go where he pleases. If you tie a horse to a stake, do you expect he will grow fat? If you pen an Indian

Chief Joseph of the Nez Percé Indians.

Lesson 44 *Using a primary source* **125**

wars. We shall all be alike—brothers of ... ther and mother, with one sky above us ... one country around us and one ... ment for all. Then the Great Spirit ... who rules above will smile upon this ... nd send rain to wash out the bloody ... made by brothers' hands upon the face ... earth. For this time, the Indian race are ... g and praying. I hope no more groans ... unded men and women will ever go to ... r of the Great Spirit Chief above, and ... ll people may be one people.

... 1885, after eight years of campaigning ... alf of his people, Joseph and the other ... Percé were allowed to return to the ... west. Unable to join the treaty bands on ... aho reservation, Joseph and the others ... scorted to the Colville Reservation in ... ington Territory. It was there that ... died in 1904, reportedly from a ... heart.

...ACTS

...ring and contrasting

9 ...y did the soldiers think that Chief ...eph was a great leader?
...ple never killed without a reason, did not burn

...oy the property of settlers, and fought only to

...themselves and their land.

...g details

10 ...er living on a reservation, where did ...ief Joseph say he wanted to take his ...ople? Why?
...oseph wanted to take his people to Canada,

...hey would not have to live on a reservation.

...ontext clues

11 ...ite the letter of the correct meaning in ...t of each word.

... retreat   a. following in order to capture

... pursuit   b. to give up

... surrender c. to go to a safe place

126 Lesson 44 *Using a primary source*

8

Word clues—Unfamiliar words are defined using context clues, such as synonyms, appositive phrases, comparisons, and details, to aid reading and comprehension.

9

After reading, students complete written activities.

10

Recalling Facts—checks students' literal comprehension of the selection. (In the *Annotated Teacher's Edition*, each question has a skill label and answer for the teacher's benefit.)

11

Vocabulary Skills—The last item in "Recalling Facts" is a vocabulary check.

12

INTERPRETING FACTS

Identifying point of view

1. For each pair of sentences, circle th
   Joseph's thoughts and opinions in
   (a) The white man can live in peace
       same law.
   b. Because so many promises have
      man and the Indian.
   a. There will be no more wars wh
   (b) There will be no more wars wh

Drawing conclusions

2. Decide whether Chief Joseph is a g
   must look carefully at Chief Josep
   are listed in order below. For each

   a. Chief Joseph first agrees to lead
      He knows that the small number of Nez Pe

   b. Chief Joseph decides to lead his
      He wants to escape the army's punishment
      put on reservations.

   c. Chief Joseph will fight the army
      He knows that the battle will end only in de

   d. Chief Joseph leads his people o
      He is trying to avoid battle and being captu

   e. During this time, Chief Joseph
      He knows that the skills of his warriors will

   f. Chief Joseph says that he will "
      reservation.
      The army has trapped them. His people hav
      They must either surrender or die.

   g. Two years later, Chief Joseph sp
      even though he led his people th
      He believes that taking away a people's fre
      live "penned up." Yet, he has given his wor

Now answer this question: Do you think that Chief Joseph was a great and honorable leader? In your answer, first tell what you mean by the words *great* and by *honorable*. Then tell why you think Chief Joseph was or was not a great and honorable leader.

Conclusions will vary, but all answers should include the following: (a) Student's definition of *great* and *honorable* and (b) student's conclusion about Chief Joseph should be consistent with their definitions of *great* and *honorable* and should cite facts in the selection and speech that led to the conclusion.

SKILL FOCUS

13

Reread Chief Joseph's speech. Pay special attention to what it tells you about Chief Joseph's feelings and motives. Then answer the questions below.

1. *Find out all you can about the primary source.*

   What type of document is this? _____ a speech _____

   Who wrote it? _____ Chief Joseph _____

   Was the author involved in the event? _____ yes _____

   When was it written? _____ 1879 _____

2. *Study the primary source to learn about a past event.*

   What facts can you learn from this document? Indian lands were being overrun by white men; many Indians were dying and being treated as outlaws.

   What was the author's opinion about what was reported? Chief Joseph believed that the Indians and white men could live in peace if all were subject to the same laws. He thought that his people would prosper if they could be moved back to the Pacific Northwest (Oregon).

▶ **Real Life Connections** Write an interesting fact or story about the history of your community. List your primary sources.

14

128 Lesson 44 *Using a primary source*

12

Interpreting Facts—checks students' comprehension on *inferential* and *critical* levels.

13

Skill Focus—checks students' understanding of the Lesson skill. In the "Skill Focus" at the beginning of the Lesson, students learned about the Lesson skill. Now students

complete a written activity that applies the skill to the reading selection.

14

Real Life Connections— asks students to apply what they have read or learned to their own lives, communities, or interests.

Brief end-of-unit Lessons follow.

Lesson 40

Main Idea and Suppo...

15

Many times in reading, you will l...
details. Details give more informati...
supporting details because they sup...

Below is a paragraph about how the brakes w...
the supporting details are listed.

Braking a car is an interesting process. I...
most cars, a liquid called brake fluid begi...
the steps that stop the moving automobil...
When the brakes are not being used, the flu...
rests in the master cylinder and the brak...

Main Idea   Braking a car is an interesti...
Supporting Details
a. In most cars, a liquid called brake flui...
   automobile.
b. When the brakes are not being used, t...
   tubes.
c. When the driver steps on the brake pe...
d. The brake shoe presses against the bra...
e. Each wheel has its own braking syster...

On the next page, write the main idea and th...

16

1. In the United States, almost everyone...
life is linked to the auto industry. Most peopl...
depend on a car, bus, or truck fo...
transportation. More than 12 million peopl...
earn their living in some part of the ca...
industry by building, shipping, servicing, c...
selling cars, buses, or trucks. These peopl...
account for about one tenth of the labor forc...
In fact, there are 500,000 automobile-relate...
businesses in the United States.
2. Several steps go into designing a ne...
car model. Automobile designers creat...
hundreds of sketches on computers. Final idea...
for the new model come from these sketche...
Then a full-sized clay model is made. Furthe...
improvements are made in the design. ...
fiberglass model is made. Finally, when ever...
part has been approved, blueprints of the ca...
are drawn so that the car can be cut out of ste...
and built.
3. Most of the early automobile builder...
were mechanics or knew about machine...

112 Lesson 40 *Identifying the main idea and supportir...*

Lesson 42

Comparing Car Ads

17

If you are interested in buying a new car, reading ads in newspapers and magazines should start you in the right direction. The details in ads can help you decide what kind of car will suit your needs and your budget. After you decide on the best car for your needs, you shop around for the best price.

Carefully read the following ads to compare the two cars.

PASHUBI: WE DESIGNED OUR CAR FOR ■ *YOU* ■ *THE* DRIVER

At Pashubi, we think you are very important. So we created the 630-X, a fully equipped luxury sports car. The 630-X surrounds the driver with more window than other sports cars. The 630-X has a steering wheel and instrument panel that can be moved up or down.

The roomy bucket seats can be easily moved and can tilt back as far as you like. And the large storage area in back lifts up to become two additional seats.

There are 30 standard equipment features, including power disc brakes, power windows, electrically heated outside rearview mirror, two-tone paint, and CD player.

At $20,025, the 630-X offers more than other imported cars. And you'll save on gas—an exceptional 43 EST HWY MPG, 28 EST MPG. Use MPG for comparison. Mileage may differ depending on conditions. Highway mileage may be less.

The 630-X. By Pashubi. It's *not* for everyone—but it is for *you*.

TILTON:
The American way to get more for your money.

You get more for your money with our cars. Take the Star, for example. This compact car uses 3,000 computer-assisted robot welds, more than any other car. This helps to create an easy-to-maintain car which will give you more for your money for years to come.

The Star gives you more for your money because it's sensibly priced. It starts as low as

$16,999*. The Star gives you more for your money with front-wheel drive. With the engine pulling in front and rack-and-pinion steering, you get the real feel of the road.

The six-passenger Star gives you more for your money with comfort.

And the Star gives you more for your money when you study the mileage figures:
41 EST HWY, 26 EST MPG.+

The Star's standard equipment includes power disc brakes, CD player, and 5-speed transmission (3-speed automatic is extra). Among the other extras are two-tone paint, luggage rack, leather steering wheel, power windows, and more.

Last year's Star was the best-selling compact car. See the Star today—and learn how to get more for your money the American way.

* $19,698 as shown in photograph

+ Use EST MPG for comparison. Mileage may vary depending on speed, trip length, and weather. Actual highway mileage lower.

116 Lesson 42 *Comparing car ads*

15
Each brief Lesson focuses on one important skill and begins with instruction.

16
Students benefit from skills practice and reinforcement without full-length reading selections. (In Levels A, B, and C, phonic skills are reviewed in the Lessons.)

17
The last Lesson in each unit is on a practical skill—such as reading a bus schedule, filling out a job application, or following directions.

(See Level A, Lessons 40 and 42)

Basic Reading Skills

Whether students are reading a story for pleasure, skimming newspapers or magazines for information, or studying a chapter in a textbook, they need the following basic reading skills.

Word Recognition: the ability to recognize words.

Comprehension: the ability to derive stated and implied meanings from printed symbols.

Reading Rate: the ability to adjust reading rate to content and purpose.

Study Skills: the ability to apply what is already understood in a new context.

Word Recognition

In *Be A Better Reader*, specific skills instruction in word recognition is designed to provide students with a variety of word attack strategies needed to read an unfamiliar word.

Phonetic Analysis: recognizing and identifying the sounds of consonants, consonant blends, and digraphs; recognizing and identifying vowel sounds and their variant spellings.

Structural Analysis: recognition of root words, prefixes and suffixes, compound words, multi-syllabic words, accent marks, and syllabication.

Context Clues: determining word meaning from a particular context clue.

Respellings, Footnotes, and Other Word Helps: using vocabulary aids typical of content-area textbooks.

Comprehension

Reading comprehension is a process that begins with word recognition, but does not end until students have derived meaning from the ideas both stated and implied in the text and have been able to evaluate these ideas. In *Be A Better Reader*, each lesson focuses on a specific reading skill that helps students recognize and understand a text pattern that is typical of a content area, as well as a variety of other reading materials that students encounter in their daily lives.

Literal Comprehension

Literal questions are included to help students process information that is stated explicitly in the text. These questions require students to recall from memory or to select from the text specific answers; in other words, to reproduce what has been stated in the text.

The literal comprehension activities and questions in the Understanding Facts and Skill Focus activities sections require students to do the following.

1. Identify stated main idea
2. Identify stated main idea and details
3. Recall details
4. Identify stated cause and effect
5. Recognize sequence of events
6. Recognize fact and opinion
7. Recognize elements of a short story (plot, character, setting, theme, etc.)
8. Recognize variety of literary types or genres (fiction, play, nonfiction, biography, primary sources, etc.)

Inferential and Critical Comprehension

Numerous activities and questions are included to encourage students to probe for deeper meanings that are implied but not explicitly stated in the text. These questions require students to think about the meanings that can be derived from their reading, not just reproduce what the text has stated. Inferential and critical comprehension begins with literal meanings, but advances to higher-level thinking and reasoning skills that require students to go beyond the printed symbol.

The inferential and critical comprehension questions in the Interpreting Facts and Skill Focus activities sections require students to do the following.

1. Infer unstated main idea
2. Infer cause and effect
3. Infer details
4. Infer conclusions
5. Infer comparisons and contrasts
6. Distinguish fact from opinion
7. Infer information about elements of a short story (plot, character, setting, theme, etc.)
8. Draw conclusions and make generalizations
9. Evaluate validity of ideas
10. Predict outcomes

Reading Rate

Studies indicate that students are ready for a variety of reading rates by the latter part of fifth grade or by sixth grade. Students who have acquired reading skills through reading fiction only need to learn that there are different rates at which they should read different content. Practice in adjusting reading rate is introduced in Level C of *Be A Better Reader*. Emphasis is placed on adjusting the rate of reading to the content and the purpose of the material.

Study Skills

An analysis of questions, exercises, explanations, visuals, and directions in the various content area textbooks reveals that certain basic study skills are called for again and again in all subject areas. Most of these skills involve using comprehension skills to study and understand information in the content area. As students work with materials in literature, social studies, science, and mathematics, *Be A Better Reader* provides instruction and practice in the following study skills.

Selecting and Evaluating Information: the ability to select items from context and evaluate them in terms of conditions or specifications.

Organizing Information: the ability to put together or organize similar ideas.

Locating Information: the ability to find information in reference books and periodicals.

Reading Visuals: the ability to understand information presented in visuals, such as diagrams, maps, and graphs.

Following Directions: the ability to follow a specific sequence of steps.

Previewing: the ability to use previewing skills to understand the meaning and organization of a selection before reading it.

Reading Special Materials: the ability to read materials other than classroom textbooks.

Selecting and Evaluating Information

Just as word recognition skills are basic to reading, selection and evaluation are basic to study skills. Textbooks in the content areas contain many questions and directions that call for selection and evaluation skills. The skill of selecting and evaluating information requires students to select a piece of information and judge its worth in meeting the specifications of an activity or question. The answers to most literal comprehension questions need only to be selected from the text. However, inferential questions require students to go beyond the selection process to evaluation, the highest level of critical comprehension. In *Be A Better Reader*, lessons on fact and opinion, primary sources, and propaganda teach students selection and evaluation skills.

Organizing Information

The skill of organizing information is important because of the frequency with which students must apply it in studying textbooks, listening in class, and writing papers and tests. This skill provides opportunity for applying comprehension of content to a different format. Organizing information calls for putting together systematically items or ideas that belong to a whole. *Be A Better Reader* includes lessons on the procedures most often used in organizing information: (1) classifying items that belong to one group or that occur in a certain order; (2) outlining to show the relationship among ideas; (3) summarizing important ideas.

Locating Information

The skill of locating information includes activities that range from using a table of contents and an index to using a dictionary, an encyclopedia, and the library database system. Skill in locating information begins with recognizing alphabetical order and advances to finding information in complex reference books. In *Be A Better Reader*, lessons on locational skills are self-contained and include representative examples of typical dictionary and encyclopedia entries, indexes, and tables of contents.

Reading Visuals

Most content-area textbooks require students to read a variety of visuals, such as maps, timelines, diagrams, and graphs. Throughout *Be A Better Reader*, in all content areas, students are taught how to extract specific information from visuals and how to compress textual information into a brief visual presentation.

Following Directions

Reading to follow directions is a fundamental skill needed in studying all content areas. In *Be A Better Reader*, students are given directions for carrying out the activities that follow the reading selections. Thus, in addition to specific lessons in following directions, students acquire abundant experience in reading and following directions throughout each level of the program.

Previewing

Previewing a selection is another organizational skill. Previewing results in an organized "picture" or understanding of the structure of the selection. In *Be A Better Reader*, students learn to preview a selection by noting headings of sections, main ideas, and visuals.

Reading Special Materials

Students must be able to read special materials that they encounter outside the classroom. The last lesson in each unit of *Be A Better Reader* provides specific directions on how to read the yellow pages, a recipe, a floor plan, a travel brochure, and so on. Practice with these materials helps students make the transition from relatively controlled classroom reading situations to everyday reading situations.

Reading research has shown that different types of content require specialized reading skills. In preparing *Be A Better Reader*, textbooks in four different content areas were analyzed.

Literature

Social Studies

Science

Mathematics

Books were analyzed for text patterns, visual programs, and study aids typical of each content area. The specific skills situations that occurred most often in each content area were selected for inclusion in *Be A Better Reader*. The situations in which the skills were used were more abstract and higher levels of thinking were required in the books intended for the higher grades, but the skills situations are basically the same at all grade levels at which each subject is taught.

Literature

The literature selections in *Be A Better Reader* were carefully selected to appeal to student interest and are written at appropriate reading levels. The basic goal of the lessons with literature selections is threefold: (1) to acquaint students with various literary genres; (2) to increase students' awareness of the literary elements; and (3) to provide practice in applying comprehension skills to reading literature. A variety of genres is included in each level of *Be A Better Reader*. In the instructional section of each lesson, an important literary concept is stressed in terms appropriate to the particular level.

Each level of *Be A Better Reader* provides a lesson that develops one of the following special skills required in understanding and appreciating literature.

Recognizing plot

Recognizing character

Recognizing conflict

Recognizing setting

Recognizing theme

Plot

Most short stories have a plot, or sequence of events. They have a beginning, a middle, and an end, and events are arranged to build to a climax. As students read stories, it is important for them to keep the events in order, to notice how one event leads to the next, and to be able to identify the climax, or turning point of the story.

Character

The characters in a story are as important as the plot. Students need to be able to identify the main character, or protagonist, in a story. They should think about what motivates characters to act as they do. They should also notice how characters develop and change by contrasting how the characters behave at the beginning of a story with how they behave at the end.

Conflict

Students should be able to recognize a story's central conflict, or problem. Most stories are built around one of three common conflicts.

1. The main character is in conflict with himself or herself.
2. The main character is in a conflict with other characters.
3. The main character is in conflict with nature, society, or some outside force over which he or she may not have any control.

Setting

Setting is the time and place of the events in a story. Awareness of setting is essential to understanding the characters and their conflicts. Students must be shown how to interpret setting and its impact on the story's characters and events.

Theme

The theme, or idea, of a story is usually the most difficult concept for students to formulate by themselves. Students need to use higher-level comprehension skills to infer the author's underlying message.

Social Studies

Social studies texts have their own characteristic text patterns that require special reading skills. For example, social studies texts include frequent references to visuals, such as maps, graphs, and pictures. These references may require students to find information in a specific visual and then combine that information with information in the text.

Students need to become familiar with the text patterns typical of social studies textbooks. *Be A Better Reader* teaches some of the skills that are necessary to aid in comprehension of the patterns.

Reading visuals, such as pictures, maps, and graphs

Recognizing cause-and-effect relationships

Understanding sequence of events

Making comparisons and contrasts
Understanding detailed statements of fact
Thinking and reading critically

Visuals

Pictures in social studies textbooks are selected to depict historical concepts and events. The ability to read pictures and captions that accompany them results in students gaining information and implied meanings that go beyond the text. Reading pictures requires close attention to detail.

Reading maps and graphs is a highly specialized kind of reading skill. Map reading requires recognition and interpretation of symbols for rivers, mountains, lakes, towns and cities, boundary lines, and such features as scales of miles, color keys, and meridians. When reading graphs, students need to know how to extrapolate data and use it to make generalizations, thereby supplementing information in the text.

Cause and Effect

While the cause-and-effect text pattern occurs to some extent in most content areas, it occurs with the highest frequency in social studies, especially history. Every major event in history comes about as the result of some cause or set of causes, and when the event happens its effect or effects are felt. Sometimes the effect of one event becomes the cause of another event. Thus, the student often encounters a chain of causes and effects. Students who are adept at recognizing cause-and-effect patterns will find this to be a valuable asset in studying social studies textbooks.

Sequence of Events

Another text pattern encountered in social studies presents events in specific time sequences accompanied by dates. Students should read this pattern for two purposes: (1) to grasp the chronological order of large periods or whole blocks of events and (2) to grasp times of important happenings within each period or block—stopping long enough to associate events with dates and to think about how each event led to others.

Social studies textbooks include several kinds of visual aids designed to help students understand time relationships. These aids include charts of events and dates, chronological summaries, timelines, outline maps with dates and events, and so on. Each of these visual aids requires special reading skills.

Comparison and Contrast

A text pattern calling for the comparison of likenesses and/or contrast of differences is common in social studies textbooks. This pattern occurs most frequently in discussions of such topics as the theories of government or policies of different leaders; physical features, products, or industries of different countries; and so on. Students who recognize a comparison and contrast chapter or section of a text can approach it with the foremost purpose of noting likenesses and differences.

Detailed Statements of Fact

Much social studies text contains many details and facts. Facts, however, are usually included within one of the characteristic text patterns already discussed. The facts in social studies textbooks are not as dense as they usually are in science textbooks, nor are they as technical. Because they are often associated with sequential events or with causes and effects, they are more easily grasped.

Critical Thinking

Many social studies texts require students to interpret material critically. Students are expected to make inferences from facts, to distinguish fact from opinion, to analyze propaganda, to interpret primary sources, to draw conclusions and make generalizations, and to answer open-ended questions. Students need specific instruction and practice in these skills if they are to probe for deeper meanings and respond to higher-level questions.

Combination of Patterns

A single chapter in social studies may contain several text patterns. For example, a chapter may contain biographical material similar to the narrative pattern, a chronology of events during a certain time period, maps and charts depicting those events, and cause-and-effect relationships. If students who start to study such a chapter have not acquired the skills necessary to recognize and process each of these text patterns and instead use the same approach in reading all of them, the resulting understandings of the concepts presented will be extremely limited.

Science

Science text, like all other types of text, calls for the use of such comprehension skills as identifying main ideas and making inferences. However, an analysis of science textbooks reveals text patterns unique to science text that call for other approaches and special reading skills.

As in social studies textbooks, science texts include frequent references to such visuals as diagrams and pictures. Students need continued practice in combining text reading with visual reading in order to process all the information that is available on a science text page.

Be A Better Reader provides lessons on the following special reading skills that are needed for science textbooks.

Understanding classification

Reading an explanation of a technical process

Recognizing cause and effect relationships

Following directions for an experiment

Understanding detailed statements of fact

Recognizing descriptive problem-solving situations

Understanding abbreviations, symbols, and equations

Reading text with diagrams

Classification

The classification pattern is characteristic of science text. In this pattern, living things, objects, liquids, gases, forces, and so on are first classified in a general grouping that has one or more elements in common. This group is further classified into smaller groups, each of which varies in certain respects from every other group in the general grouping. Students who recognize the classification text pattern will concentrate on understanding the basis of the groupings and the chief characteristics of each one.

Explanation of a Technical Process

Another text pattern particularly characteristic of science is the explanation of a technical process. Explanation is usually accompanied by diagrams, necessitating very careful reading of text with continuous references to diagrams. The diagrams themselves require students to use special reading skills in addition to those needed to grasp the text explanations.

Cause and Effect

A text pattern sometimes encountered in science textbooks, but not unique to science, is the cause-and-effect pattern. In this pattern the text gives information that explains why certain things happen. In reading this type of pattern, students first read to find the causes and effects. A careful rereading is usually necessary to determine how and why the causes had the effects that they did.

Following Directions for an Experiment

This text pattern consists of explicit directions or instructions that must be carried out exactly. The common study skill of following directions is essential in reading this science pattern, but experiments also call for the mental activities of making discriminating observations, understanding complex explanations, and drawing considered conclusions.

Detailed Statements of Fact

Another pattern frequently encountered in science textbooks is detailed statements of fact. This pattern in science differs from factual text in the other content areas in two respects: (1) the facts are more dense and (2) they frequently lead to or embody a definition or a statement of a principle.

In reading this text pattern, students can make use of the reading skill of finding the main ideas and supporting details. Students first locate the most important thought or main idea in each paragraph, then proceed to find details that reinforce the main idea— noting particularly any definitions or statements of principles.

Descriptive Problem Solving

This text pattern describes problem-solving situations by taking the reader through a series of scientific experiments conducted by one or by many people. Students should approach this pattern with the idea of finding out what each successive problem was and how it was solved.

Abbreviations, Symbols, and Equations

Another science text pattern that requires a special kind of reading makes liberal use of abbreviations, formulas, and equations. For example, grasping the meaning of the symbol $°$ (degree) and the formula $CaCO_3$ (calcium carbonate) when they are integrated with words in the text calls for special recognition skills in addition to the usual recognition of word symbols. This pattern is still further complicated when symbols and abbreviations are involved in equations or number sentences.

Diagrams

Science textbooks usually contain many diagrams. Students need to learn how to go from the text to the diagrams and back to the text if they are to understand the meaning of scientific concepts. Reading diagrams requires an understanding of the purpose of diagrams, ability to interpret color and other visual devices used to highlight parts of a diagram, and comprehension of labels.

Combination of Patterns

As in social studies textbooks, a single chapter of a science text at the higher levels may contain several text patterns. If students who start to study such a chapter have not acquired the skills necessary to recognize and process each of these patterns and instead use the same approach in reading all of them, then the resulting understandings of the concepts presented will be extremely limited.

Mathematics

The reading skills needed for reading mathematics are sharply different from the skills needed in other content areas. Many students who read narrative with relative ease have great difficulty in reading mathematics, especially word problems and abstract mathematical symbols. The mathematics selections in *Be A Better Reader* are not included for the purpose of teaching mathematics. Their function is threefold: (1) to develop in students an awareness of the difference between reading mathematics texts and reading other texts; (2) to give students practice in reading the different types of text and symbols used in mathematics textbooks; and (3) to apply basic reading skills to mathematics text.

One of the special characteristics of mathematics text is compactness. Every word and every symbol is important. Unlike reading in other content areas, skipping an unfamiliar word or guessing its meaning from context will impair students' progress in mathematics. Students should be aware of this difference.

Another adjustment students have to make in reading mathematics is a change in basic left-to-right eye movement habits. Mathematics text often requires vertical or left-directed eye movements for rereading portions of the text for better understanding or for selecting certain numbers or symbols. While some students read mathematics more rapidly than others, text patterns in mathematics are not appropriate for speed reading.

Reading in mathematics makes heavy demands on the comprehension skills that call for interpretation, critical reading, and creative reading. Many mathematical situations call for a careful weighing of relationships. Of great importance is the ability to discover principles as a result of studying pictures and diagrams.

The inferential reading skills and the study skills of reading pictures and diagrams emphasized throughout *Be A Better Reader* should transfer to the following skills and attitudes specifically needed in working with mathematics.

> **Reading word problems**
>
> **Reading mathematical terms, symbols, and equations**
>
> **Reading graphs and other mathematical visuals**
>
> **Reading explanation for processes or principles, such as fractions, decimals, and percents**

Word Problems

Because problem solving is a priority in mathematics and closely related to basic reading skills, the Seventh Edition of *Be A Better Reader* includes in each level two lessons on problem solving. A five-step strategy is introduced in the first problem-solving lesson and used throughout the series. The steps in the strategy closely parallel the steps used in most mathematics textbooks. However, *Be A Better Reader* emphasizes the reading and reasoning skills necessary to solve word problems.

While the problem-solving strategy remains the same throughout the series, each succeeding lesson focuses on slightly more sophisticated problems. For example, the first problem-solving lesson focuses on problems that involve one mathematical operation. At a later level, problems are introduced in which two operations are necessary.

Terms, Symbols, and Equations

In mathematics, students must read sentences composed of word symbols and number symbols, such as equations. Recognizing and understanding symbols of various types is reading and should be taught as such in mathematics.

In reading equations, students have to recognize the meaning of the entire mathematical sentence, as well as the symbols $+$, $-$, $\times$, $\div$, and $=$. They also have to recognize and understand the symbols x and n, just as they have to learn to recognize and grasp the meaning of a new word in reading.

Students have to learn to recognize and understand the properties of geometric figures, such as the octagon, pentagon, prism, cube, cylinder, and pyramid. Parentheses, $>$, $<$, and other symbols are used frequently.

Graphs and Charts

Other distinctive text patterns in mathematics are graphs, such as bar graphs and circle graphs. While these visual aids are used in social studies, science, and other subjects, they almost always represent mathematical concepts.

To get the most information from a graph, students should: (1) read the title to determine exactly what is being compared; (2) read the numbers or labels to determine what the figures or labels stand for; (3) study the graph to compare the different items illustrated; and (4) interpret the significance of the graph as a whole. Due to the prevalence of graphs and similar mathematical visuals in most content area textbooks, most students profit from instruction in reading these types of text patterns.

Explanation

The explanation text pattern in mathematics texts is similar to the explanation text pattern in science textbooks, except that in mathematics text explanations describe a mathematical principle or process rather than a scientific process. Mathematical explanations are comparatively short and often contain symbols other than words. They are usually accompanied by or are preceded by a series of exercises or questions designed to guide students in discovering the principle or process. This text pattern calls for very careful reading and rereading until the process is understood.

Assessment tests for Level A are designed to measure students' level of achievement in each of the important comprehension and study skills that receive emphasis in *all* levels of **Be A Better Reader**. The tests may be used as pre-tests and/or post-tests, depending on students' needs and your particular classroom management style. Combined with an overview of student performance on each lesson, the tests should enable you to refine your assessment of students' performance and determine students' readiness to advance to the next level.

The four tests in Level A can be administered separately or at one time, depending on time available. Because directions are provided for each test, students should be able to take the tests independently. However, enough time should be allowed for each student to complete the tests.

The skill for each test item is identified in the answer key below. Following the skill is the number of the lesson or the lessons in Level A where that skill is treated as a Skill Focus. To simplify the scoring process, you can use the answer key to make a scoring mask, which when placed over the answer sheet reveals only those items that are correct. The total score is equal to the number of correct items. Criterion scores are not specified, as the individual class or group situation should determine the appropriate criterion.

Answer Key and Skills Correlation

Test 1

1. c Understanding character (43)
2. a Understanding character (43)
3. a Understanding character (43)
4. b Understanding character (43)
5. b Recognizing sequence of events (1)
6. a Recognizing sequence of events (1)
7. c Recognizing sequence of events (1)
8. c Recognizing sequence of events (1)
9. b Identifying setting (13)
10. c Identifying setting (13)
11. b Identifying setting (13)
12. b Identifying setting (13)
13. a Identifying conflict and resolution (24)
14. b Identifying conflict and resolution (24)
15. b Identifying conflict and resolution (24)
16. b Identifying conflict and resolution (24)
17. c Inferring theme (33)
18. a Inferring theme (33)
19. a Inferring theme (33)
20. c Inferring theme (33)
21. b Making inferences (49, 57)
22. a Making inferences (49, 57)
23. a Making inferences (49, 57)
24. b Recognizing multiple meanings of words (59)
25. b Using comparison context clues (13)
26. c Using detail context clues (33, 44, 45)

Test 2

27. b Identifying cause and effect (2, 26)
28. a Identifying cause and effect (2, 26)
29. c Identifying cause and effect (2, 26)
30. c Comparing and contrasting (25)
31. b Comparing and contrasting (25)
32. b Comparing and contrasting (25)
33. c Comparing and contrasting (25)
34. a Using synonym context clues (1, 24, 25, 26, 43, 46)
35. c Distinguishing fact from opinion (39)
36. c Distinguishing fact from opinion (39)
37. b Distinguishing fact from opinion (39)
38. a Distinguishing fact from opinion (39)
39. a Making inferences (49, 57)
40. b Making inferences (49, 57)
41. a Making inferences (49, 57)
42. c Making inferences (49, 57)
43. b Making inferences (49, 57)
44. c Identifying the main idea (6, 17, 18)
45. a Identifying the main idea (6, 17, 18)
46. b Identifying the main idea (6, 17, 18)
47. b Identifying the main idea and supporting details (40, 45)
48. a Identifying the main idea and supporting details (40, 45)
49. b Identifying the main idea and supporting details (40, 45)

50. c Recognizing multiple meanings of words (59)
51. b Recognizing multiple meanings of words (59)
52. c Recognizing multiple meanings of words (59)
53. b Using a primary source (44)
54. a Using a primary source (44)
55. c Using a primary source (44)
56. a Using a primary source (44)
57. b Using a map (14, 54, 56)
58. b Using a map (14, 54, 56)
59. c Using a map (14, 54, 56)
60. b Using a map (14, 54, 56)
61. a Using a map (14, 54, 56)

Test 3

62. a Identifying cause and effect (2, 26)
63. a Identifying cause and effect (2, 26)
64. b Identifying cause and effect (2, 26)
65. c classifying (3)
66. a classifying (3)
67. b classifying (3)
68. a Using appositive context clues (15, 56)
69. c Reading text with diagrams (15, 35)
70. b Reading text with diagrams (15, 35)
71. c Reading text with diagrams (15, 35)
72. a Reading text with diagrams (15, 35)
73. a Identifying the main idea (6, 17, 18)
74. c Identifying the main idea (6, 17, 18)
75. b Identifying the main idea (6, 17, 18)

76. a Identifying the main idea and supporting details (40, 45)
77. b Identifying the main idea and supporting details (40, 45)
78. c Recognizing multiple meanings of words (59)
79. a Recognizing multiple meanings of words (59)
80. b Solving word problems (4)
81. c Solving word problems (4)
82. a Solving word problems (4)
83. b Solving word problems (4)

Test 4

84. a Using a dictionary entry (52)
85. a Using a dictionary entry (52)
86. b Using a dictionary entry (52)
87. b Using a dictionary entry (52)
88. b Using an encyclopedia (62)
89. a Using an encyclopedia (62)
90. c Using an encyclopedia (62)
91. c Using an encyclopedia (62)
92. a Recognizing root words (29)
93. c Recognizing root words (29)
94. b adding suffixes to words (29, 61)
95. a adding suffixes to words (29, 61)
96. b adding prefixes to words (29, 60)
97. a adding prefixes to words (29, 60)
98. b adding prefixes to words (29, 60)
99. a Dividing words into syllables (31, 38, 47, 48)
100. c Dividing words into syllables (31, 38, 47, 48)

T16

Be A Better Reader

Level A

Seventh Edition

Nila Banton Smith

Globe Fearon Educational Publishers
A Division of Simon & Schuster
Upper Saddle River, New Jersey

Pronunciation Key

Symbol	Key Word	Respelling
a	act	(akt)
ah	star	(stahr)
ai	dare	(dair)
aw	also	(awl soh)
ay	flavor	(flay vər)
e	end	(end)
ee	eat	(eet)
er	learn	(lern)
	sir	(ser)
	fur	(fer)
i	hit	(hit)
eye	idea	(eye dee ə)
y	like	(lyk)
ir	deer	(dir)
	fear	(fir)
oh	open	(oh pen)
oi	foil	(foil)
	boy	(boi)
or	horn	(horn)
ou	out	(out)
	flower	(flou ər)
oo	hoot	(hoot)
	rule	(rool)
yoo	few	(fyoo)
	use	(yooz)

Symbol	Key Word	Respelling
u	book	(buk)
	put	(put)
uh	cup	(kuhp)
ə	a as in along	(ə lawng)
	e as in moment	(moh mənt)
	i as in modify	(mahd ə fy)
	o as in protect	(prə tekt)
	u as in circus	(ser kəs)
ch	chill	(chil)
g	go	(goh)
j	joke	(johk)
	bridge	(brij)
k	kite	(kyt)
	cart	(kahrt)
ng	bring	(bring)
s	sum	(suhm)
	cent	(sent)
sh	sharp	(shahrp)
th	thin	(thin)
z	zebra	(zee brə)
	pose	(pohz)
zh	treasure	(treszh ər)

Be A Better Reader, Level A, Seventh Edition
Nila Banton Smith

Copyright © 1997 by Globe Fearon Educational Publisher. One Lake Street, Upper Saddle River, New Jersey 07458. All rights reserved. No part of this book may be kept in any information storage or retrieval system, transmitted or reproduced in any form or by any means without the prior written permission of the publisher.

Printed in the United States of America
6 7 8 9 10   98 99 00 01

C12
ISBN 0-8359-1916-1

Acknowledgments
We wish to express our appreciation for permission to use and adapt copyrighted materials.

The dictionary definitions in this book are reprinted with permission of Macmillan General Reference USA, a Division of Simon & Schuster Inc., from WEBSTER'S NEW WORLD DICTIONARY, Basic School Edition. Copyright © 1983 by Simon & Schuster Inc.

Harold Courlander for the play adaptation of "Anansi's Fishing Expedition." From The Cow-Tail Switch and Other West African Stories, by Harold Courlander and George Herzog. Holt, Rinehart and Winston, 1947. Copyright © 1947, 1973 by Harold Courlander and George Herzog. Used by permission of the authors.

Photo Credits
p. 8: Wide World Photos; p. 18: W. Gregory Brown/Animals, Animals; p. 19: (left) E. R. Degginger/Animals, Animals, (right) DPI/© John H. Gerard; p. 51: David Madison; p. 95: The Bettmann Archive; p. 96: Lee Snider/Image Works; p. 97: M. Siluk/Image Works; p. 125: Smithsonian Institution; p. 130: Laurence Gould/Animals, Animals; p. 140: The Bettmann Archive; p. 157: AFZAI/Photo Researchers; p. 162: DPI/Leonard Lee Rue III.

Contents

For more than thirty years, **Be A Better Reader** has helped students improve their reading skills. **Be A Better Reader** teaches the comprehension and study skills that you need to read and enjoy all types of materials—from library books to the different textbooks that you will encounter in school.

To get the most from **Be A Better Reader**, you should know how the lessons are organized. As you read the following explanations, it will be helpful to look at some of the lessons.

In each of the first four lessons of a unit, you will apply an important skill to a reading selection in literature, social studies, science, or mathematics. Each of these lessons includes the following seven sections.

Skill Focus

This section teaches you a specific skill. You should read the Skill Focus carefully, paying special attention to words that are printed in boldface type. The Skill Focus tells you about a skill that you will use when you read the selection.

Word Clues

This section teaches you how to recognize and use different types of context clues. These clues will help you with the meanings of the underlined words in the selection.

Reading a Literature, Social Studies, Science, or Mathematics Selection

This section introduces the selection that you will read and gives you suggestions about what to look for as you read. The suggestions will help you understand the selection.

Selection

The selections in the literature lessons are similar to those in a literature anthology, library book, newspaper, or magazine. The social studies selec- tions are like chapters in a social studies textbook or encyclopedia. They often include maps and tables. The science selections, like a science textbook, include special words in boldface type and sometimes diagrams. The mathematics selections will help you acquire skill in reading mathematics textbooks.

Recalling Facts

Answers to the questions in this section—the first of three activity sections—can be found in the selection. You will sometimes have to reread parts of the selection to do this activity.

Interpreting Facts

The second activity includes questions whose answers are not directly stated in the selection. For these questions, you must combine the information in the selection with what you already know in order to *infer* the answers.

Skill Focus Activity

In the last activity, you will use the skill that you learned in the Skill Focus section at the beginning of the lesson to answer questions about the selection. If you have difficulty completing this activity, reread the Skill Focus section.

The remaining lessons in each unit give you practice with such skills as using a dictionary, an encyclopedia, and other reference materials; using phonics and syllabication aids in recognizing new words; locating and organizing information; and adjusting reading rate. Other reading skills that are necessary in everyday experience are also covered, such as reading a bus schedule and a menu.

Each time that you learn a new skill in **Be A Better Reader**, look for opportunities to use the skill in your other reading at school and at home. Your reading ability will improve the more you practice reading!

Lesson 1
Sequence of Events

Reading a Literature Selection

▶ **Background Information**

Have you ever dreamed of going around the world? The Robertson family did, and they decided to make their dream a reality.

"Broken Voyage" is a true story about their trip. They set sail from England in a 43-foot sailboat named the *Lucette*. They made their way halfway around the world to the Pacific Ocean. For part of the trip, the Robertsons sailed in a small raft and finally in a rowboat. Look at the map on page 7 to see just how far the Robertson family traveled. In this selection, you will read about a dangerous adventure that the Robertsons had on the Pacific Ocean.

▶ **Skill Focus**

As you read a story, pay close attention to the **sequence of events**. One way you can keep track of the plot, or sequence of events in a story, is to think about the story as having three parts: a **beginning**, a **middle**, and an **end**. Most stories follow the same plot

sequence. You can think of a story's sequence of events as a mountain. The most exciting part of the story occurs at the top of the peak.

The following questions may help you to identify the three parts.

Beginning
1. What are the people doing when the story begins?
2. What problems do the people have at first?

Middle
3. What is the most exciting event of the story?
4. What happens as a result of this event?

End
5. What is the most serious problem the people face?
6. How do the people solve this problem by the end of the story?

▶ **Word Clues**

When you read a word that you do not know, look for context clues to help you understand it. Context clues are words near the unknown word that make its meaning clearer. Read the following sentences.

It was thirteen-year-old Neil's turn to wash dishes and clean the <u>galley</u> after breakfast. The boat's kitchen was very small, but it had everything they needed.

If you do not know the meaning of the word *galley*, the word *kitchen* in the next sentence can help you. The words *kitchen* and *galley* are synonyms. A galley is a ship's kitchen.

Look for **synonym** context clues to find the meaning of the three underlined words in the selection.

▶ **Strategy Tip**

As you read the story, keep track of the sequence of events. Think about which events happened in the beginning, middle, and end of the story. When you finish, you should be able to recall the important events.

Broken Voyage

The first two days of sailing on the Pacific had been stormy. On the third day, the Robertson family was happy to see the sun rise through the clouds. They had bravely battled the waves of the Pacific in their small sailboat, and they needed a rest.

Their 43-foot sailboat was named the *Lucette*. It had carried the Robertsons from their home in England across the Atlantic and into the Pacific on their journey around the world. They had just left the Galapagos Islands off the northwest coast of South America.

During the last six months, they had sailed the *Lucette* through many storms, but they agreed that the last two days were the worst they had seen. As the Robertsons ate breakfast, they talked happily about the day of quiet sailing ahead.

"But now we have work to do," said Mr. Robertson.

It was thirteen-year-old Neil's turn to wash dishes and clean the galley after breakfast. The boat's kitchen was very small, but it had everything they needed. Neil's twin sister Sandy gathered the broken fishing gear to repair it. Douglas, their older brother, was already at the wheel in the cockpit, keeping the *Lucette* on <u>course</u>. It was his responsibility to make sure that they were going in the right direction.

On deck, Mrs. Robertson picked up the rubbish left by the storm. Below, Mr. Robertson checked the *Lucette's* course. He read the <u>charts</u> to make sure they were on course. According to the maps, the Robertsons were 3,000 miles from the islands where they planned to stop next.

In the galley, Neil washed the last pan and put the towel out to dry. He had finished his work for the morning, and now he planned to read a book. As he headed for the cabin, he could hear the water gently slapping against the sides of the boat. It was a comfortable sound. Neil, who had lived all his life on a farm in England, now called this sailboat his home.

He climbed into his bunk and leaned back to enjoy his book. He had just started to read

> *"Yes! Get ready to abandon ship!" shouted Mr. Robertson.*

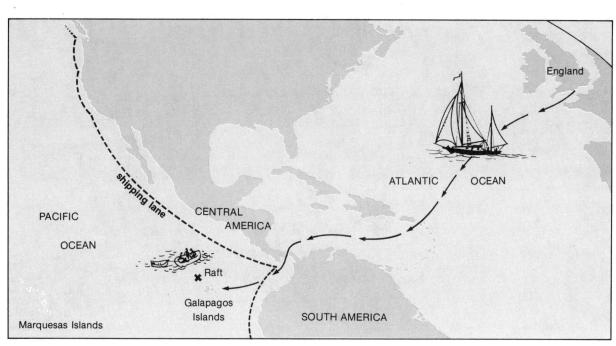

The map shows the course of the Robertson family on the *Lucette* and on the raft.

PACIFIC OCEAN

CENTRAL AMERICA

ATLANTIC OCEAN

England

shipping lane

Raft

Galapagos Islands

SOUTH AMERICA

Marquesas Islands

when something hit the side of the boat. Neil was thrown across the cabin and against the far wall. The *Lucette* was rolling wildly from side to side. Neil was on the floor. His ears were ringing and his shoulder hurt.

As he tried to stand up, Neil heard his family shouting outside. Then he heard his mother yell, "Killer whales!" A moment later, she ran into the cabin. "Neil, put on your life jacket and get on deck."

The whales had punched a huge hole in the *Lucette's* side, and water was rushing in. As Neil left the cabin, the water already covered the floorboards. He heard his brother Douglas call, "Are we sinking, Dad?"

"Yes! Get ready to abandon ship!" shouted Mr. Robertson. He picked up a knife as he dashed out of the galley. He then cut the ropes to free the small rowboat tied to the mast. "Get the raft ready. We'll need that too," he cried.

The boys pulled down the raft. Douglas pressed the button to fill it with air. Then he and Neil turned to help their father free the rowboat. The sea was nearly up to the *Lucette's* deck. She was sinking fast. The rubber life raft swiftly filled with air. Douglas looked at his father. "When do we lower the raft, Dad?"

"Now! And tie the rowboat to the raft." Mr. Robertson shouted as he ran into the galley.

Water was rolling over the sailboat's decks as Mr. Robertson returned with a bag of food. He had thrown bread, biscuits, sugar, candy bars, and other foods into the bag. He gave it to Neil. "Put this in the raft and tell everyone to get in. Hurry! She's going under."

Mr. Robertson made one last trip into the galley. He returned with two bags of oranges, lemons, and onions. He tossed them into the rowboat, now tied to the raft. Then he took a last look around. His family waited in the raft. Behind it, the sea stretched as far as he could see. The killer whales were nowhere in sight. The Robertsons were alone. Mr. Robertson jumped into the water and began swimming to the raft. A moment later, the *Lucette* began sinking into the deep, dark heart of the Pacific.

That afternoon, Neil wrote on a piece of sail: *June 15. Neil's log in the lifeboat.* Lucette *sunk by killer whales. Very sad. She went down in 2 minutes.*

The Robertson family aboard the tuna boat that rescued them.

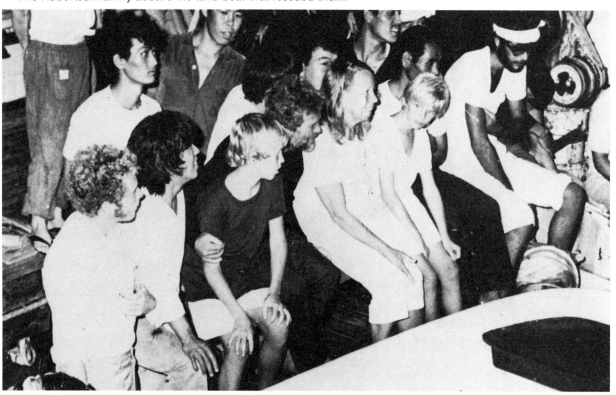

The Robertson family aboard the tuna boat that rescued them.

The Robertsons were lucky to be alive. As the sun went down, they wondered about their chances of staying alive. They had no radio. They were hundreds of miles away from a shipping lane and 3,000 miles from their next port. They would not be missed for at least five weeks.

That night, each person had a piece of biscuit, a sip of water, and a small piece of candy. They divided one orange among them.

A week passed on the lonely Pacific. The rubber life raft had tiny pinholes in the sides. Soon it had to be blown up every hour. High waves forced the Robertsons to bail the raft regularly. After almost three weeks, the family knew that the raft would soon sink. They moved to the tiny rowboat.

The five members of the family crowded together in the little boat. Everyone knew that a sudden movement might cause the boat to tip over. No one moved without warning the others.

Their two greatest problems were thirst and hunger. Their mouths always felt like cotton. Because most of the food from the *Lucette* was gone, they were always hungry. Also, their skin was raw from the burning sun and the stinging salt water.

But as long as the rowboat could carry them, they could stay alive on the dangerous sea. During storms, they caught rain water with a rubber sheet. They filled all the cans they had with water. But each person drank only a little water each day. They did not know when another rain might come. By the time their food was gone, they had learned to catch fish with hooks of wire. Sometimes big turtles poked their heads up next to the boat. Douglas and his father pulled them aboard and quickly slit them open with a knife. The turtle meat would keep them all alive for another day.

The tiny rowboat crept along the course the Robertsons had set for South America. Five weeks had passed since they had abandoned the *Lucette*. "With luck we should make the coast in about three weeks," said Mr. Robertson, "but I'm afraid the wind's changing. So we may have to start rowing . . ."

Suddenly, he stopped talking and stared straight ahead. The others looked at him. "A ship," he said. "There's a ship!"

"Where?" they asked, and everyone turned to look.

"Keep still!" shouted Mr. Robertson. "We don't want to tip over now. I must signal the ship. Neil, hand me a flare from that box."

Carefully standing up, he lit the <u>flare</u> and held it high overhead until it burned his fingers. Then he threw it into the air.

The family watched him, hardly breathing. Mr. Robertson stood frozen, eyes fixed on the distant ship. Moments passed. Then he looked at his family and quietly said, "She's seen us. She's changed course. We're saved."

A passing Japanese tuna boat picked up the Robertsons on July 22. Mr. Robertson was the last to climb on board. He was surprised to see that his family was sitting on the deck. Suddenly, he realized why. Living for 38 days on a raft and in a rowboat had weakened his legs, too. Four days later, the Robertson family was back on land.

RECALLING FACTS

Write the answers to the following questions on the lines provided. If necessary, you may go back to the selection to find an answer.

Recalling details
1. Who are the members of the Robertson family?

The members of the Robertson family are Mr. and

Mrs. Robertson, the twins, Neil, Sandy, and Douglas.

Recalling details
2. What course did the Robertsons sail?

The Robertsons sailed from England, across the

Atlantic Ocean, and into the Pacific Ocean.

Recalling details
3. At what point in the Robertsons journey does this story begin?

The Robertsons had just left the Galapagos Islands

off the northwest coast of South America.

4. Tell what work each member of the Robertson family had to do after breakfast.

Mrs. Robertson picked up rubbish on the deck.

Mr. Robertson read the charts to make sure that they were on course.

Sandy repaired fishing gear.

Neil washed dishes and cleaned the galley.

Douglas was at the wheel in the cockpit.

Recalling details

5. What did Neil do after he finished cleaning the galley?

Neil went to his cabin and started to read.

Identifying cause and effect

6. What caused the *Lucette* to sink?

Killer whales punched a huge hole in the side of the boat.

Recalling details

7. What are the two most serious problems that the Robertsons faced at sea?

The most serious problems were thirst and hunger.

Recalling details

8. How did the Robertsons get fresh drinking water?

During storms, they used rubber sheets to catch rain.

Recalling details

9. How did they get food?

They caught fish with hooks of wire.

Recalling details

10. Why did Mr. Robertson tell the family to keep still when he saw a ship?

He was afraid the rowboat would tip over.

Identifying cause and effect

11. What effect did living at sea for 38 days have on the Robertsons?

Their legs were so weak that when they were rescued they could not stand up right away.

Using context clues

12. Write the letter of the correct meaning in front of each word.

b course   a. maps used by sailors

a charts   b. the direction taken by a ship

c flare   c. a bright light used to signal for help

INTERPRETING FACTS

Not all questions about a story are answered directly in the story. For the following questions, you will have to figure out answers not directly stated in the story. Write the answers to the questions on the lines provided.

Making inferences

1. At what time of day did the *Lucette* sink? How do you know?

The *Lucette* sank at mid-morning. Neil had finished cleaning the galley after breakfast; in the afternoon he wrote about the *Lucette*'s sinking.

Making inferences

2. Why did the Robertsons take the rowboat with them?

In case something happened to the raft, they could use the other boat.

Making inferences

3. Why did the Robertsons use the raft instead of the rowboat?

The raft was larger and more comfortable.

4. Put a check mark before the words that describe the Robertson family.

_____ playful   _____ lazy

✔ responsible   ✔ cooperative

✔ helpful   _____ nervous

5. What is the meaning of the title "Broken Voyage"?

The journey was interrupted when the *Lucette* sank.

_____

_____

_____

SKILL FOCUS

Below are some of the events in "Broken Voyage." On the numbered lines, write the events in the sequence in which they took place. Which events happened at the beginning of the story? in the middle? at the end? Then on the blank lines, fill in a different incident that occurs during each part of the story.

    a. Killer whales hit the *Lucette*.

    b. The Robertsons are alone with little food and water.

    c. The Robertsons get into the rubber raft and watch the *Lucette* sink.

    d. A passing ship rescues the Robertsons.

    e. The Robertsons hit storms in the Pacific.

    f. The Robertsons look forward to a quiet day of sailing.

Beginning

1. e. The Robertsons hit storms in the Pacific.

2. f. The Robertsons look forward to a quiet day of sailing.

Answers will vary.

Middle

3. a. Killer whales hit the *Lucette*.

4. c. The Robertsons get into the rubber raft and watch the *Lucette* sink.

Answers will vary.

End

5. b. The Robertsons are alone with little food and water.

6. d. A passing ship rescues the Robertsons.

Answers will vary.

▶ **Real Life Connections** Imagine being on board the *Lucette* as it starts to sink. What is the first thing that you might do to help the situation?

Cause and Effect

__Reading a Social Studies Selection __

▶ **Background Information**

Whales have been hunted for many centuries and in many parts of the world. As a result of their being hunted, many types of whales are extinct. These whales no longer exist. Other types of whales are endangered. There are so few of these types of whales that if they are not protected, they may soon become extinct. Laws in the United States now prohibit people from hunting certain types of whales. However, some countries around the world still allow people to hunt them.

As you read "The Whaling Industry," you will find out when the whaling industry started and what caused it to grow. You will also find out about the two kinds of whales that whalers hunted most often. After reading the selection, you will know what caused the end of the American whaling industry.

When reading textbooks, you may find words that are difficult to say, or pronounce. Sometimes these words are *respelled* to help you pronounce them. Sometimes

the meaning of the word is explained in a *definition*. In this selection, the first word that is respelled is *baleen* (bə LEEN). As you read, look for other words that are respelled. Try saying each word quietly to yourself.

▶ **Skill Focus**

Many events that you read about in textbooks are connected by **cause and effect.** When events are connected in this way, it means one event or condition (the cause) made another event happen (the effect). Look at the following example.

Cause: People needed food and oil.

Effect: They hunted whales for food and oil.

Because people needed food and oil, they hunted whales. The cause and effect are connected.

When you read this article, try to find the conditions and events that are connected in this way. When you come to an important event, think about what caused it to happen.

▶ **Word Clues**

Read the sentences below. Look for context clues that explain the underlined word.

By 1700, whales had become very important for their blubber, whalebone, and meat. Blubber is the fat under the skin of the whale.

If you do not know the meaning of the word *blubber* in the first sentence, read on. The second sentence states what the word *blubber* means. A word meaning that is stated directly can often be found before or after a new word.

Use **definition** context clues to find the meaning of the three underlined words in the selection.

▶ **Strategy Tip**

Before you read "The Whaling Industry," look at the headings in heavy type. Look at the pictures and read their captions. As you read the article, remember to look for the important events and what caused them.

The Whaling Industry

People have hunted whales for food and oil since early times. Even before there were whaling voyages, people killed whales that they found washed up on beaches. Later, people used boats to hunt whales. They killed whales with hand-thrown underline harpoons. A harpoon is a spear with a line attached to it. Today many countries are against commercial whaling.

The Early Days of Whaling

The people of southern France and northern Spain hunted whales during the 1200s. They made the first whaling voyages. They used large ships in the part of the Atlantic Ocean called the Bay of Biscay. Each ship carried small boats in which whalers set out to kill whales. When whales no longer came close to shore, the whalers went farther out to sea. During the 1500s, they hunted whales across the Atlantic Ocean as far as Newfoundland.

In the 1600s, Dutch and English sailors found many whales in the Arctic waters. Soon a group of islands north of Norway became the center of Arctic whaling.

At the same time, American Indians were also hunting whales. They hunted whales in much the same way as the first whalers. Shortly after the American colonists arrived in the 1600s, they hunted whales off the Atlantic coast. Lookout towers were built in many New England towns along the coast. When whales were sighted from the towers, the whalers launched their boats.

The "Right" Whale to Hunt

The whales that were hunted up to this time had no teeth. They are called baleen (bə LEEN) whales.

Baleen whales have whalebone, or baleen, instead of teeth. They have about four hundred thin plates of baleen in their mouths. Through these plates, baleen whales filter sea water to strain out the small fish they feed on.

There are many kinds of baleen whales. The whalers, however, hunted for the kind that swam slowly, was easily overtaken, floated when dead, and provided great quantities of oil and whalebone. Because this whale was the right kind to hunt, whalers called it the right whale. Today the whale is still called by that name.

By 1700, whales had become very important for their blubber, whalebone, and meat. Blubber is the fat under the skin of the whale. Nearly two hundred gallons of whale oil could be gotten from one ton of melted blubber. This oil was used for cooking and lighting lamps. Whalebone was used for fishing rods, buggy whips, and umbrellas. Whale meat was cooked and eaten.

Discovery of the Sperm Whale

In 1712, an American whaling ship was caught in a storm at sea and blown off course. The whalers came upon a school of whales, killed one, and brought it back to shore. To the whalers' surprise, the whale, unlike a right whale, had teeth.

Whales with teeth are called toothed whales. The New England whalers had discovered the largest of the toothed whales, the sperm whale. The sperm whale was larger and stronger than the right whale. This discovery started the American whaling industry.

The Golden Age of American Whaling

✔ The sperm whale soon became the prime catch of the American whalers. By 1800, Americans were hunting sperm whales throughout the Atlantic Ocean. The town of New Bedford in Massachusetts became the whaling capital of the world. Nantucket, Salem, and other New England cities with harbors also became centers for large whaling fleets. By 1835, Americans were whaling in the Pacific Ocean. San Francisco became an important whaling center.

✔ Whalers got three valuable substances from sperm whales. The first was sperm oil, used for lamps and cooking. It was better than the oil of the right whale. Another important substance was spermaceti (sper mə SET ee). Spermaceti is a pure wax found in the whale's head. It was used in making candles. A third substance, called ambergris (am ber GREES), was used for perfumes. The high value of sperm oil, spermaceti, and ambergris more than made up for the absence of whalebone in the sperm whale.

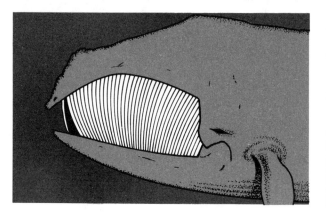

Baleen hangs from the upper jaw of baleen whales.

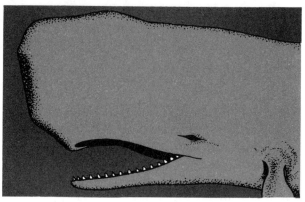

Teeth grow from the lower jaw of most toothed whales.

The Decline of the Whaling Industry

The American sperm whaling industry grew until about 1850. Whale oil had become the chief lamp fuel. However, when gold was found in 1848, many whalers left their ships to search for gold in California. During the Civil War, the Confederate navy sunk many whaling ships. With fewer whalers and ships, whaling began to suffer. The discovery of oil in the ground hurt whaling most of all. It led to the start of a new industry. Soon it was cheaper to use this oil for lamps than to use sperm oil.

> *Whales spend most of their life on the surface of the water and are able to swim up to 35 miles per hour.*

Whaling in the Twentieth Century

During the first half of the 1900s, whaling fleets killed large numbers of whales. As a result, they reduced the world's whale population and endangered many kinds of whales. Nevertheless, whale oil and sperm oil are still used in making cosmetics and soaps. Ambergris is still used in making perfumes. Whalebone is often ground up and used as meal for livestock. People in Japan and Norway, still eat the meat of baleen whales.

To prevent the extinction of certain whales, several nations met in 1946 and formed the International Whaling Commission. This commission decides the length of the whaling season, limits the number of whales that may be killed each year, and does not allow the killing of certain whales. Because the whale population continued to decline, the commission placed a ban on commercial whaling, which was supported by twenty-five nations and began in 1986. Other antiwhaling groups have since tried to limit further or to ban whaling altogether.

RECALLING FACTS

Write the answers to the following questions on the lines provided. You may go back to the selection to find an answer. Use the headings in the selection to help you find information.

Recalling details

1. Who were the first whalers?

The people of southern France and northern Spain

were the first whalers.

Recalling details

2. What is baleen?

Baleen is whalebone that the whale uses to filter sea

water.

Recalling details

3. Why did the early whalers hunt for the right whale?

They hunted for the right whale because it swam slowly,

was easily overtaken, floated when dead, and provided

great quantities of oil and whalebone.

4. Name the two groups of whales.

The article discusses the baleen and toothed whales.

5. What discovery caused the beginning of the whaling industry in America?

The discovery of the sperm whale caused the

beginning of the whaling industry.

6. Name one difference between right whales and sperm whales.

Right whales have no teeth; sperm whales have teeth.

7. What parts of the right whale were valuable?

The meat, blubber, and whalebone of the right whale

were the most valuable.

8. What parts of the sperm whale were valuable?

The sperm oil, spermaceti, and ambergris of the

sperm whale were the most valuable.

9. Tell one event that caused the decline of whaling in America.

The discoveries of gold and oil; (or the Civil War)

contributed to the decline of whaling in America.

10. Number the following events in the order in which they happened.

_2_ The islands north of Norway became the center of Arctic whaling.

_4_ The discovery of ground oil hurt the whaling industry.

_1_ Whalers hunted whales in the Bay of Biscay.

_3_ New Bedford, Massachusetts, became the whaling capital of the world.

_5_ Twenty-five nations supported a ban on commercial whaling.

11. Two paragraphs have check marks next to them. Reread both paragraphs. Then underline the sentence that tells what each paragraph is about.

12. Write the letter of the correct meaning in front of each word.

_b_ harpoons   **a.** a pure wax found in the head of sperm whales

_a_ spermaceti   **b.** spears used to kill whales

_c_ ambergris   **c.** a substance found in sperm whales that is used in making perfume

INTERPRETING FACTS

Not all questions about a selection are answered directly in the selection. For the following questions, you will have to figure out answers not directly stated in the selection. Write the answers to the questions on the lines provided.

1. Why was the sperm whale more valuable than the right whale?

Sperm oil was better for cooking and lighting lamps

than oil from right whales. The sperm whale also

provided wax for making candles and ambergris

for perfumes. These substances were more valuable

than the right whale's meat, blubber, and whalebone.

Inferring cause and effect

2. Why was the discovery of ground oil one of the major causes of the decline of whaling in America?

Ground oil was cheaper, more economical, and more in

demand than whale oil.

_____

_____

Answers will vary. Students should state facts to

support their conclusions.

_____

_____

_____

_____

Drawing conclusions

3. Do you think whaling should be outlawed? Write a paragraph using facts from the selection to support your opinion.

_____

_____

_____

_____

SKILL FOCUS

Match each cause with its effect. You may need to reread the selection.

Cause

1. __e__ Because whales no longer used the Bay of Biscay as a feeding ground,

2. __h__ Because the Dutch and English found Arctic waters filled with whales,

3. __a__ Because whale meat, blubber, and whalebone were valuable,

4. __g__ Because American whalers were hunting whales throughout the Atlantic,

5. __b__ Because whalers were able to get valuable sperm oil, spermaceti, and ambergris from sperm whales,

6. __d__ Because there was an abundance of whale oil,

7. __f__ As a result of the California Gold Rush, the Civil War, and the discovery of oil,

8. __i__ As a result of whaling fleets' killing large numbers of whales in the early 1900s,

9. __c__ Because the number of whales declined,

Effect

a. whales became very important.

b. the sperm whale became the prize catch of American whalers.

c. a ban was placed on commercial whaling.

d. whale oil became the chief source of lamp fuel.

e. the first whalers went farther out to sea.

f. the whaling industry in the United States rapidly declined.

g. many New England cities became whaling centers.

h. the islands north of Norway became the center of Arctic whaling.

i. there is a smaller whale population today.

▶ **Real Life Connections** Do you think that whaling should be outlawed in all parts of the world? Tell why or why not.

Classifying

Reading a Science Selection

▶ Background Information

The ocean covers more than 70 percent of the earth's surface. However, until recently the ocean has been largely a mystery to us. Oceanography–the study of the ocean–has come a long way since it started thousands of years ago.

In ancient Greece, the ocean was a subject of great interest. The Greeks did not have the instruments available to unlock many of the secrets of the ocean. Since then, people have been studying the ocean. In the 1800s, exploration of the ocean reached new heights. S.C.U.B.A. gear, underwater breathing equipment, and underwater laboratories have made the study of the ocean easier. People now have the ability to explore all but the deepest bottoms of the ocean. There are hopes that this exploration will lead to discoveries that may help better humankind.

While there are still many mysteries of the deep, many discoveries have been made. The ocean is rich with many kinds of life. Many varieties of plants and animals live beneath the surface of the ocean. Of course, these differences (and similarities) are what allows scientists to classify these animals. Aquatic animals are classified into three different groups, which you will read about in this selection.

▶ Skill Focus

Sometimes information is organized by **classifying** similar objects or ideas into groups. It is then easier to see similarities and differences among these groups. Classifying is very helpful for people who work with a great number of objects, as scientists often do.

When scientists classify plants and animals, they take large groups and break them up into smaller groups. The members of each smaller group are similar in some way. Goldfish and sharks are similar—they are both in the group called *fish*. Clams live in the water, but they belong to a different group than goldfish and sharks. Lobsters and crabs live in the water like fish, but they belong to yet another group.

When reading about groups, notice the important details. Ask yourself questions like the following.

1. What is similar about the animals that scientists put in the same group?
2. How are the animals in one group different from the animals in another group?

▶ Word Clues

Pictures can be used as context clues. Sometimes pictures help you with the meaning of a word. Look at Figure 1 on page 18. The picture helps you understand the meaning of the word *haddock*.

Use pictures to find the meaning of the two underlined words in the selection.

▶ Strategy Tip

When reading a science selection, it is helpful to look at the words that are printed in heavy, or **boldface**, type. These words are the most important in the selection. Look at the three headings in the selection. Each heading tells you the name of a group of ocean animals.

Three Groups of Water Animals

The Group Called Fish

Haddock, codfish, and mackerel are all fish. The body of a fish has a backbone and a skeleton. Animals that have backbones are known as **vertebrates** (VER tə brats). The bodies of most fish are covered with flat scales, like shingles on a roof. Fish can breathe underwater through gills. Most fish also have air bladders inside their bodies. These air bladders are filled with gases. By changing the amount of gas in its air bladder, a fish can move up or down through the water.

A fish uses its tail to push itself through the water. The shape of its body helps it move through the water easily. Most fish have fins that they use for balancing, steering, and braking.

Sharks are fish, but they do not have true backbones or air bladders. Some sharks are dangerous to people. The great white shark can be as much as 7.6 meters long. White sharks have attacked swimmers as far north as Cape Cod on the Atlantic coast. Other dangerous sharks are the hammerhead shark and the tiger shark.

Fish are a very important food for people. Hundreds of millions of dollars' worth of fish are sold every year. Scientists are helping to feed the people of the world by finding new ways to raise fish.

The Group Called Mollusks

Oysters, scallops, clams, snails, squids, and octopuses are all **mollusks** (MAH lusks). The word *mollusk* means "soft-bodied." All mollusks have soft bodies. Many have tough, hard shells for protection. Clams, oysters, and scallops have two-piece shells that are connected by a hinge of muscle. Their soft, fleshy bodies are used as food by many people.

Mollusks have no backbones, but they do have gills. Mollusks are sometimes called shellfish, but they are not really fish.

For protection, the squid depends not on a heavy shell, but on its ability to swim quickly. The octopus does not have a shell either. It can also move quickly. The octopus has eight arms, and the squid has ten arms.

You may have heard "sea-monster" stories of giant squids and octopuses. However, most squids and octopuses are not giants. They swim away when they see a large creature. They can also squirt a black fluid that forms a dark cloud in the water. This makes it more difficult for their enemies to find them.

Scallops move through the water in an interesting way. These mollusks "clap" their two shells together. The large muscle that closes the scallop shell is enjoyed as a food by many people. The rest of the body is thrown away.

Oysters are a very good food. Some oysters grow pearls inside their shells. In Japan people make oysters grow pearls by placing single grains of sand inside the oysters' shells. The pearls grow around these grains of sand. After several years, the oysters produce a very valuable crop of pearls.

The Group Called Crustaceans

Another group of animals that live mostly in salt water is called the **crustaceans** (krus TA shənz). Crustaceans are covered with a heavy crust or hard shell. They

Figure 1. The rock cod above, along with haddock and mackerel, belongs to the group called fish.

have gills for breathing underwater. Their bodies have many joints and sections but no backbones. Most of them move by crawling. <u>Lobsters</u>, crabs, and shrimp are all crustaceans.

Lobsters are caught in wooden or metal traps called lobster pots. When alive, lobsters are a greenish-blue color. When they are cooked, their shells turn a bright red.

Many kinds of crabs are found along the seashore. Among these are the blue crab, the rock crab, the hermit crab, and the fiddler crab. Crabs that have shed their hard shells are called soft-shelled crabs. The soft-shelled blue crab is used for food.

Shrimps found in salt water have narrower bodies than crabs. Like lobsters and crabs, shrimps are valued as a food. Every year, large numbers of shrimps and other crustaceans are sold frozen or canned at stores or fresh at fish markets.

Figure 2. The giant clam belongs to the group called mollusks.

Figure 3. The lobster belongs to the group called crustaceans.

Recalling facts

Write the answers to the following questions on the lines provided. You may go back to the selection to find an answer.

Recalling details

1. Name three kinds of fish.

The codfish, mackerel, and haddock are all fish.

Recalling details

2. How does a fish use its tail?

A fish uses its tail to push itself through the water.

Recalling details

3. How does the shape of a fish help it?

The shape of a fish's body helps it move through

water easily.

Recalling details

4. Name three ways in which a fish uses its fins.

A fish uses its fins to balance, to steer, and to brake.

Identifying cause and effect

5. What is one way a fish moves up through the water?

It changes the amount of gas in its air bladder.

Identifying cause and effect

6. Octopuses can squirt a black fluid. What effect does the fluid have on their enemies?

It makes it more difficult for their enemies to find them.

7. What do clams and oysters have that protect them from their enemies?

Their shells protect them.

8. Do mollusks have backbones?

Mollusks do not have backbones.

9. How do people make oysters grow pearls?

They place a single grain of sand inside the shell of a

young oyster.

10. What word can you find in the word *crustacean* that helps you to remember something important about these animals?

The word *crust* tells something important about

these animals.

11. Do crustaceans have backbones?

Crustaceans do not have backbones.

12. Name four kinds of crabs.

The blue crab, rock crab, hermit crab, and fiddler crab

are four kinds of crabs.

13. How is a soft-shelled crab different from a hard-shelled crab?

It is a crab that has shed its hard shell.

14. How do these creatures move?

a. fish

Fish push themselves through the water with their tails.

b. scallops

Scallops clap their two shells together.

c. most crustaceans

Most crustaceans crawl.

15. What does the squid rely on to protect itself?

The squid relies on its ability to swim quickly for

protection.

16. Write the letter of the correct definition on the line in front of each word.

__b__ lobster   a. an animal covered by a hard shell

__a__ scallop   b. an animal with two claws and many legs

INTERPRETING FACTS

Not all questions about a selection are answered directly in the selection. For the following questions, you will have to figure out answers not directly stated in the selection. In questions 1 and 2, circle the letter of the best answer.

1. What would be the effect of more gas in a fish's air bladder?

a. The fish would move up.

b. The fish would move down.

2. Why would an oyster form a pearl around a grain of sand?

a. The sand chills it.

b. The sand irritates it.

c. The sand makes it hungry.

3. Why might a shark sink when it stops swimming?

A shark does not have an air bladder.

Write answers to the questions in the following table. The first one has been started for you.

	What are their bodies like?	What covers their bodies?
Fish	Fish have backbones and skeletons.	Flat scales cover their bodies.
Mollusks	Mollusks have soft, fleshy bodies.	Tough, hard shells cover their bodies.
Crustaceans	Crustaceans have many joints and sections.	Heavy crusts or hard shells cover their bodies.

Oysters, snails, crabs, codfish, clams, lobsters, mackerel, scallops, haddock, and shrimps are all water animals. Write the name of each animal under the heading where it belongs.

Fish	Mollusks	Crustaceans
codfish	oysters	crabs
mackerel	snails	lobsters
haddock	clams	shrimps
	scallops	

▶ Real Life Connections Work with a partner to research the following question: Why are fish an important food for the world?

Lesson 4

Word Problems

Reading a Mathematics Selection

▶ Background Information

You might wonder why you have to learn how to do word problems. You've probably said to yourself, "I'll never ever need to know that!" Sometimes you may even be right.

However, sometimes the skills that you learn at school can be used each and every day of your life. Being able to do word problems is one of these skills that you will definitely need to know.

For example, let's say that your mother gives you $10 to go to the grocery store to buy a quart of milk ($.99), a dozen eggs ($1.29), and a pint of ice cream ($3.49). You may not know it, but this is a word problem.

What if this example were changed around to look like this?

A quart of milk costs $.99. A dozen eggs costs $1.29. A pint of ice cream costs $3.49. Greg's mother asks him to buy these three items at the grocery store. What will Greg's change be if his mother gives him $10? 20?

You see, everyone uses word problems. Doctors use them to diagnose patients. Police officers use them to solve crimes. Scientists use them to learn about ocean animals, plants and rocks. In "Solving Word Problems," you will read about a five-step process for solving word problems.

▶ Skill Focus

There are five steps you should follow in solving a word problem.

First, read the problem. Be sure that you are familiar with all the words, especially the labels that are used with each number. For example, meters, dollars, and kilometers are some commonly used labels. Think about what question is being asked. Try to picture the information that is given. Read the problem again to be sure that you understand it.

Second, decide how to find the answer. It may be helpful to draw a picture of the information that is given. Should you add, subtract, multiply, or divide? Look for key words in the last sentence.

Third, estimate the answer. Use rounded numbers to make an estimate.

Fourth, carry out the plan. Do the arithmetic that will give you the answer.

Fifth, reread the problem. Is the answer logical? How close is it to your estimate?

Be sure that your answer includes the correct label(s). Without the correct labels, your answer is incomplete.

▶ Word Clues

Certain words can give you a clue to how to find the answer in a word problem. For example, words, such as *in all, total, together,* and *sum,* often show that you have to combine groups, or add, to find the answer. Words, such as *difference, more, shorter, longer, less, left, change,* and *part,* often show that you have to compare, or subtract, to find the answer. Look for these word clues in the last sentence of a problem.

▶ Strategy Tip

Scientists use numbers in word problems to learn about ocean animals, plants, and rocks. In this selection, you will learn how to use five steps in solving word problems.

Solving Word Problems

Scientists have learned a great deal about the ocean by measuring and counting the things found there. Knowing how to work with different number facts can help you answer questions. Suppose these two facts about whales are known.

A humpback whale is 18 meters long.

A blue whale is 31 meters long.

One question that can be asked is "What is the difference in length between the blue whale and the humpback whale?" How can the facts be used to answer this question? Follow the five steps below.

READ THE PROBLEM

A humpback whale is 18 meters long. A blue whale is 31 meters long. What is the difference in length between the blue whale and the humpback whale?

Read the problem again. Be sure that you know the label that is used with each number fact. Are there any words that you do not know? If so, look them up to find their meanings. What question does the problem ask? Often the question is asked in the last sentence: *What is the difference in length between the blue whale and the humpback whale?*

DECIDE HOW TO FIND THE ANSWER

It is helpful to make a drawing or diagram.

31 Meters
———————————————— Blue Whale

18 Meters
———————— Humpback Whale

Should the numbers be added, subtracted, multiplied, or divided to answer the question? *They should be subtracted because you are comparing lengths.* The key word *difference* tells you that you need to subtract.

ESTIMATE THE ANSWER

Use rounded numbers to help make an estimate. Round to the nearest ten and then subtract.

$$30 - 20 = 10$$

Your estimate is 10.

CARRY OUT THE PLAN

Do the arithmetic.

$$31 - 18 = 13$$

REREAD THE PROBLEM

After rereading the problem, write the complete answer.

The blue whale is 13 meters longer.

Does the answer make sense? How close is your answer to your estimate? If the answer is not close to your estimate, you should start all over.

These five steps can be used to help solve all word problems.

1. Read the problem.
2. Decide how to find the answer.
3. Estimate the answer.
4. Carry out the plan.
5. Reread the problem.

Read: Mt. Pico is 6,100 meters from the ocean bottom to sea level. Then it rises 2,300 meters above the sea. What is the total height of Mt. Pico?

Decide:

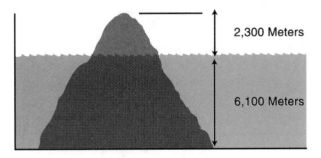

2,300 Meters

6,100 Meters

To find the answer to this problem, you need to combine the two number facts. The word *total* is a clue to use addition. Add the numbers to put the two measurements together.

Estimate: Round each number to the nearest thousand and add.

$$2,000 + 6,000 = 8,000.$$

Carry Out: $2,300 + 6,100 = 8,400$

Reread: After reading the problem, write the complete answer: Mt. Pico is 8,400 meters tall. Does this answer make sense? How close is this answer to your estimate?

RECALLING FACTS

Write the answers to the following questions on the lines provided.

Recalling details

1. What label is used in the example problem on page 23?

The label *meter* is used in the problem.

Recalling details

2. What should you do if your answer is quite different from your estimate?

Check your work and go through the five steps again.

Recognizing sequence of events

3. Write the five steps for solving word problems.

a. Read the problem.

b. Decide how to find the answer.

c. Estimate the answer.

d. Carry out the plan.

e. Reread the problem.

Recalling details

4. What technique does the selection suggest for finding the answer to a word problem.

It suggests making a drawing or diagram.

INTERPRETING FACTS

Not all questions about a selection are answered directly in the selection. For the following questions, you will have to figure out answers not directly stated in the selection. Write the answers to the questions on the lines provided.

Making inferences

1. Why is making an estimate important in problem solving?

It will help you find out whether your answer is correct.

Making inferences

2. If your estimate is 100 and your answer is 104, why might your answer be correct?

The answer might be correct because it is close to the estimate.

Making inferences

3. If your estimate is 4 and your answer is 8, why might your answer be incorrect?

The answer might be incorrect because it is double the estimate.

SKILL FOCUS

Use the five steps to solve these word problems. The first one is started for you. If necessary, draw pictures or diagrams on another sheet of paper to help you with the second step.

1. Read: In May a tuna weighs 181 kilograms. By September it has gained 136 kilograms. What is the tuna's total weight in September?

Decide: Add to put the two weights together.

Estimate: 130 + 180 = 310

Carry Out: 181 + 136 = 317

Reread: The tuna weighs 317 kilograms in September.

2. Read: Most deep sea divers can go only 40 meters under water. Some divers can go 21 meters deeper. How deep can the best divers go?

Decide: Add to find the total depth.

Estimate: 40 + 20 = 60

Carry Out: 40 + 21 = 61

Reread: The best divers can dive 61 meters.

3. Read: A blue marlin swims 48 kilometers per hour. A dolphin swims 40 kilometers per hour. What is the difference between the two speeds?

Decide: Subtract to compare the two speeds.

Estimate: 50 − 40 = 10

Carry Out: 48 − 40 = 8

Reread: There is a difference of 8 kilometers per hour.

4. Read: The highest ocean mountain is 9,693 meters tall. The highest land mountain is 8,840 meters. How much lower is the land mountain?

Decide: Subtract to compare the two heights.

Estimate: 10,000 − 9,000 = 1,000

Carry Out: 9,693 − 8,840 = 853

Reread: The land mountain is 853 meters lower.

5. Read: The Pacific Ocean covers 166,000,000 square kilometers, the Atlantic Ocean covers 87,000,000 square kilometers, and the Indian Ocean covers 73,000,000 square kilometers. What is their area all together?

Decide: Add to find the total area.

Estimate: 170,000,000 + 90,000,000 + 70,000,000 = 330,000,000

Carry Out: 166,000,000 + 87,000,000 + 73,000,000 = 326,000,000

Reread: The total area is 326,000,000 square kilometers.

6. Read: The Java Trench is 7,125 meters deep. The Mariana Trench is 10,924 meters deep. How much deeper is the Mariana Trench?

Decide: Subtract to compare two lengths.

Estimate: 11,000 − 7,000 = 4,000

Carry Out: 10,924 − 7,125 = 3,799

Reread: The Mariana Trench is 3,799 meters deeper.

▶ **Real Life Connections** Estimate the number of students in your school. Then find out the exact number. What's the difference? How close was your estimate?

Lesson 5

Consonants

Say each picture name. Listen to the beginning sound. On the line, write the letter that stands for the **consonant** sound you hear at the beginning of the picture name.

1. t table
2. f fish
3. jar — j
4. m monkey
5. b bed
6. l lamp
7. w wagon
8. s sun
9. k kite
10. n needle
11. r ring
12. z zebra
13. d dog
14. h hand
15. p pencil
16. violin — v

Say each picture name. Listen to the ending sound. On the line, write the letter that stands for the **consonant** sound you hear at the end of the picture name.

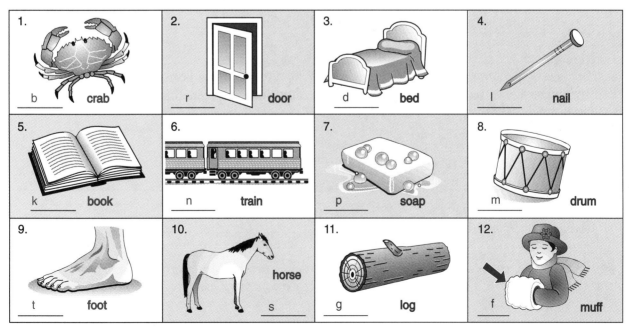

1. b crab
2. r door
3. d bed
4. l nail
5. k book
6. n train
7. p soap
8. m drum
9. t foot
10. s horse
11. g log
12. f muff

26 Lesson 5 *Recognizing consonants*

Main Idea

In many of the paragraphs that you read, one sentence is more important than the others. This sentence states the main idea of the paragraph. The main idea is the idea that is most important in the paragraph. It tells what the paragraph is about. Finding the sentence with the main idea will be helpful to you in all your studies.

Read the following paragraphs. Below each one are three sentences from the paragraph. Underline the sentence that is the main idea of the paragraph.

Oysters

1. The largest supply of oysters in the world is found in Atlantic waters. Oysters live in quiet, shallow waters. They like bays and river mouths. The Atlantic coast has quiet bays. This is why so many more oysters are found along this coast than in any other waters.
   a. Oysters live in quiet, shallow waters.
   b. The Atlantic coast has quiet bays.
   c. <u>The largest supply of oysters in the world is found in Atlantic waters.</u>

2. Oysters like warm waters. They grow best in temperatures between 66°F and 70°F. In southern waters they grow to full size in two to three years. In the north, it takes about four years for them to grow.
   a. <u>Oysters like warm waters.</u>
   b. In southern waters they grow to full size in two to three years.
   c. In the north, it takes about four years for them to grow.

3. Oysters are grown as a crop. People who fish for oysters rent underwater beds from the government. They clean the rubbish from the beds. Then they place seed oysters in the beds. They feed and care for the oysters until the crop is ready to harvest.
   a. They clean the rubbish from the beds.
   b. <u>Oysters are grown as a crop.</u>
   c. Then they place seed oysters in the beds.

4. Fine pearls come from "pearl oysters." Once in a while, a pearl is found in an edible oyster, but it is a low-grade pearl. Pearl oysters grow in the warm waters of southern seas.
   a. Once in a while, a pearl is found in an edible oyster, but it is a low-grade pearl.
   b. Pearl oysters grow in the warm waters of southern seas.
   c. <u>Fine pearls come from "pearl oysters."</u>

5. Oysters have many enemies. Boring snails bore a hole through oysters' shells and eat the oysters. Crabs attack small and weak oysters and kill them. Fish with sharp teeth crush and eat young oysters.
   a. Crabs attack small and weak oysters and kill them.
   b. <u>Oysters have many enemies.</u>
   c. Fish with sharp teeth crush and eat young oysters.

6. Oysters have been valuable to people for hundreds of years. Early people prized beautiful pearls for jewelry. They considered oysters to be an important source of food.
   a. Early people prized beautiful pearls for jewelry.
   b. <u>Oysters have been valuable to people for hundreds of years.</u>
   c. They considered oysters to be an important source of food.

Which sentence in each paragraph has the main idea? The first sentence contains the main idea.

Following Directions

Flight attendants on airplanes show passengers how to use safety and emergency devices, such as seat belts and oxygen masks. If the plane is flying over an ocean or other large body of water, the flight attendants also show how to use life jackets. Cards with directions and drawings for using life jackets are in the seat packets for each passenger to read.

Below are the steps for using a life jacket. Each step is numbered and illustrated. The directions are given in English and Spanish. Study the directions carefully, as well as the illustrations, so that you will understand how a life jacket works.

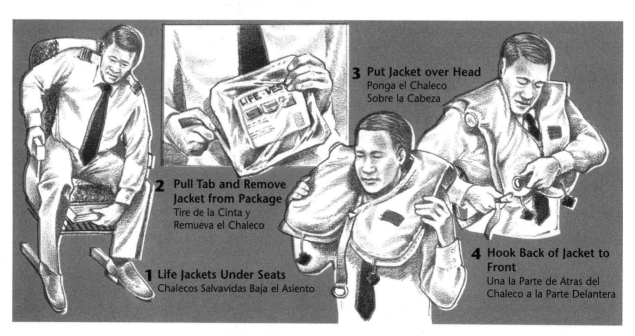

3 Put Jacket over Head
Ponga el Chaleco
Sobre la Cabeza

2 Pull Tab and Remove Jacket from Package
Tire de la Cinta y
Remueva el Chaleco

4 Hook Back of Jacket to Front
Una la Parte de Atras del
Chaleco a la Parte Delantera

1 Life Jackets Under Seats
Chalecos Salvavidas Baja el Asiento

A. Below, in the incorrect order, are the steps to follow when using a life jacket. Write 1 in front of the step to follow first, 2 in front of the step to follow next, and so on.

__3__ Put the life jacket on over your head, keeping the tabs in front.

__5__ Tighten the belt around your waist by pulling the ends of the belt.

__7__ If the life jacket does not fill up with air, blow into the tubes to inflate it.

__1__ Get the package containing the life jacket from under your seat.

__6__ After leaving the plane, pull down on the tabs to inflate the life jacket.

__4__ Buckle both ends of the belt to the center ring on the front of the life jacket.

__8__ If it is dark outside, pull down on the center tab for light.

__2__ Pull the tab to open the package and remove the life jacket.

B. Choose one of the topics listed below and write directions for it. Make sure that your directions are clear enough for other students to follow them.

1. how to play your favorite game

2. how to make your favorite sandwich or dessert

3. how to build a model car, airplane, or boat

4. how to use your personal computer

Students directions should show a clear and logical sequence of steps.

_____

_____

_____

_____

_____

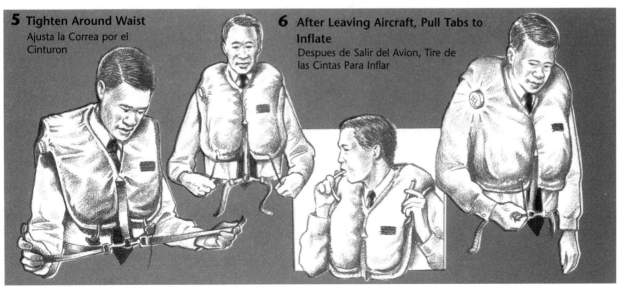

5 Tighten Around Waist
Ajusta la Correa por el Cinturon

6 After Leaving Aircraft, Pull Tabs to Inflate
Despues de Salir del Avion, Tire de las Cintas Para Inflar

7 Oral Inflation Tubes
Tubos Para Inflar con la Boca

8 If Dark, Pull Center Tab to Activate Light
Si esta Obscura, Tire de la Cinta del Centro Para Activar la Linterna

Consonant Blends

Many words begin with the sound of just one consonant. Some words have two consonants at the beginning. If you hear the consonant sounds that both letters stand for, the two letters are called a **consonant blend**. The following are called *r* blends.

br   cr   dr   fr   gr   pr   tr

Say each picture name. Listen to the beginning sounds. On the line, write the blend listed above that stands for the consonant sounds that you hear at the beginning of the picture name.

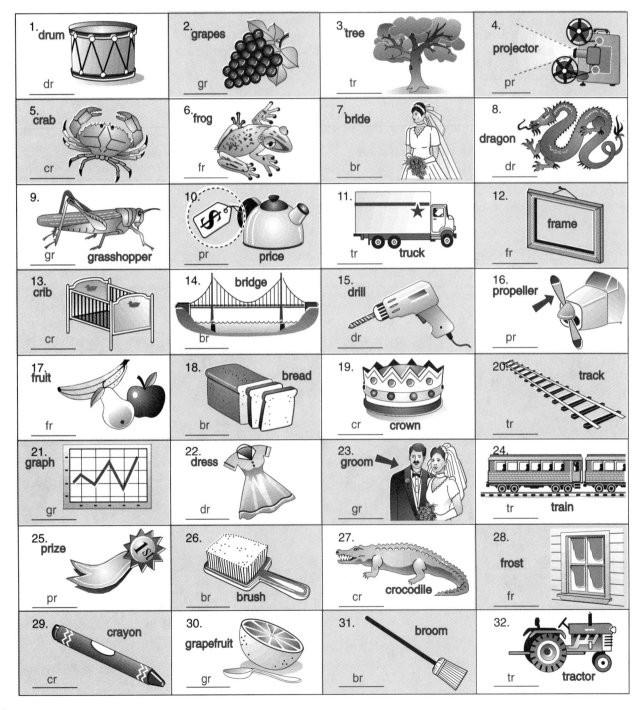

1. drum — dr
2. grapes — gr
3. tree — tr
4. projector — pr
5. crab — cr
6. frog — fr
7. bride — br
8. dragon — dr
9. grasshopper — gr
10. price — pr
11. truck — tr
12. frame — fr
13. crib — cr
14. bridge — br
15. drill — dr
16. propeller — pr
17. fruit — fr
18. bread — br
19. crown — cr
20. track — tr
21. graph — gr
22. dress — dr
23. groom — gr
24. train — tr
25. prize — pr
26. brush — br
27. crocodile — cr
28. frost — fr
29. crayon — cr
30. grapefruit — gr
31. broom — br
32. tractor — tr

Consonant Blends

A **consonant blend** is two or more consonant letters that blend together in such a way that the consonant sound each stands for is heard. Here are some *l* blends.

bl   cl   fl   gl   pl   sl

Say each picture name. Listen to the beginning sounds. On the line, write the blend listed above that stands for the consonant sounds that you hear at the beginning of the picture name.

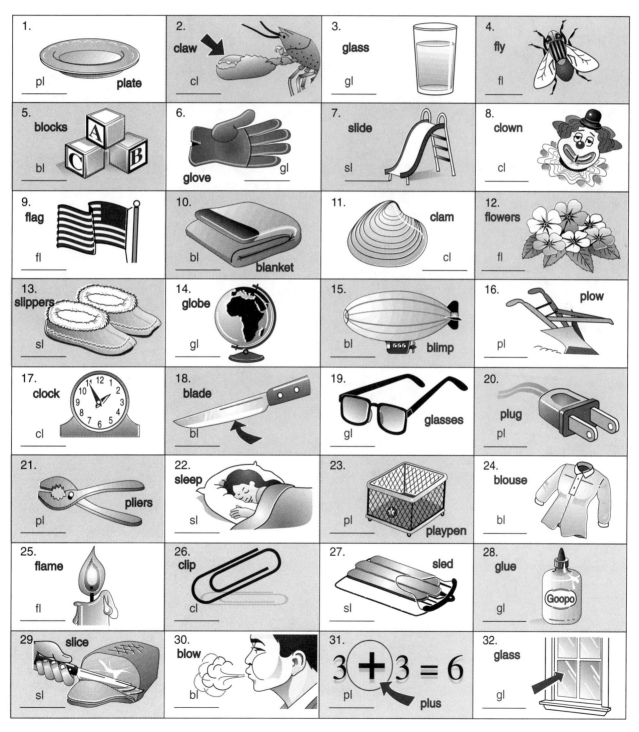

1. pl _____ **plate**

2. **claw** cl _____

3. **glass** gl _____

4. **fly** fl _____

5. **blocks** bl _____

6. gl _____ **glove**

7. **slide** sl _____

8. **clown** cl _____

9. **flag** fl _____

10. bl _____ **blanket**

11. **clam** cl _____

12. **flowers** fl _____

13. **slippers** sl _____

14. **globe** gl _____

15. bl _____ **blimp**

16. **plow** pl _____

17. **clock** cl _____

18. **blade** bl _____

19. gl _____ **glasses**

20. **plug** pl _____

21. **pliers** pl _____

22. **sleep** sl _____

23. pl _____ **playpen**

24. **blouse** bl _____

25. **flame** fl _____

26. **clip** cl _____

27. **sled** sl _____

28. **glue** gl _____

29. **slice** sl _____

30. **blow** bl _____

31. pl _____ **plus**

32. **glass** gl _____

Consonant Blends

Some words have two consonants at the beginning of them. If you hear the sounds that both of these letters stand for, the two letters are called a **consonant blend**. Here are some *s* blends.

sc   sm   sn   sp   st   sw

Say each picture name. Listen to the beginning sounds. On the line, write the blend listed above that stands for the consonant sounds that you hear at the beginning of the picture name.

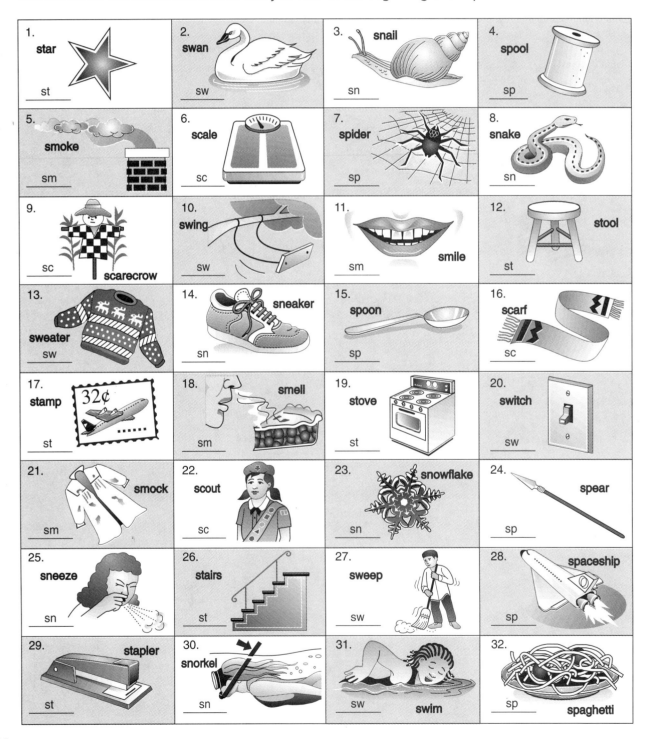

1. star — st	2. swan — sw	3. snail — sn	4. spool — sp
5. smoke — sm	6. scale — sc	7. spider — sp	8. snake — sn
9. scarecrow — sc	10. swing — sw	11. smile — sm	12. stool — st
13. sweater — sw	14. sneaker — sn	15. spoon — sp	16. scarf — sc
17. stamp — st	18. smell — sm	19. stove — st	20. switch — sw
21. smock — sm	22. scout — sc	23. snowflake — sn	24. spear — sp
25. sneeze — sn	26. stairs — st	27. sweep — sw	28. spaceship — sp
29. stapler — st	30. snorkel — sn	31. swim — sw	32. spaghetti — sp

Lesson 11

Long and Short Vowel Sounds

Say the word *apple*. Listen to its beginning sound. The sound you hear at the beginning of the word *apple* is called the short sound of *a*. Other **short vowel sounds** are *e* as in *egg, i* as in *it, o* as in *on*, and *u* as in *umbrella*. Most dictionaries do not mark short vowel sounds.

Long vowel sounds give the name of the vowel, as *a* in *age, e* in *eagle, i* in *ice, o* in *open*, and *u* in *unit*. Most dictionaries mark long vowel sounds with a macron (‾) above the vowel letter. Example: āge.

Words Ending in *e*

Look at each picture. Read the words. Write the word that names the picture.

pin or pine?
pine

rob or robe?
robe

cub or cube?
cube

can or cane?
cane

Write a one-word answer to each question in the headings. Then complete Guide 1.

	Is the first vowel sound long or short?	*Is there an* e *at the end of the word?*	*Is the* e *silent or sounded?*
1. page	long	yes	silent
2. ice	long	yes	silent
3. globe	long	yes	silent

Guide 1: When a word contains two vowels, one of which is final ___e___, the first vowel is usually ___long___, and the final *e* is ___silent___.

Words That Do Not End in *e*

Write a one-word answer to each question in the headings. Then complete Guide 2.

	Is the first vowel sound long or short?	*Is there a vowel at the end of the word?*
1. sand	short	no
2. bend	short	no
3. rock	short	no

Guide 2: When a word contains only one vowel, and that vowel is not at the end of the word, the ___vowel___ is usually ___short___.

Long and Short Vowel Sounds

The two guides that you have learned to help you decide whether the vowel sound in a one-syllable word is long or short are given below with a word missing in each one. Write a word on the line to complete each guide.

Guide 1: When a word contains two vowels, one of which is final *e*, the first vowel is usually ———— long ————, and the final *e* is silent.

Guide 2: When a word contains only one vowel, and that vowel is not at the end of the word, the vowel is usually ———— short ————.

Decide how to pronounce each word below. On the line, write the number of the guide that you used to make your decision. Mark each long vowel with a macron (–). Do not mark the short vowels.

	Guide No.		Guide No.		Guide No.
1. māke	1	15. shīne	1	29. gāme	1
2. leg	2	16. clam	2	30. man	2
3. smīle	1	17. plāce	1	31. bīte	1
4. grin	2	18. mīle	1	32. lock	2
5. hot	2	19. hit	2	33. flāme	1
6. mūle	1	20. rāke	1	34. slip	2
7. land	2	21. mīce	1	35. grand	2
8. deck	2	22. pot	2	36. lāte	1
9. ship	2	23. cūbe	1	37. stōve	1
10. hill	2	24. thēse	1	38. set	2
11. tīme	1	25. brīde	1	39. rūle	1
12. hōse	1	26. sun	2	40. crab	2
13. flag	2	27. rōpe	1		
14. shut	2	28. bed	2		

Setting

Reading a Literature Selection

▶ **Background Information**

Have you ever heard of a hang glider? Do you know what it does? A hang glider is a large sail, like a giant kite. The sail has a metal bar connected to it. The wind lifts the sail into the air, and the bar drops down below. A person is held up by a harness or belt attached to the sail. The "pilot" can fly the hang glider by moving the bar. In this story, Angela wants to take a ride on a hang glider.

▶ **Skill Focus**

Setting is the place and time of the events in a story. Setting tells where and when the events occur. Events can happen in any place and at any time. A story can take place on the streets of a city, in the fields of a farm, or high in the mountains. A story can take place in the present, a hundred years ago, or a hundred years from now. Whatever the setting, it must fit the events in the story.

In some stories, the setting is crucial to the plot. In others, the setting creates an atmosphere, or feeling.

A writer can describe the setting at the beginning of a story or reveal it slowly as the plot develops. As you read, look for words that tell about the setting. Try to picture the place and time of the story.

The following questions will help you understand setting. Ask yourself questions such as the following as you read a story.

1. Where does the story take place?
2. When does it take place?
3. Does the setting fit the events in the story?
4. Why does the setting fit?

▶ **Word Clues**

The words *like* or *as* can signal a context clue. The words provide a comparison that will help you understand the new word or words. Notice the clue to the meaning of the word *dunes* in the following sentence.

The road ended in sandy white <u>dunes</u> that looked like snowdrifts above the beach.

If you do not know the meaning of the word *dunes*, the phrase *like snowdrifts* can help you. The dunes are compared to snowdrifts using the word *like*. From reading the sentence, you can picture dunes as high piles of white sand that look something like snowdrifts.

Use **comparison** context clues to find the meaning of the three underlined words in the selection.

▶ **Strategy Tip**

Setting is one of the most important elements of a story. When you read a literature selection, it is important that you understand the story's setting.

As you read "Angela's First Flight," think about whether Angela could hang glide if she lived somewhere else or if she lived many years ago. What are some of the features of the setting that are necessary for hang gliding?

Angela's First Flight

Angela Holland slammed the screen door. "That Paul Daniel!" she shouted. "I can't stand that creep!"

Her mother stood by the kitchen counter. She was slicing bread for lunch. She glanced at Angela.

"Now what happened?" she asked.

Angela flopped down on a kitchen chair.

"He won't let me try his hang glider." Angela rolled her eyes. "You'd think I never had a hang gliding lesson."

"But Angela, you've only had two lessons. You've never flown more than a few feet off the ground."

"But I have my own helmet and gloves. Besides, Paul could teach me. He's been hang gliding for a long time now. And he's had plenty of lessons."

Her mother set the bread and a jar of peanut butter on the table. As Angela sliced a banana for her peanut butter sandwich, her mother listened to her and shook her head.

"Hang gliding is really great, Mom! Once you catch the wind, you glide along on waves of air just like a bird." Angela took a big bite of her sandwich.

When Angela finished her sandwich, she jumped up from the chair, grabbed her helmet and gloves, and headed for the door.

"Thanks for lunch, Mom," she said.

"Where are you going?" her mother asked. "I want you back here by 4:00 to help weed the garden."

"Okay, I'll be back to help." Angela opened the screen door. "I'm going to ride down to the beach."

"Don't do anything foolish, Angela."

As the screen door clapped shut behind her, Angela thought, "There must be some way to get a ride on that glider."

Angela climbed on her bicycle and rode for ten minutes to the beach. All the way she tried to think of ways to get Paul to let her use his glider.

The road ended in sandy white dunes that looked like snowdrifts above the beach. With her equipment in hand, Angela walked to the edge of the dunes. The land dropped off in a steep slope to the beach below. On most days, the wind came in off the ocean. Blowing across the beach, it hit the sandy cliff and rose higher. The rising air was just right for hang gliding.

"Oh no! Are you back?" said Paul. He was standing a little way down the slope.

Angela said nothing as she put on her helmet and gloves. She crossed her legs and sank down on the sand.

The bright blue and green glider lay on the sand next to Paul. He put on his safety helmet. Paul then put on his harness and fastened it to the frame of the glider. Once securely hooked to the glider, Paul lifted it so that the harness straps were tight and tugging at his body. He was now attached to the glider. When the glider took off, he would hang in the air just behind the guide bar.

Paul grabbed the bar and then swung the big wing up over his head and pointed it down the slope. As fast as he could go, Paul ran down the slope, trying all the while to maintain his balance. He was building speed and taking longer and longer strides.

Angela held her breath. The sail filled with air. Within seconds Paul's feet were off the ground. He was lifted higher as the wind caught the hang glider. And then—he sailed

along the slope, keeping the glider pointed into the wind and the control bar in the flying position.

Angela cheered and said to herself, "I just have to do it."

Suddenly the nose of the sail pointed up. The back dipped low. The glider had "stalled." Paul and the glider dropped down, bouncing on the sand. He unhooked his harness and took off his helmet. Pulling the glider behind him, Paul <u>trudged</u> up the slope like a tired pack mule.

"What happened?" Angela called out, grinning. "Haven't you learned to fly yet?"

The sun was beating down. Paul was hot, and he was tired from so much gliding. He didn't like people watching him. He had good flights while Angela was away at lunch.

Like an angry lion, Paul <u>glared</u> at Angela. "I bet you couldn't even lift it."

"What!" Angela ground her teeth.

Paul dragged himself up the steep slope. The glider came to a stop. Paul took off his harness and sat down in the sand.

"Bet I can," Angela yelled, jumping up. She grabbed the harness and slipped it on. Then she ran down to the glider and hooked the harness to the frame as her instructor had

shown her. She lifted the glider off the ground. With the control bar in the flying position, Angela began running down the slope.

Paul shouted, but Angela didn't hear what he said. The glider wasn't heavy, but it tipped to one side. She lost her footing and tumbled to the ground. The glider dug into the sand and tipped over.

Angela's mouth was full of sand. Sand was in her eyes and hair, too. She heard Paul laughing from up the slope. He cupped his hands and shouted, "How's it taste?"

Angela jumped up, brushing the sand from her face. She grabbed the glider's bar.

"Hey, you had a chance! Beat it!" shouted Paul. But Angela had the glider over her head and was running down the slope again. The wind rushed past her face. The ocean roared in her ears. She remembered what her instructor had said: "Don't think about flying. Think about running to the bottom of the hill."

Paul's voice came after her. "Tear that sail and you'll pay for it!"

Angela raced down the slope. She was going fast. Each step got longer and longer. Her legs could barely keep up. She started to stumble again. Then she felt a strong tug on the handle. Her feet came off the ground. She was in the air!

The world seemed to fall away. Angela floated slowly along the face of the cliff. The ocean's roar seemed far off. A seagull drifted by right next to her.

Angela leaned toward the ocean side. The wing tipped that way and began a slow, silent turn over the beach.

Angela tried to remember how to land. But it was too late.

Angela could hardly breathe. Her heart pounded with excitement. She loved this feeling of freedom. And flying was so easy.

The glider turned back toward the cliff. Suddenly, Angela was afraid. She had never landed from such a height. Her instructor had warned about wind currents and rotors. Angela felt her fear turning to panic.

The glider was heading straight for the sandy cliff. Angela tried to remember how to land. But it was too late. The wing tip dug into the sand with a <u>jolt</u> as sudden as a flash of lightning. Angela hit the sand hard before coming to a stop.

Angela shook her head and opened her eyes. Her side hurt. Slowly, she looked around. She saw Paul running down the slope toward her and his glider. He glared at Angela and then turned to check the sail.

"You're lucky, Angela," said Paul. "Everything was fine until you landed. You need more lessons. Maybe I can give you some tips."

Paul started to explain to Angela what she did wrong. "You must remember this rule: If you try to keep the hang glider on the ground as you run down the hill, you will have a better takeoff. If you try to keep the hang glider in the air as you land, you will have a good landing."

Angela listened to Paul attentively. He was absolutely right about takeoffs and landings. She knew that once she finished her lessons, Paul would give her another try. She realized now how foolish she had been to take Paul's glider. She was lucky that she hadn't been seriously hurt. Next time, though, her landing would be perfect.

RECALLING FACTS

Recalling details

1. What is a hang glider?
A hang glider is a large sail with a metal bar connected

to it.

Recalling details

2. How does it fly?
The wind lifts the sail into the air, and the bar drops

down. By holding on to the bar, a person can fly the

hang glider.

Recalling details

3. How many hang gliding lessons has Angela had?
She has had only two lessons.

Recalling details

4. What equipment must a hang glider pilot have?
A helmet, gloves, and harness are all items that a hang

glider pilot must have.

Recalling details

5. Why is the beach a good place for hang gliding?
At the beach, the air blows off the ocean, hits the steep

cliffs, and rises. When the glider catches the wind, it

quickly lifts off the ground and "glides."

Recalling details

6. What drifts right by Angela on her flight?
A seagull flies past Angela during her flight.

Comparing and contrasting

7. Was Angela's second attempt to hang glide more or less successful than her first? Explain.
Her second attempt was more successful. Angela did

fly, even if only for a short while. The glider took off,

and Angela was flying. However, the glider crashed,

and Angela hit the sand again.

Recalling details

8. What must Angela do before Paul will let her have another ride on his glider?
Angela must finish taking her flying lessons.

Using context clues

9. Complete each sentence with the correct word from below.

glared   jolt   trudged

a. Robert had trouble pulling the sled as he _____trudged_____ through the snow.

b. The _____jolt_____ of the car hitting a tree threw the driver forward in his seat.

c. Lisa _____glared_____ at her brother when he used her computer without permission.

INTERPRETING FACTS

Making inferences

1. How does Mrs. Holland feel about Angela's wanting to hang glide?
She's very concerned about Angela's wanting to fly because she knows that Angela hasn't finished her flying lessons.

Drawing conclusions

2. Do you think Paul is a selfish person? Explain.
Yes. He won't share his glider with anyone. No. He's cautious and concerned about friends using his glider when they

don't know how to control it.

Making inferences

3. How does Angela feel about her first flight with a hang glider?
She loves the feeling of freedom it gave her; she can't wait to try it again.

Drawing conclusions

4. How could hang gliding be dangerous?

It could be dangerous if the person flying wasn't trained or if he or she didn't have the right equipment.

Drawing conclusions

5. Do you think that Angela would try new sports as she discovered them? Explain.

Yes. Angela seems adventurous and willing to try almost anything.

Identifying point of view

6. a. Describe what you would see if you were flying the hang glider over the beach.

One would see the beach and ocean below, as well as seagulls and other birds. One might also see ships at

sea and people on the beach.

b. Would a person on the ground watching you see the same things? Explain.

No. The person on the ground could not look down on the beach and ocean and could not see ships far out

at sea.

Drawing conclusions

7. Could Angela have gone hang gliding if she lived in an inland city? Explain.

No. Hang gliding needs high, open places where one can run until the wind lifts the sail.

SKILL FOCUS

Below are the questions you were asked to think about as you read the story. Write your answers on the lines provided.

1. Where does the story take place?

The story takes place near and at the beach.

2. When does it take place?

The story takes place probably during summer, in the afternoon, and in the present.

3. Does the setting fit the events in the story?

Yes, the setting fits the events in the story.

4. Why does the setting fit?

Hang gliding needs a high, open place (usually near a beach where there are mountains or cliffs) where one can run

until the wind lifts the sail.

5. Could you hang glide where you live? Why? Why not?

Answers will vary. Students should consider wind and high, open places as essential to hang gliding.

▶ **Real Life Connections** Would you like to try hang gliding? Why or why not?

Reading a Map

Reading a Social Studies Selection

▶ Background Information

For years, Russia and the United States have competed with one another to be the first country in space and the first country to land on the moon. The competition began when Russia launched its first unmanned satellite, *Sputnik I*, meaning *traveler*, into space on October 4, 1957.

In 1961, a Russian cosmonaut and an American astronaut were the first people to travel in space. Yuri Gagarin was the first to go into orbit around Earth. Alan Shepard's flight was about a month later. Since that time, there have been many historic space flights. In 1969, American astronaut Neil A. Armstrong climbed out of Apollo II to the moon's surface. He was the first human to set foot on the moon. In 1975, the United States and Russia cooperated on their first joint mission—an Apollo spacecraft docked with a Soyuz craft in space. During the *Atlantis-Mir* mission in 1995, Americans and Russians soared together in space again.

▶ Skill Focus

When reading about different parts of the world, you may want to use a globe to see where these places are located. A globe, however, may not be nearby. That is why some of your textbooks include **maps**. A map can show you the whole world at one time or only a part of the world.

There are many important things to look for on a map. You should first look at the **title** of the map or the caption under the map. The caption or title tells what the map shows. Another important feature is the **compass**, which shows the directions north, south, east, and west. A compass tells you the direction from one place on the map to another.

On a map of the world, also be sure to look for the **equator**. The equator is an imaginary circle around the earth that divides the world into the Northern Hemisphere and the Southern Hemisphere.

You can often find other information on maps, such as the names of cities, countries, bodies of water, and so on. Together, the map and the selection give you more information than either one could provide alone.

▶ Word Clues

Read the sentences below. Look for the context clues that explain the underlined word.

> Then they joined in a celebration and exchanged offerings. These gifts included flowers, fruit, and chocolates from *Atlantis*. *Mir* offered the traditional Russian gifts of bread and salt.

If you do not know the meaning of the word *offerings* in the first sentence, read the next sentence. The words *these gifts* explain the meaning of *offerings*.

Use **definition** context clues to find the meaning of the three underlined words in the selection.

▶ Strategy Tip

When you read a social studies selection, such as "The *Atlantis-Mir* Mission," it is important to look at the maps. Look at the map on page 43. Read the title and the compass. Also locate the equator.

The *Atlantis-Mir* Mission

Robert Gibson had his hand on a <u>joystick</u>, a control stick in the craft. His eyes were on a television screen. Everything had to go just right. Even a few inches made a difference.

Gibson was 245 miles above Earth. He was commander of the American space shuttle *Atlantis*. And his spacecraft was moving toward the Russian space station *Mir*. If all went well, the two orbiting spacecrafts would soon dock in space. When spacecrafts <u>dock</u>, they join in space. But if *Atlantis* bumped *Mir* too hard, both of the spaceships and the people aboard could be in danger.

Gibson gently moved *Atlantis* into position. *Atlantis* had a camera in the middle of its docking fixture. This technology allowed Gibson to watch what was happening on a TV screen. *Atlantis* floated toward *Mir*, foot by foot, inch by inch. Latches and hooks locked into place. And an American spaceship and a Russian one flew in space together.

Gibson had brought the two crafts together within two seconds of the planned time. Linked together, they became the largest structure people had ever placed in orbit. Millions watched the docking on live television. Both spacecrafts were beaming pictures back to Earth. Pictures from *Mir* showed *Atlantis* astronauts waving through overhead windows as the spaceships moved closer together.

Atlantis had left Cape Canaveral, Florida, on June 27, 1995. About two days later, the successful docking took place. The spaceships docked over central Russia, near the Russian and Mongolian border.

Mir had been in orbit since 1986, but the crew of the space station had been <u>rotated</u>. When crews are rotated, a spaceship brings a new crew to the craft and returns the old crew to Earth.

Russian–American Teams

Americans and Russians had begun working together even before the docking took place. *Atlantis* and *Mir* each carried American astronauts and Russian cosmonauts.

The American aboard *Mir* was Dr. Norman Thagard. After training in Russia, he had spent three months on *Mir* before the docking with *Atlantis*. The Russians aboard *Mir* were Commander Vladimir Dezhurov and Gennady Strekalov.

In addition to Commander Gibson, *Atlantis* carried four other Americans, two women and two men. They were Ellen Baker, Bonnie Durbar, Charles Precourt, and Greg Harbaugh. The Russians on *Atlantis* were Anatoly Solovyev and Nikolai Budarin.

Anniversary in Space

After docking, crew members spent the first two hours checking for leaks. Then Gibson opened a hatch to meet Commander Dezhurov. The Russian grabbed Gibson's hand as he greeted him joyfully.

The crews could now go back and forth in a passageway between the two crafts. Because there is no gravity in space, people are weightless. The crews could simply float as they moved about the spacecrafts. The men gathered in the *Mir* to take pictures. Then they celebrated their joint mission and exchanged offerings. These gifts included flowers, fruit, and chocolates from *Atlantis*. *Mir* offered the traditional Russian gifts of bread and salt.

This celebration was not just for the successful docking. It was also an anniversary. Twenty years before, in 1975, Americans and Russians docked in space for the first time. On that mission, the U.S. Apollo docked with the USSR Soyuz. The two crews worked together for two days.

Now, at the second docking in space, Gibson spoke in Russian. "Today we're reaffirming our friendship after the flight of *Apollo-Soyuz*," he said. "Together we will build a future based on cooperation, mutual trust and friendship."

> *Atlantis* and Mir *each carried American astronauts and Russian cosmonauts.*

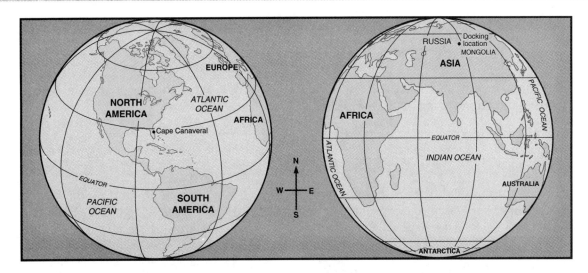

Working Together in Space

After the celebrations, the crews got to work. First, they carried food and water from the *Atlantis* to the *Mir* to replace the *Mir's* supplies. Then they began the experiments that they would do during their five days together.

The shuttle's Spacelab module held a laboratory about the size of a bus. This lab was used for many tests to study how space flight affects the body. All ten people were tested, especially those on the *Mir*. Because they had been in orbit several months, both crews were tested for the long-term effects of space flight.

The crews also hoped they would learn information that would help people on Earth. For example, many people suffer from a bone condition called osteoporosis (OSS tee o pə RO səs). People with this condition lose bone mass. The bones then break very easily. While astronauts are in space, where there is no gravity, they lose bone mass. Because calcium builds bones, tests were done on how the body uses calcium while weightless. Scientists would be able to use the information from the tests as they studied bone conditions on Earth.

The *Atlantis-Mir* mission was an important first step in a long-term plan. The United States and Russia will continue to work together on missions in space. *Mir* remained in orbit, and several more *Atlantis-Mir* dockings are planned. There are also plans for a new space station, with other countries joining the effort.

Undocking

After five days in space, the two spaceships were ready to undock. Before separating, they exchanged some crew members. The crew on *Mir*, including Dr. Thagard, came aboard the *Atlantis*. The two Russians on *Atlantis* boarded the *Mir*. They would continue in orbit until they were replaced by another crew.

The astronauts and cosmonauts were almost tearful as they said good-bye. Charles Precourt said, "I feel very small . . . when I look back at Earth through the window, I see a giant planet. Together we can do anything. . . . We can even fly to Mars."

Return to Earth

After the undocking, *Atlantis* returned to Cape Canaveral. The eight people landed safely on July 7, 1995. Dr. Thagard had been in space for nearly four months. He had set a new record for the longest space flight for an American. President Clinton called from the White House to congratulate him.

NASA doctors expected Dr. Thagard to be wobbly after his long flight. But they were surprised when he walked from the space shuttle. The doctors tested Dr. Thagard and his two crewmates from *Mir* for nearly a month. The tests, along with those done in space, will help them study the effects of long space flights.

President Clinton also spoke with Commander Gibson. "This is truly the beginning of a new era of cooperation in space between the United States and Russia," President Clinton said. "We're doing things together, and I think what you and your team and . . . the Russians did together symbolize that more than anything that I could ever say."

Along with congratulations, one astronaut received a special treat. Dr. Thagard had been promised ice cream. And that is what he got after his long journey into space.

Recalling details

1. Tell the names of the American space shuttle and the Russian space station.

The American space shuttle was the *Atlantis*.

The Russian space station was the *Mir*.

Recalling details

2. How many miles above Earth were the spaceships?

The spaceships were 245 miles above Earth.

Recalling details

3. How could Commander Gibson watch what was happening as he prepared for docking?

The *Atlantis* had a camera in the middle of its docking

fixture. This technology allowed him to watch what was

happening on a TV screen.

Recalling details

4. Was this the first time Americans and Russians had docked in space? Explain.

No; the first time was twenty years before, in 1975.

Identifying cause and effect

5. What caused the crews to float in space?

They floated because there is no gravity in space; the

absence of gravity made them weightless.

Recalling details

6. What was Spacelab used for?

It was used to study how space flight affects the body.

Recalling details

7. Why were the people on the *Mir* tested?

They had been in orbit several months; they were

tested for the long-term effects of space flight.

Recalling details

8. Tests were done on how the body uses calcium while weightless. How could scientists use these tests to help people on Earth?

Scientists would be able to use the information from

the tests to study bone conditions on Earth.

Recognizing sequence of events

9. Tell, in order, the main events that occurred after the crews had spent five days in space.

Crew members were exchanged; undocking took place;

Mir remained in orbit; *Atlantis* returned to Cape

Canaveral.

Using context clues

10. Write the letter of the correct meaning in front of each word.

_c_ joy stick   **a.** join

_a_ dock   **b.** brought something new to replace something else

_b_ rotated   **c.** control stick

Making inferences

1. Think about the astronauts and cosmonauts who worked together in space. What qualities did they need to have?

They needed to be skilled, efficient, cooperative, adventurous, courageous, and self-disciplined.

Making inferences

2. How do you think the astronauts and cosmonauts felt as they prepared to undock?

They felt sad to say good-bye to one another; they were happy with the success of the mission; they looked forward

to more cooperative efforts; they looked forward to returning home to relatives and to the comforts on Earth.

3. When Dr. Thagard walked from the shuttle at Cape Canaveral, he was not wobbly as doctors had expected. What conclusions can you draw about the effect of several months in space on the astronaut?

Several months in space had not harmed the astronaut in any noticeable way; he returned in better condition than

doctors expected.

S KILL   FOCUS

Use the maps of the world on page 43 to answer these questions. If necessary, look back at the selection.

1. Find the point on the map from which *Atlantis* started. What is the name of this place?

Atlantis began its mission from Cape Canaveral.

2. On what continent is this place located?

Cape Canaveral is located in North America.

3. What ocean is nearby?

The Atlantic Ocean is nearby.

4. *Atlantis* and *Mir* docked in space above a place shown on the map. What is the name of this place?

The name of this place is Russia.

5. On what continent is this place located?

Russia is located on the continent of Asia.

6. What ocean is to the east of this continent?

The Pacific Ocean is located to the east of the Asian continent.

7. What continent is to the southwest?

Africa is located to the southwest of Asia.

8. What continent is to the southeast?

Australia is located to the southeast of Asia.

9. Did the spaceships dock north or south of the equator?

The spaceships docked north of the equator.

10. Use the maps to plan a docking in space. Choose a place over which the spaceships will dock. Tell the name of the continent and its location in relation to oceans, other continents, and the equator.

Answers will vary.

▶ **Real Life Connections** Name another endeavor in which you feel the Americans and the Russians could work together today. Give reasons for your response.

Diagrams

Reading a Science Selection

▶ Background Information

Whoosh! The hot-air balloon rises. You float silently above the earth. How does the balloon work? How can hot air keep hundreds of pounds up in the sky? This selection uses both words and diagrams to show how balloons work.

As you read "Balloons and Airships," look carefully at the diagrams. Remember to go back and forth between the paragraphs and the diagrams.

▶ Skill Focus

Drawings, or **diagrams**, are often used in textbooks to show what the words in a selection explain. Diagrams are usually called Figure 1, Figure 2, and so on. When reading a selection with diagrams, read the text first. Then look at the diagram that shows what the words explain.

When you read diagrams, be sure to read the **labels.** Labels name the parts of the diagram. Often a **caption** will appear with a diagram. Read it before you study the diagram. It will often be helpful to read the explanation in the selection again. Going back and forth from the words in the selection to the diagram will help you to understand the ideas.

When you read a selection that has diagrams, use the following steps.

1. Read the paragraph before each diagram. Then study the diagram and read the caption that goes with it. If there are labels, read them while studying the diagram. The paragraph below the diagram may explain what is pictured. Read that paragraph, too.

2. Slowly read the rest of the paragraphs. Look back at the diagrams when you think they will help you.

3. After you have finished reading and studying the diagrams, look away from the selection. Try to picture what you have read and the details in the diagrams. If you cannot do this, read the paragraphs and study the diagrams again.

4. Continue to work in this way until you understand all the ideas in the selection.

▶ Word Clues

Read the sentence below. Look for context clues that explain the underlined word.

> Every material has a certain density, or thickness of matter.

If you do not know the meaning of the word *density*, the phrase *thickness of matter* can help you. Density is thickness of matter. The phrase *thickness of matter* is an appositive phrase. An appositive phrase explains a word coming before it and is set off from the word by commas or dashes and the word *or*.

Use **appositive phrases** to find the meaning of the three underlined words in the selection.

▶ Strategy Tip

When reading a science selection it is particulary helpful to look carefully at the diagrams. As you read "Balloons and Airships," remember to go back and forth between the paragraphs and the diagrams.

BALLOONS AND AIRSHIPS

How Do Things Float?

A balloon is known as a "lighter-than-air craft." How can this be? We know that air is lighter than almost anything. A balloon—cloth, rope, wood, steel, and other things—must be heavier! A balloon can't really be "lighter" than air. So, what keeps it up?

Every material has a certain density, or thickness of matter. This term means that the basic building blocks—the molecules—can be closer together or farther apart. Air is not very dense. Rocks and steel are quite dense.

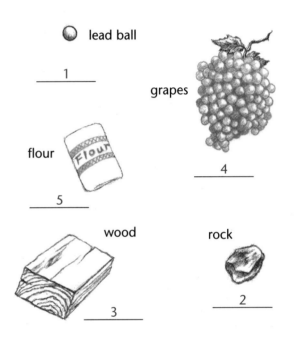

Figure 1. This diagram shows various materials and how much space a kilogram of each material will take up.

Imagine a pound of air and a pound of rocks. Which one would be bigger? In Figure 1, you can see pictures of several items. They all weigh the same. Which is the biggest? Which is the smallest? Which is the most dense? Which is the least dense?

If you heat up air, it becomes less dense. The molecules move around a lot more when the air is hot. The moving molecules take up more space. If you fill a balloon with hot air, the air in the balloon is less dense than the air outside the balloon. What happens? Figure 2 shows that denser air around the balloon

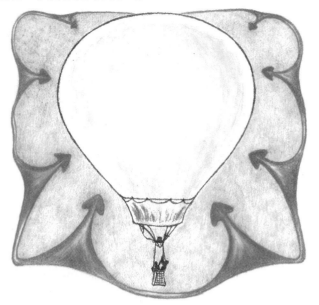

Figure 2. The air around the balloon is denser. It tries to move into the space that the balloon takes up. The balloon is forced upward because it is lighter than the amount of air that would fill the same space.

pushes in against it and forces it upward. If the upward force is more than the weight of the balloon and the air inside it, the balloon will float upward.

How Does a Hot-Air Balloon Work?

A hot-air balloon has several parts, as you can see in Figure 3. The **bag** is made of strong cloth like nylon. The cloth is covered with rubber to keep it from leaking. A net of ropes on the outside of the bag helps to keep its shape

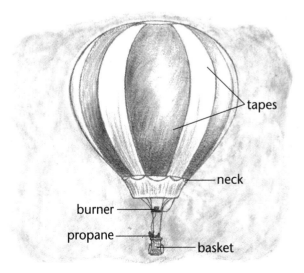

Figure 3. Parts of a hot-air balloon.

and supports the **basket** or **gondola** below. The bottom of the balloon is called the **neck**. Hanging inside the neck is a propane burner for heating the air.

A balloonist makes the balloon rise by heating the air at the neck. The hot air is less dense and rises into the bag. As hot air enters the bag, the colder air inside is forced out of the neck. When the bag has expanded enough, it begins to float. Soon the balloon, with its burner, basket, and passengers, rises into the air. The balloonist can then shut off the burner.

✔ As the air in the balloon begins to cool, the air in it takes up less space. The air around the balloon has less to push on, so the balloon begins to come down. <u>The balloonist can control the rising and sinking of the balloon very precisely by running the burner and shutting it off.</u> Short bursts of hot air can keep the balloon at one level. Longer bursts can make it rise.

How Does a Gas Balloon Work?

Some gases are much less dense than air. <u>Helium</u>—or a relatively expensive gas—is much less dense than air. It is suitable for use in balloons. In Figure 4, you can see a helium balloon. It looks a lot like the hot-air balloon. What parts are the same? What parts are different? The balloonist cannot control the temperature of the gas. How does the balloon go up and down?

Once the helium gas is pumped into the bag, the balloon begins to rise. <u>Ballast</u>, or weights that control the height of the balloon,

hang around the outside of the basket to weigh it down. The balloonist dumps some of the sand to make the balloon rise. When the balloon is at the right height, the balloonist can open a **valve** at the top of the bag to spill out some of the gas. The open valve makes the balloon stop rising.

The balance between the gas and the weight of the balloon is very fine. If the balloonist dumps out a few handfuls of sand, the balloon will rise very quickly. If the balloonist opens the valve for just a few seconds, the balloon will sink very quickly.

How Do You Steer a Balloon?

If you let a toy helium balloon go, it will rise and be carried away by the wind. The same thing happens with hot-air and gas balloons. Balloonists must plan carefully. They get weather reports and make sure that the wind will carry them where they want to go. You can imagine that balloons are not very efficient for transportation.

There are other kinds of balloons, called **airships.** Airships have motors and propellers on them so that they can go in any direction. A <u>dirigible,</u> or an airship that can be steered, was once a means of transportation. Some dirigibles even crossed the ocean. Now they are used mostly to carry advertising or to provide a bird's-eye view at sporting events.

Figure 5 shows several types of balloons and airships. Which ones are dirigibles? Which ones can carry passengers?

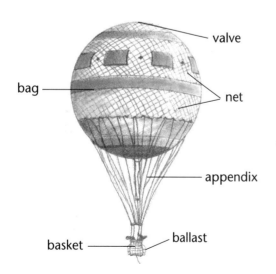

Figure 4. Parts of a gas balloon.

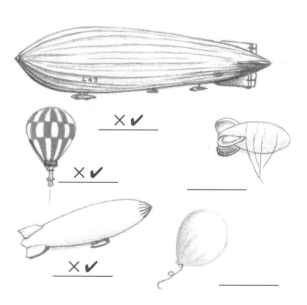

Figure 5. Different kinds of balloons and airships.

RECALLING FACTS

Recalling details

1. Which is denser, feathers or wood?
Wood is denser than feathers.

Identifying cause and effect

2. What happens when you heat air?
The air becomes less dense; it takes up more space.

Identifying the main idea

3. Find the paragraph that has a check mark next to it. Underline the sentence that tells the main idea.

Using context clues

4. Write the meaning of each word.
helium _is a gas that is less dense than air and_ _is used in balloons._

dirigible _is an airship that can be steered._

ballast _weights carried to control the height_ _of a gas balloon._

INTERPRETING FACTS

Making inferences

1. What advantage does a dirigible have over a hot-air balloon?
A dirigible can be steered and can move against the wind.

Inferring cause and effect

2. What would limit the amount of time you could spend on a hot-air balloon ride?
The amount of gas available for the burner and how much you would need to burn to maintain altitude; or, the

coldness of the weather and its cooling effect on the air in the balloon would limit the amount of time that you could

spend in a hot-air balloon ride.

Inferring cause and effect

3. What would limit the amount of time you could spend on a helium balloon ride?
The amount of helium and how much you would need to spill in order to maintain altitude would limit the amount of

time you could spend on a helium balloon ride.

SKILL FOCUS

1. In Figure 1, number the materials according to how dense they are. Use *1* for the densest material.

2. List any items in Figure 3 that are missing from Figure 4. propane, burner, neck, tapes

3. List any items in Figure 4 that are missing from Figure 3. valve, ballast, bag, net, appendix

4. In Figure 5, put an **X** by the balloons that can be steered. Put a check mark by the balloons that can carry people.

▶ **Real Life Connections**   In your opinion, are hot-air balloons safe? Tell why or why not.

Lesson 16

Metric Terms and Symbols

Reading a Mathematics Selection

► Background Information

Did you know that in 1670, Frenchman Gabriel Mouton proposed a decimal system. One year later, Jean Picard, a French astronomer proposed that the unit of measure be based on the swing of a pendulum. Over the next 120 years, many others propsed various systems.

In 1790, Thomas Jefferson suggested that the United States use a decimal measurement system. Congress rejected this recommendation. At the same time in France, the metric system was being created.

In 1821, Secretary of State John Quincy Adams also thought that the United States should convert to a decimal system. However, at the time, the United States traded mostly with Canada and Great Britain. The United States, Canada, and Great Britain all used the English System. At the time, these three countries believed that there was no need to change their system.

You are already familiar with the English system. This system began in the 1200s in England. The problem with the English system is that it is haphazard; it doesn't follow a specific pattern. For instance, twelve inches equals one foot, while three feet equals one yard. Unless a person is familiar with the system, it is very difficult to follow.

Since 1790, the world has gradually converted to the metric system. Canada and Great Britain were among the last countries to change over to this system. Once this took place, the United States evaluated the situation and decided on a gradual shift to the metric system. This is why it is important for you to learn the metric system.

► Skill Focus

A group of French scientists created the metric system in the 1790s. Why did they decide to use the metric system? Until that time, each country had its own language of measurement. This made it difficult for scientists from different countries to communicate. Finally, some scientists decided to make one system of measurement. This made it easier to compare the work of scientists from different countries.

The metric system is simple to use. To change from one unit of length to the next smaller unit in the metric system, divide by 10. To go from one unit to the next larger unit, multiply by 10.

► Word Clues

When working with metric measurements, you will come across the following three words: *meter, gram,* and *liter.* Prefixes can be added to these words to change their meanings. Some of these prefixes are *kilo, hecto, deca, deci, centi,* and *milli.*

► Strategy Tip

The **metric system** is a system of measurement that is used around the world. You know many of the labels that are used in the English system, such as inches, feet, pounds, and miles. The metric system also has special labels that you need to know. In "Metric Base Units and Prefixes," you will learn some of those words and some special prefixes.

Metric Base Units and Prefixes

Base Units

There are seven base units in the metric system. Most everyday measurements can be done with only three of these units.

To measure length, use the **meter.** A meter is about the length of a baseball bat.

To measure weight, use the **gram.** A gram is about the weight of a dollar bill.

To measure volume, use the **liter.** A liter of milk is about as much as a quart of milk.

Metric Prefixes

Larger and smaller units in the metric system are named by adding prefixes to the base units. You know that a prefix can change the meaning of a root word. In the metric system, several prefixes are used with each of the three base units. Prefixes are added to the units meter, gram, and liter to change their meanings. Following are six prefixes for you to learn. Knowing these prefixes can help you unlock the meaning of most words in the metric system.

kilo	1,000 times larger
hecto	100 times larger
deca	10 times larger
deci	10 times smaller
centi	100 times smaller
milli	1,000 times smaller

A **hectometer** (HEK tə meet ər) is 100 times longer than a meter. That means that a hectometer is about the length of 100 baseball bats put end to end. A hectometer is a little longer than a football field.

A **milliliter** (MIL ə leet ər) is 1,000 times smaller than a liter. A milliliter of water is only a few drops.

A **kilogram** (KIL ə gram) is 1,000 times heavier than a gram. A brick weighs about one kilogram.

Symbols

There are symbols that stand for the metric units and the prefixes. This means that the whole word does not have to be written each time. Notice that the symbols do not have periods after them. Notice also that only the symbol for liter is capitalized.

Prefixes				*Units*	
kilo	**k**	deci	**d**	meter	**m**
hecto	**h**	centi	**c**	liter	**L**
deca	**da**	milli	**m**	gram	**g**

The symbols for the prefixes and units can be combined. The symbol for kilogram is *kg,* the symbol for **decaliter** (DEK ə leet ər) is *daL,* and so on.

As you learn to use the metric system, these units will be easier for you to recognize. For now, the most important thing is to remember what each unit measures and to get a feeling for the size of the measures.

RECALLING FACTS

1. How many base units are in the metric system?

   There are seven units in the metric system.

Recalling details

2. How many base units are commonly used for measurements?

   There are three base units that are commonly

   used for measurements.

Recalling details

3. What are the names of the three base units in the metric system?

   meter ___ gram ___ liter ___

Recalling details

4. Many metric words are formed by adding

   a ___prefix___ to a base unit.

Recalling details

Put a check mark next to the words that complete each of the following sentences.

5. When the prefixes *kilo*, *hecto*, and *deca* are added to a base unit, the measurement is

   ___ the same as the base unit.

   ✔ larger than the base unit.

   ___ smaller than the base unit.

Recalling details

6. When the prefixes *deci*, *centi*, and *milli* are added to a base unit, the measurement is

   ___ the same as the base unit.

   ___ larger than the base unit.

   ✔ smaller than the base unit.

INTERPRETING FACTS

Drawing conclusions

1. All the prefixes that make the base unit smaller end in what letter? ___i___
Drawing conclusions

2. All the prefixes that make the base unit larger end in what letters? ___a, o___
Drawing conclusions

3. How does knowing the meaning of the prefix *kilo* help you understand the word *kilometer*?
   If you know *kilo* means "1,000," you can figure out that *kilometer* means "1,000 meters."

Making inferences

4. What might happen if a country chose not to use the metric system?
   Scientists in that country might have difficulty sharing information with other countries.

SKILL FOCUS

A. Write *meters*, *liters*, or *grams* on the lines provided.

1. In 1903, an airplane flew for 12 seconds. It flew about 37 ___meters___.

2. The Lockheed C-5A Galaxy can carry 110,000 kilo ___grams___ of cargo.

3. The Hindenberg was about the length of 30 buses, about 245 ___meters___.

4. The steward served 200 milli _____liters_____ of coffee to each passenger.

5. In 1908, an airplane flew for 1 minute and 28 seconds. It flew about 1 kilo _____meter_____.

6. The fuel gauge showed the pilot that she had 47 _____liters_____ of fuel left.

B. Write the symbol for the following measures on the lines provided. Remember that only the symbol *L* is capitalized. You may look back at the selection to find an answer.

1. kilometer _____km_____ **4.** decagram _____dag_____ **7.** milliliter _____mL_____

2. milligram _____mg_____ **5.** centimeter _____cm_____ **8.** kilogram _____kg_____

3. deciliter _____dL_____ **6.** hectoliter _____hL_____ **9.** decameter _____dam_____

Write the word for each symbol on the lines provided.

10. mm _____millimeter_____ **13.** daL _____decaliter_____ **16.** cL _____centiliter_____

11. cg _____centigram_____ **14.** hm _____hectometer_____ **17.** hg _____hectogram_____

12. kL _____kiloliter_____ **15.** dg _____decigram_____ **18.** dm _____decimeter_____

C. Circle the unit that you would use to measure each of the things pictured.

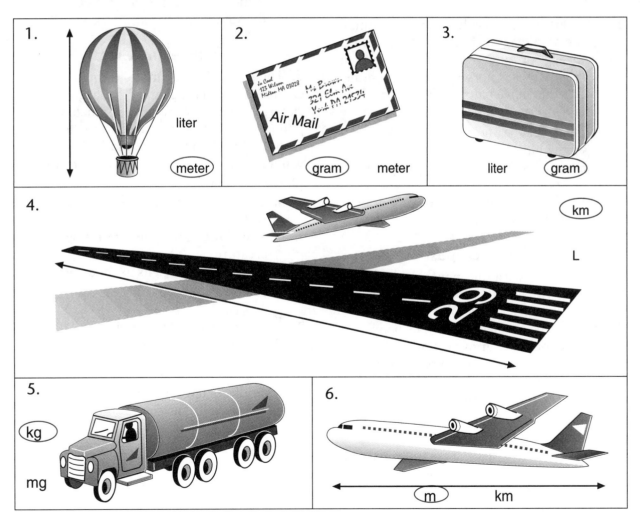

1. liter / meter

2. Air Mail — gram / meter

3. liter / gram

4. km / L

5. kg / mg

6. m / km

▶ **Real Life Connections** How many meters is it from your room to the refrigerator?

Main Idea

The main idea of a paragraph is not always found in the first sentence. It is sometimes found in the last sentence.

Read the following paragraphs. Below each one are three sentences from the paragraph. Circle the letter of the sentence that is the main idea of the paragraph.

The Sea Horse

1. The sea horse isn't like most fish. Its head looks like that of a pony. The sea horse has hard, spiny skin. Its tail looks like that of a monkey. It has one fin that isn't much help in swimming. Sea horses drift upright in the water.

   a. The sea horse has hard, spiny skin.
   b. Its tail looks like that of a monkey.
   (c.) The sea horse isn't like most fish.

2. The father sea horse has a pocket somewhat like a kangaroo's pouch. He carries the mother's eggs around in this pouch. He even carries the baby sea horses around for some time after they have hatched. The father sea horse takes very good care of his young.

   a. The father sea horse has a pocket somewhat like a kangaroo's pouch.
   b. He carries the mother's eggs around in this pouch.
   (c.) The father sea horse takes very good care of his young.

The Octopus

3. The octopus has a soft, pouchlike body. It has a head with eyes that look like human eyes. Instead of having fins like a fish, it has eight long arms coming out from its body. Some octopuses have arms nine or ten feet long. Each arm is lined with cuplike suckers. Like the sea horse, the octopus's shape is different from that of most fish.

   a. It has a head with eyes that look like human eyes.
   (b.) Like the sea horse, the octopus's shape is different from that of most fish.
   c. Some octopuses have arms nine or ten feet long.

4. The octopus uses its arms to get food. It moves along the ocean floor looking for something to eat. When it finds a crab, lobster, or fish, the octopus wraps its arms around the victim. The suckers on the octopus's arms hold the animal as the arms draw the food to the mouth.

   a. When it finds a crab, lobster, or fish, the octopus wraps its arms around the victim.
   (b.) The octopus uses its arms to get food.
   c. It moves along the ocean floor looking for something to eat.

The Giant Clam

5. The giant clam is an interesting sea creature. The giant clam is the largest of all clams. It sometimes weighs as much as 500 pounds. Its shell may measure four feet across. This clam is not found in American waters. It lives in the warm waters of the Indian and Pacific oceans.

   a. This clam is not found in American waters.
   (b.) The giant clam is an interesting sea creature.
   c. It sometimes weighs as much as 500 pounds.

6. The giant clam's shell consists of two parts. Each part is used as a huge storage area for water and food. The clam can snap the two parts of its shell together with great force. It is said that divers have been caught and injured in this great shell. The clam's shell is both useful and dangerous.

   (a.) The clam's shell is both useful and dangerous.
   b. The giant clam's shell consists of two parts.
   c. It is said that divers have been caught and injured in this great shell.

Lesson 18

Main Idea

In many paragraphs you read, the main idea is in the first or last sentence of the paragraph. However, the main idea doesn't always appear in these sentences. It can sometimes be found in any of the sentences in between.

Read the following paragraphs. Below each one are three sentences from the paragraph. Circle the letter of the sentence that is the main idea of the paragraph.

1. Birds are alike in many ways. All of them are vertebrates because they have backbones. All birds have two legs and two wings. All birds have feathers and lungs. Birds are warmblooded. *Warmblooded* means "their bodies are warm even when the weather is cold."

    a. All birds have feathers and lungs.
    (b.) Birds are alike in many ways.
    c. Birds are warmblooded.

2. Some birds, like the ostrich, are taller and heavier than a person. Some are very small, like the hummingbird. Some hummingbirds are the length of a person's finger. Many birds, such as swallows and ducks, are good flyers. Some birds cannot fly at all. The penguin's wings cannot lift the penguin off the ground. There are many different kinds of birds.

    a. Some birds, like the ostrich, are taller and heavier than a person.
    b. The penguin's wings cannot lift the penguin off the ground.
    (c.) There are many different kinds of birds.

3. The outer feathers of birds form a smooth covering for their bodies. The down feathers next to their bodies help to keep in body heat. Their wing feathers are used for flying. Their tail feathers help them in balancing or in steering. Not only does each feather type have a purpose, but the feathers can be replaced. Birds usually shed their old, worn-out feathers in the fall and grow a new set. Shedding of feathers is known as molting.

    (a.) Not only does each feather type have a purpose, but the feathers can be replaced.
    b. Shedding of feathers is known as molting.
    c. Their wing feathers are used for flying.

4. Birds weigh very little because their bones are thin-walled and hollow. Their feathers are also very light. Flying birds have powerful muscles attached to the breastbone. The bodies of most birds are built for flying.

    a. Birds weigh very little because their bones are thin-walled and hollow.
    b. Their feathers are also very light.
    (c.) The bodies of most birds are built for flying.

5. Birds' eggs must be kept warm. The baby bird grows inside the egg, eating up the food stored in the egg. By the time the food is used up, the bird fills the whole egg. Then it comes out of the egg, or hatches. All birds develop in eggs. Large birds, such as ostriches, lay eggs that are often as large as six inches long. Tiny birds, such as hummingbirds, lay eggs that are each only a quarter of an inch long.

    (a.) All birds develop in eggs.
    b. Birds' eggs must be kept warm.
    c. Tiny birds, such as hummingbirds, lay eggs that are each only a quarter of an inch long.

6. Certain birds serve as symbols. For example, many people regard the owl as a symbol of wisdom. The dove is often a symbol of peace. The eagle can be a symbol of political and military power. The bald eagle, which lives only in North America, is the national symbol of the United States.

    a. The dove is often a symbol of peace.
    (b.) Certain birds serve as symbols.
    c. The bald eagle, which lives only in North America, is the national symbol of the United States.

Consonant Blends

Some **consonant blends** have three letters. Three consonants are blended together in such a way that the consonant sound each stands for is heard.

scr   shr   spl   spr   squ   str   thr

Say each picture name. Listen to the beginning sounds. On the line, write the blend listed above that stands for the consonant sounds that you hear at the beginning of the picture name.

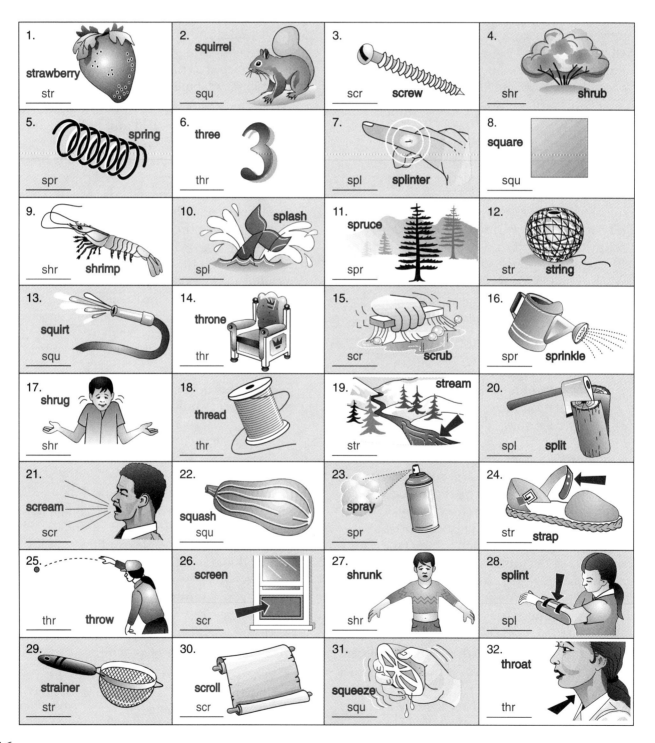

1. strawberry
   str

2. squirrel
   squ

3. screw
   scr

4. shrub
   shr

5. spring
   spr

6. three
   thr

7. splinter
   spl

8. square
   squ

9. shrimp
   shr

10. splash
    spl

11. spruce
    spr

12. string
    str

13. squirt
    squ

14. throne
    thr

15. scrub
    scr

16. sprinkle
    spr

17. shrug
    shr

18. thread
    thr

19. stream
    str

20. split
    spl

21. scream
    scr

22. squash
    squ

23. spray
    spr

24. strap
    str

25. throw
    thr

26. screen
    scr

27. shrunk
    shr

28. splint
    spl

29. strainer
    str

30. scroll
    scr

31. squeeze
    squ

32. throat
    thr

Consonant Digraphs

Say the word *shadow* and listen to its beginning sound. You hear only one sound at the beginning of the word. When two letters stand for one sound, as in *sh*, the two letters are called a **consonant digraph**.

ch   ph   sh   th   wh

Say each picture name. Listen to the beginning sound. On the line, write the digraph listed above that stands for the sound that you hear at the beginning of the picture name.

1. <u>sh</u> sheep	2. <u>ch</u> chair	3. <u>wh</u> wheel	4. <u>th</u> thermometer
5. phone <u>ph</u>	6. <u>wh</u> whistle	7. <u>th</u> thimble	8. <u>sh</u> shell
9. <u>ch</u> cheese	10. <u>ph</u> photograph	11. <u>wh</u> whale	12. <u>sh</u> shoe
13. <u>ch</u> chicken	14. <u>ph</u> phonograph	15. thumb <u>th</u>	16. <u>sh</u> shark

Say each picture name. Listen to the ending sound. On the line, write the digraph listed above that stands for the sound that you hear at the end of the picture name.

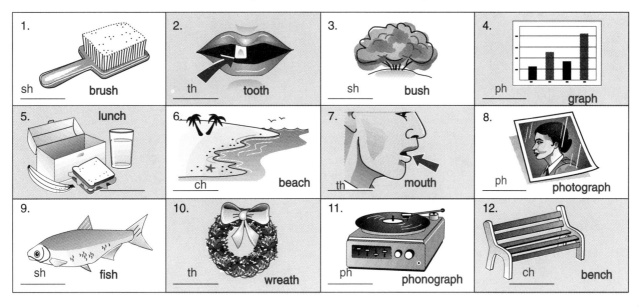

1. <u>sh</u> brush	2. <u>th</u> tooth	3. <u>sh</u> bush	4. <u>ph</u> graph
5. lunch	6. <u>ch</u> beach	7. <u>th</u> mouth	8. <u>ph</u> photograph
9. <u>sh</u> fish	10. <u>th</u> wreath	11. <u>ph</u> phonograph	12. <u>ch</u> bench

Long Vowel Sounds

You have had practice in working with one-syllable words with and without a final *e.* You have learned two guides to use in deciding whether the first vowel sound in such words is long or short.

There is another guide that you can use to decide if a vowel is long. See if you can discover this guide for yourself.

Words with Two Vowels Together

Write a one-word answer to each question. The first one has been done for you.

	How many vowels are there together?	*Which vowel has a long sound?*	*Which vowel is silent?*
1. boat	two	first	second
2. real	two	first	second
3. wait	two	first	second
4. heal	two	first	second
5. roast	two	first	second
6. soap	two	first	second

Fill in the words necessary to complete the following guide.

> **Guide 3:** When two ___vowels___ come together in a word, the first ___vowel___ is usually ___long___, and the second is usually ___silent___.

Read each sentence below. Look for a word in each sentence that has two vowels together. Say this word softly. Circle the vowel that has a long sound.

1. Tom went to Maine to spend the summer months.

2. He liked the sea.

3. He can swim and he can float.

4. His father has a boat.

5. They often went for a sail.

6. One day Tom invited some children to a party at the beach.

7. It started to rain but stopped by lunchtime.

8. They had a corn roast.

9. Afterward, they had fresh peaches.

10. Finally, they had vanilla ice cream.

Long and Short Vowel Sounds

The three guides that you have learned to help you decide whether the vowel sound in a one-syllable word is short or long are given below with a word or words missing in each one. Write a word on each line to complete the three guides.

Guide 1: When a word contains two vowels, one of which is a final *e*, the first vowel is usually _____long_____, and the final *e* is silent.

Guide 2: When a word contains only one vowel, and that vowel is not at the end of the word, the vowel is usually _____short_____.

Guide 3: When two vowels come together in a word, the first vowel is usually _____long_____, and the second vowel is usually _____silent_____.

Decide how to pronounce each word below. On the line, write the number of the guide that you used in making your decision. Mark each long vowel with a macron (–). Do not mark the short vowels.

	Guide No.		*Guide No.*		*Guide No.*
1. wāge	1	13. grāin	3	25. rīde	1
2. drōve	1	14. rōad	3	26. hōme	1
3. truck	2	15. rush	2	27. lōad	3
4. bēan	3	16. tāke	1	28. while	1
5. grāpe	1	17. ēat	3	29. gāin	3
6. pēa	3	18. rāin	3	30. trim	2
7. man	2	19. tank	2	31. fēast	3
8. thēse	1	20. tīme	1	32. sāme	1
9. ēach	3	21. shed	2	33. rēap	3
10. īce	1	22. job	2	34. still	2
11. fresh	2	23. mēal	3	35. lāke	1
12. tēam	3	24. lāte	1	36. flōat	3

Using a Train Schedule

Many people travel to work every day on trains. Most commuter trains follow a **schedule,** a printed timetable of arrivals and/or departures. People who commute every day at the same time do not need to think much about train schedules. However, shoppers, visitors, and workers without fixed work times often look at a train schedule so that they can plan their travel.

Study the portion of a train schedule below. It gives information about trains that travel from Franklin to Boston, Massachusetts. The headings at the top of each column tell what kind of information is given in each column. Notice the abbreviations and special symbols. Explanations are listed at the bottom of the schedule.

INBOUND	Train No.	700	702	704	706	708*	752
READ DOWN		A.M.	A.M.	A.M.	A.M.	A.M.	A.M.
Dep: Forge Park	O	5:15	5:45	6:15	6:33	7:06	
Franklin	O	5:22	5:52	6:22	6:42	7:13	
Norfolk		5:29	5:59	6:29	6:49	7:20	
Walpole	O	5:35	6:05	6:35	6:55	7:27	
Windsor Gardens		5:39	6:09	6:39	7:01	7:31	
Norwood Central	O	5:43	6:13	6:43	7:05	7:36	7:58
Norwood Depot		5:46	6:16		7:08		8:01
Islington		5:49	6:19		7:11		8:04
Dedham Corporate Ctr.		5:52	6:22	6:48	7:14	7:42	8:07
Endicott		5:55	6:26		7:18		8:11
Readville		6:00	6:29		7:21		8:15
Ruggles	T			7:00	7:32	7:56	
Back Bay	T, O		L6:43	L7:04	L7:36	L8:00	
Arr: South Station, Boston	T, O	6:20	6:48	7:09	7:41	8:05	8:35

SYMBOLS

    L: Regular stop to discharge or pick up passengers but train may leave ahead of schedule.

    O: Ticket outlet is located at or near station.

    T: Subway connection.

    Handicapped accessibility at Forge Park, Norfolk, Norwood Central, Norwood Depot, Dedham Corporate Ctr., Ruggles, Back Bay, and South Station.

    Train 706 stops at Plimptonville at 6:38 A.M.

Shaded portion denotes peak service.

    * Train does not operate on Martin Luther King Day, Columbus Day, and Veterans Day.

A. Write the answer to each question on the line.

    1. What is the number of the earliest train you can take from Forge Park? _____700_____

    2. At which stations can you connect with the subway system? Ruggles, Back Bay, and South Station

_____

    3. At what station does Train 752 begin? _____Norwood Central_____

    4. What is the number of the train that is not in the peak service area? _____700_____

    5. What time does Train 704 leave Walpole? _____6:35 A.M._____

6. What is the number of the train that leaves Endicott at 7:18 A.M.? _____706_____

7. Which train can't you take on Veterans Day? _____708_____

8. At which station could a train leave early? _____Back Bay_____

9. Where can you connect with the subway but not buy tickets? _____Ruggles_____

10. Which train makes the fewest stops? _____752_____

11. What time do you have to leave Franklin to get to South Station before 7:00 A.M.? _____5:52 A.M._____

12. If you leave Norfolk at 6:49 A.M., what time will you arrive at South Station? _____7:41 A.M._____

13. Plimptonville is between which two towns? _____Forge Park and Franklin_____

B. Underline the correct answer to each question.

1. How long does it take to get from Franklin to Norfolk?
   a. <u>7 minutes</u>   **b.** 3 minutes   **c.** 6 minutes

2. How many trains stop at all stations?
   a. 2   **b.** 5   **c.** <u>1</u>

3. At which of these stations can you *not* buy train tickets?
   a. Franklin   **b.** <u>Islington</u>   **c.** Back Bay

4. Which of these stations should you avoid if you are in a wheelchair?
   a. Norwood Central   **b.** <u>Endicott</u>   **c.** Ruggles

5. You have an important breakfast meeting near South Station at 7:45 A.M. It takes about ten minutes to walk from the station to your meeting. What is the latest you could leave Walpole to be at your meeting on time?
   a. 6:05 A.M.   **b.** <u>6:35 A.M.</u>   **c.** 6:55 A.M.

6. How long does it take to go from Forge Park to South Station on Train 700?
   a. <u>65 minutes</u>   **b.** 55 minutes   **c.** one hour

7. Which town do you think is closest to Walpole?
   a. Franklin   **b.** Norfolk   **c.** <u>Windsor Gardens</u>

8. If you miss the first train out of Readville, how long will you have to wait for the next train?
   a. <u>29 minutes</u>   **b.** 20 minutes   **c.** 5 minutes

9. How many trains stop at Norwood Depot?
   a. <u>4</u>   **b.** 3   **c.** 6

10. Which train takes the least time to make the entire trip?
    a. 702   **b.** <u>704</u>   **c.** 706

11. Which stations have the most trains leaving from them?
    a. <u>Norwood Central and Dedham Corporate Ctr.</u>
    b. Walpole and Dedham Corporate Ctr.
    c. Forge Park and Norwood Central

12. How often do the first three trains of the day run?
    a. every hour   **b.** every fifteen minutes   **c.** <u>every half hour</u>

Lesson 24

Conflict and Resolution

Reading a Literature Selection

▶ **Background Information**

In this story, 16-year-old Keema feels angry and confused after she moves to a new neighborhood and leaves her old friends behind. Keema and her family live in Harlem, which is a section of New York City located in northern Manhattan. Harlem was founded in 1658. Around 1910 many African Americans begin settling there. Soon it became one of the largest African American communities in the United States. After World War II, many Latin Americans moved to East Harlem, or Spanish Harlem.

In the 1920s, many African American artists, writers, and musicians came to Harlem to work and live. Some of the most famous writers from this period are Langston Hughes and Zora Neale Hurston. The jazz music, paintings, novels, and poetry created by these artists is now world famous. This period is called the Harlem Renaissance.

▶ **Skill Focus**

Characters are the people in a story. Usually one of the characters in a story faces a problem. The struggle to solve this problem is called the **conflict**.

There are three types of conflict in stories.

Conflict with Self A character in this type of conflict may have to struggle with his or her feelings. You might find this conflict in a story about a person who overcomes a fear of heights by climbing a mountain.

Conflict with Another Character In this type of conflict, one character may have a problem with another character. This conflict is often found in detective stories when a police officer is after a person who has broken the law.

Conflict with Nature A character in this type of ، conflict may come face-to-face with some danger or outside force over which he or she has no control. A story about people living in a town hit by an earthquake or a family lost at sea usually confronts this type of conflict.

Every character who faces a conflict tries to solve this problem. The solution to a story's problem, or conflict, is called the **resolution**. The resolution usually comes at the end of the story.

▶ **Word Clues**

Read the sentences below. Look for context clues that explain the underlined word.

As much as she missed her old neighborhood, Keema loved the bustle of this busy street. Everywhere she looked the street was bursting with activity. ،

If you do not know the meaning of the word *bustle*, the word *activity* in the next sentence can help you. The words *bustle* and *activity* are synonyms.

Use **synonym** context clues to find the meaning of the three underlined words in the selection.

▶ **Strategy Tip**

As you read "Something to Cheer About," pay special attention to the problem that Keema faces and how she solves it. What type of conflict does she face? What is the resolution?

Something to Cheer About

Nothing was going the way that 16-year-old Keema Watkins thought it would. After her family moved to Harlem in August, her life changed completely. "It's like my whole world turned upside down," Keema thought to herself. "One day I'm walking around my old neighborhood talking to my best friend, Marisa. And the next day, here I am. A new house, a new school, and no best friend."

Early one afternoon, Keema was walking down Amsterdam with her younger brother Jamal. It was a <u>crisp</u> October day. The cool, sharp air felt good after the hot, rainy summer. As much as she missed her old neighborhood, Keema loved the bustle of this busy street. Everywhere she looked the street was bursting with activity. Skaters on in-line skates whizzed by them. Shoppers crowded the busy stores. Music blared at Keema and Jamal from a dozen radios. Street <u>vendors</u> sold everything from hot dogs to CD's. One of these street sellers held out a steaming hot dog to Jamal. "The best in New York," he said, grinning. "And there's no charge for the mustard, either."

But Jamal and Keema didn't have time to stop. They were looking for a hardware store so that they could buy house paint for their mother. This weekend, the whole family was going to paint the living room of their new house. The house was another thing that Keema couldn't quite get used to. It was great having a room to herself. In her old apartment, Keema had shared a bedroom with her mother. But fixing up an old house took a lot of time and work. Sometimes Keema wished that she just could shut her eyes and wake up in her old apartment again. More than anything, she missed her old life.

Jamal looked up at Keema. "Hey, stop daydreaming," he said. "If we don't find that hardware store, we are going to be in serious trouble. You know how important painting the house is to Mom." Jamal said, grinning.

Keema sighed and shook her head. "Tell me about it," she said. "Look, there's the hardware store. It's right next to the subway." As they crossed the street, a girl waved to Keema and called her name.

"Who's that?" Jamal asked, as they entered the hardware store.

"Maria Hernandez," Keema answered "She's in some of my classes."

Ten minutes later Keema paid for the paint while Jamal loaded it into their shopping cart.

"You two must be new to the neighborhood," the store manager said. "I've worked here almost forty years. I must know everyone in the area. Where do you live?"

"On West 13th Street—right near Sixth Avenue," Keema said without thinking.

The store manager looked surprised. "Then you sure are a long way from home," he said. "That's at the other end of the city."

Suddenly, Keema felt <u>embarrassed</u>. "I mean, we live on Hamilton Place," she said, looking uncomfortable. "We just picked up and moved here two months ago."

"Well, stop by again," the manager said as Keema and Jamal left the store. "Welcome to the neighborhood," he called after them.

"Hey, big sister," Jamal said, grinning. "I know you're not too happy about moving and

everything. But you at least can learn our new address. I think it's kind of a cool place to live."

Before Keema could answer, Maria Hernandez walked up to them. "I thought I saw you go into the hardware store," she said to Keema. "A couple of us are going in-line skating in the park this afternoon. Why don't you come along?"

Keema shook her head. "Thanks, but I promised my mom that I'd help her around the house today. Maybe some other time."

"Okay," Maria said. "See you in school on Monday."

As Maria walked away, Jamal turned to Keema. "She seems nice," he said.

Keema walked on without answering.

"Hey," Jamal yelled, as he tried to catch up with her. "What's wrong with you? At least help me with this shopping cart. This paint is heavy."

When Keema and Jamal carried the cans of paint into the living room, their mother was waiting for them. "Just in time," she said with a grin. "I've plastered every crack in this room. Now I can't wait to get my hands on a paint brush. Who's going to help me stir this paint?"

"Mom, I'm going to change into my old jeans," Keema said. "I'll be down in a minute." As Keema ran upstairs, Jamal looked at his mother and shrugged his shoulders.

The walls of Keema's bedroom were covered with pictures of her friends from her old high school. A banner that said "Washington Irving High School" hung above her bed. Keema looked at a photograph from last year's class party. She and Marisa grinned at the camera surrounded by all their friends. "It just isn't the same without you guys," Keema said to herself.

Keema was still thinking about her old friends on her way to school Monday morning. As she got off the crowded subway car and hurried down the street, she remembered what her mother had said to her at breakfast. "Honey, you have to give your new school a fair chance. You'll make new friends. Once you do, you'll like your new home as much as Jamal does. You'll see."

"Face it, Keema," she said to herself.

"Mom's right. So you had to move because of her great new job. What's the big deal? Lots of people move every day of the year. And that job was important to mom. So is owning a home. You really haven't given Park East a chance. Today is going to be different."

But when Keema walked into Park East High School, she didn't feel any different. All around her, groups of students were talking and laughing. Keema waved to a few students she knew on her way to the locker room. She didn't stop to talk to any of them. She was putting away her jacket when she saw Maria Hernandez.

"I'm glad I ran into you," Maria said. "I'm having a party this Friday night, and I'd love you to come. A lot of the kids from school will be there."

Keema wanted to say "yes." But the thought of going to a party with a bunch of kids she didn't know really scared her.

"Thanks for asking me, Maria," she said. "But this Friday, I'm seeing some friends from my old school. It's kind of a class party. They invited me weeks ago." Keema was trying so hard to sound natural that her words came out in a rush. It was all a lie and Maria knew it. Keema could tell by her look that Maria didn't believe her. And the strange thing was, Keema felt bad about lying to Maria.

On her way to her math class, Keema saw Maria walking down the hall ahead of her. For a second, Keema felt like telling her how she really felt; how she was the only one in her family who didn't like moving to a new neighborhood; how weird it was to walk to class without anyone to talk to or laugh with; and how she didn't really feel like Keema any more. "Forget it, Keema," she thought to herself. "Maria won't know what you're talking about."

That night, Keema and Jamal were washing the dinner dishes when the phone rang. It was Marisa.

As soon as she heard her friend's voice, Keema felt better. "Let's go to a movie this Friday," she said. "Maybe hang out with Lee and Josh afterward."

"I can't," Marisa said. "Don't you remember? We're going on a class trip this weekend. We won't be back until Sunday night."

Keema tried to hide the disappointment in her voice. "Oh sure," she said. "I forgot that it was this weekend. We went on a class trip the same time last year."

"This one won't be the same without you. We really miss you," Marisa said.

Keema smiled, but she felt like crying, too, and she wasn't sure why. "Let's do something when you guys get back," she said.

"Don't forget. We'll be seeing you in two weeks," Marisa said. "Our basketball team plays Park East at the end of this month. I'll save a seat for you on our side of the court."

For the next two weeks, Keema kept thinking about what her "side of the court" really was. She missed Marisa and her friends from her old high school. Still, Keema was starting to feel more at home in her new school.

The day before the big basketball game, Keema walked to English class with Maria. They were laughing about a really bad movie that they both had seen. "You're the only person who likes bad movies as much as I do," Keema said.

"I really got into them when I transferred to Park East last spring," Maria said.

"I thought you had been here since ninth grade," Keema said.

Maria shook her head. "Nope. I'm a newcomer, just like you. So, I know what it's like leaving your old friends behind." she said. Then she and Keema walked into English class together.

That Friday night, the gym was filled with students from Park East and Washington Irving. When Keema and Jamal walked into the gym, she heard Marisa call her name. The two friends hugged.

"I have so much to tell you," Keema said. "I don't know where to begin."

Marisa pointed to an empty seat beside her. "Come sit with us."

Keema looked across the court. She could see Maria and her new friends waving to her. Then she turned back to Marisa. "You know how much you all mean to me. But tonight, I want to cheer for Park East. It's where I belong now." Then she and Jamal sat down next to Maria.

The crowd roared as the basketball players took their places on the court. Keema and Jamal started cheering, too. For the first time in a long time, she had something to cheer about.

Comparing and Contrasting

1. How do Keema and Jamal feel about moving to their new neighborhood?

Keema doesn't like moving there, but Jamal enjoys the

new neighborhood.

Recognizing sequence of events

2. What happens after Maria sees Keema and Jamal come out of the hardware store?

She invites Keema to go in-line skating with a group of

friends.

Recognizing cause and effect

3. Why did Keema and Jamal move to Harlem?

Their mother moved there because she started

a new job.

Recalling details

4. How does Keema react when she arrives at school on Monday?

Although she wants to behave differently, she still doesn't

talk to any of the students she sees in the hallway.

Understanding character

5. Why doesn't Keema accept Maria's invitation to her party?

The thought of going to a party with people she doesn't

know scares her.

Recalling details

6. Why can't Marisa go to the movies with Keema?

Marisa and her friends are going away on a class trip.

Comparing and contrasting

7. In what ways are Keema and Maria alike?

They both transferred to Park East.

Identifying plot

8. What is the resolution of the conflict?

Keema sits with her friends from Park East and cheers

for their basketball team.

Using context clues

9. Decide if each statement is true or false. Write true or false on the lines provided.

a. When the air feels crisp, the temperature is cool and dry.

____true____

b. A vendor is someone who sings and dances.

____false____

c. If a person feels embarrassed, he or she is very self-confident.

____false____

Inferring details

1. Why do you think Keema gives the wrong address when the store manager asks her where she lives?

Answers may vary. She still thinks of West 13th Street as

her home, so she automatically gives that address to the

store manager.

Drawing conclusions

2. Why do you think Keema walks away from Jamal after he says that Maria Hernandez seems nice?

Answers may vary. She is angry because she misses her

old friends and isn't ready to be friends with Maria yet.

Inferring comparison and contrast

3. Why do you think Keema and her brother Jamal react so differently to the move to a new neighborhood?

Answers may vary. Keema is older and has already

started high school. She is unable to adjust as easily as

her younger brother.

Drawing conclusions

4. Why do you think Keema feels bad about lying to Maria?

Answers may vary. Keema knows Maria is trying to be

nice to her. Rejecting her invitation makes her feel guilty.

5. Why do you think Keema feels like crying when she talks to Marisa on the phone?

Answers may vary. She is sad because she realizes that

her old friends are doing things without her this year.

6. How do you think Maria feels when Keema turns down her invitation to go in-line skating and to attend her party?

Answer may vary. She is sorry that Keema doesn't want

to meet her friends. However, she also understands how

Keema feels about starting a new school.

SKILL FOCUS

Think about the conflict that Keema Watkins faces and how she solves it. Write your answers on the lines below.

1. Reread the three kinds of conflict described on page 62. What kind of conflict does Keema Watkins face?

She faces conflict with herself.

2. What causes this conflict?

Keema and her family move to Harlem because her mother is starting a new job. Keema has to transfer to a new school

and make new friends.

3. How does Keema feel about this conflict?

After her mother talks to her, she tries to act differently. However, she still feels shy and turns down Maria's party

invitation.

4. How is this conflict resolved?

Keema begins to feel more at home at her new school and becomes friends with Maria. When the basketball teams from

Washington Irving and Park East play against each other, Keema cheers for the Park East team.

5. What does Keema learn from her experience?

She realizes that she's a part of Park East now and is beginning to make friends with the students there.

6. How do you think Keema will change as a result of this experience?

She will probably be more open and accepting of change in the future. She will be more willing to give new people and

new places a chance.

▶ **Real Life Connections** Put yourself in Keema's shoes. Describe what you would do at the basketball game. Which side would you sit on?

Comparing and Contrasting

Reading a Social Studies Selection

▶ Background Information

Do you like animals? Have you ever considered becoming an animal doctor? It doesn't matter whether you live in the city or in the country. Veterinarians are needed in both places. But don't expect the job to be the same! The jobs of city vets and country vets are alike in some ways, but quite different in others.

The selection you are about to read describes the work of two veterinarians, one a country vet and one a city vet.

▶ Skill Focus

When reading a textbook, you will often need to compare two or more people, places, or events. To **compare** is to point out what is the same. To make a comparison, look for similarities. To **contrast** is to point out what is different. To find contrasts, look for differences. Sometimes people, places, or events are both similar and different at the same time.

There are two ways writers give information when comparing and contrasting two topics. The first way is to tell several details about one topic and then tell details about the other. The information about each topic is usually given in separate paragraphs.

Another way is to cover two topics point by point, detail by detail. Information that compares or contrasts details about both topics is given in the same paragraph. When you read this type of paragraph, you have to sort out the details that belong to each topic. Looking for details will help when comparing and contrasting.

As you read "City Vets, Country Vets," try to determine which method of comparing and contrasting the author used.

▶ Word Clues

Read the sentence below. Look for context clues that explain the underlined word.

Dr. Catherine Ling, an <u>urban</u> vet, sometimes sees in her city practice such unusual patients as chameleons, parrots, ferrets, and snakes.

If you don't know the meaning of the word *urban*, the word *city* in the same sentence will help you. The words *city* and *urban* are synonyms. Urban areas are cities.

Context clues can come before or after the unknown word. When you come across a word that you don't know, be sure to look for the context clues in the sentence before and after the word, as well as in the same sentence.

Use **synonym** context clues to find the meaning of the three underlined words in the selection.

▶ Strategy Tip

In "City Vets, Country Vets," the lives and practices of a city vet and country vet are compared and contrasted on the basis of three points: the work that they do, the places where they work, and their specialities.

As you read each section, you will find information comparing the two topics—city vets and country vets. Knowing how information is organized will help you find the details about each topic.

City Vets, Country Vets

1. Veterinarians weren't always around. In fact, the first veterinary schools weren't started until the late 1700s. Before that time, animals were cared for by the people who worked with them—shepherds, blacksmiths, farmers, stable hands, and others. These people depended on their experience and sometimes folk wisdom, rather than science, to treat their animals. The first trained veterinarians generally treated only large animals, such as cows, horses, sheep, goats, and pigs. These animals were very important in a farm-based economy. Vets who specialized in treating small animals, mainly pets, were unheard of at that time. But then cities grew, and society and the economy changed. More people started owning pets. Gradually, more and more veterinarians began setting up small-animal practices.

The Work Vets Do

2. Today Dr. Wendell Jordan and veterinarians like him—those who work in small towns and rural areas—usually have a mixed practice. These country vets still treat horses and <u>livestock</u>, such as dairy cows and pigs, but they also treat wildlife and pets. Dr. Jordan usually spends the morning in his office taking care of small animals that are brought in. Often these are pet cats and dogs that need checkups, shots, or medicine. That part of his practice is like a city vet's. Sometimes, however, a small patient turns out to be a wild animal like an injured fawn. That's not to say that a city vet's practice is dull! People living in cities often have exotic pets. Dr. Catherine Ling, an urban vet, sometimes sees in her city practice such unusual patients as chameleons, parrots, ferrets, and snakes.

3. Dr. Jordan's practice differs from Dr. Ling's mainly in that he spends a good part of the day traveling around to ranches, farms, and stables. He must often treat more than one animal at a time, something city vets don't usually do. For example, he must test or treat a whole herd of dairy cows to prevent the spread of disease. The treatment of entire herds is important because farmers and ranchers depend on the health of their livestock to make a living. Diseases among livestock can wipe out not only a farmer's own animals but also those on neighboring farms. Some of these diseases, such as brucellosis, can also affect humans. Both country vets and city vets help prevent the spread of animal diseases to people.

4. An important part of every veterinarian's practice is emergency care for badly injured or very sick animals. The need for emergency care is especially true for country vets, because farmers and ranchers often treat their own animals. Sometimes, farmers and ranchers call Dr. Jordan only when an animal is quite sick, limiting his ability to treat the animal successfully. By contrast, pet owners in the city generally don't treat their own animals or wait until the animal is very sick. Dr. Ling is therefore likely to spend much of her day in routine health care. Such tasks include

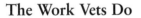

regularly cleaning teeth and ears and testing for heartworms.

Where Vets Work

5. Like many other city veterinarians, Dr. Ling works with a team of vets in a clinic. Generally large animal clinics and hospitals are equipped like human hospitals. Most anything the vets need to do—whether taking X rays of broken bones, performing eye surgery, or running laboratory tests—can be done where they work. Working in teams is helpful because the vets can see a greater number and variety of patients. They can then share valuable information.

✔ 6. The workplace is quite different for a country vet. Once Dr. Jordan leaves his office, his examining room or operating room may be a pasture or a barn stall. Equipment has to be portable, small enough to be carried in a truck or van. Unlike Dr. Ling, he does not have with him a laboratory that can do tests. He must depend on his own knowledge and experience to determine what a problem is. If he needs special equipment or must do complicated surgery, then Dr. Jordan must arrange to use a clinic. And when his visits are done, his workday is not necessarily over. Country vets are often "on call" and receive phone calls day and night. City vets like Dr. Ling, on the other hand, usually take turns covering emergencies after office hours.

The Specialists

✔ 7. Vets like Dr. Jordan and Dr. Ling have a general practice. They see all kinds of animals and treat all kinds of problems. There are country and city vets, however, who have a special practice. Some country vets, for instance, specialize in treating horses. These equine vets keep quite busy vaccinating their patients, treating them for worms, and helping them when they give birth. Similarly, some city vets specialize in treating cats or birds. Others may specialize in an area of medicine such as dermatology (for skin problems), dentistry, and ophthalmology (for eye problems). Because a vet may be the only specialist in the city, he or she may travel from one clinic to another to see patients.

R ECALLING FACTS

Recalling details

1. Before there were trained veterinarians, who took care of farm animals?

The people who worked with the farm animals took care

of them.

Identifying cause and effect

2. Why did the first veterinarians treat only large animals?

They treated only large animals because these animals

were important to a farm-based economy.

Recalling details

3. Why did veterinarians begin to set up small-animal practices?

As more people began owning pets, there was a need

for small-animal vets.

Recalling details

4. How do both country vets and city vets help human beings?

They help prevent the spread of animal diseases to

people.

Comparing and contrasting

5. List one area in which a city vet's practice differs from a country vet's practice.

Answers may vary. Possible answer: A country vet spends

most of his or her day traveling; a city vet can do most

things that need to be done right where he or she works.

Identifying the main idea

6. Two paragraphs have check marks before them. Reread each one and underline the sentence that states the main idea.

7. Underline the word that best completes each sentence.

   a. A country vet treats dairy cows, pigs, and other _____livestock_____.

      herds   wildlife   livestock

   b. Some vets might specialize in one type of animal, such as horses. These

   ___equine___ vets treat injuries and diseases that affect only horses.

   equine   bovine   feline

   c. A country vet's equipment has to be

   _____portable_____, or easy to carry.

   portable   exotic   valuable

INTERPRETING FACTS

Inferring the unstated main idea

1. Circle the letter of the statement that best expresses the main idea of the whole selection.

   a. Country vets must treat a greater variety of animals than city vets.

   ⓑ The jobs of city vets and country vets are alike in some ways, but quite different in others.

   c. The work of veterinarians has changed greatly since the late 1700s.

Distinguishing fact from opinion

2. Put a check mark before each statement that can be supported with a fact from the selection.

   ✔ People's attitudes about pets have changed greatly since veterinarians first began to practice.

   ___ Farmers and ranchers don't value a veterinarian's skill as much as city pet owners do.

   ___ Country vets need more training than city vets.

   ✔ City vets can sometimes treat problems faster than country vets.

Inferring comparisons and contrasts

3. What important job does a country vet have that a city vet doesn't?

   Answers may vary. Possible answer: Country vets must prevent the spread of disease among livestock.

Inferring comparisons and contrasts

4. Name one advantage that a city vet has over a country vet.

   Answers may vary. Possible answer: If a city vet runs into a problem, he or she can ask another vet in the clinic for help.

SKILL FOCUS

Country vets and city vets have jobs that are alike in some ways and different in others. Use the similarities and differences between them to answer the following questions.

1. Reread paragraphs 2–4 under the heading "The Work They Do." Notice that each paragraph compares and contrasts the work of country vets and city vets. List one similarity and one difference mentioned in each paragraph.

Paragraph 2:

Alike: _____ They both treat cats and dogs.

Different: _____ Country vets treat wild animals. City vets might treat exotic pets.

Paragraph 3:

Alike: ——————— They both help prevent the spread of animal diseases to people. ———————

——

Different: ——————— Country vets often treat more than one animal at a time. ———————

——

Paragraph 4:

Alike: ——————— Emergency care is important in both practices. ———————

——

Different: ——————— City vets spend more time in routine health care. ———————

——

2. Reread paragraphs 5 and 6 under the heading "Where They Work." On the lines below, summarize the differences in the ways in which city vets and country vets work.

City Vets: ——————— City vets work together in a clinic or hospital. They can do almost everything where they work and can share information. They cover for each other.

Country Vets: ——————— Country vets work alone. Because they travel, their equipment must be portable. They may not be able to do some things that city vets can do because they are not at a clinic. They are "on call" day and night.

3. Reread the text under the last heading, "The Specialists." What do some country vets and some city vets have in common?

They have a special practice. Both country vets and city vets may specialize in treating one kind of animal.

——

4. Look at the chart below. Decide whether each detail in the first column describes a city vet, a country vet, or both. Then put a check mark under the appropriate heads.

	City Vet	Country Vet
Treats livestock		✔
Treats pets	✔	✔
Helps prevent spread of disease	✔	✔
Often does routine work like cleaning teeth	✔	
Often travels		✔
May treat only a particular kind of animal	✔	✔

▶ **Real Life Connections** If possible, conduct an interview with a local veterinarian. How is the veterinarian the same as or different from Dr. Ling and Dr. Jordan?

Cause and Effect

Reading a Science Selection

▶ Background Information

A wide variety of food crops is grown on farms in the United States. Because of the different climates, some states are better than others for growing a particular food crop. In Florida, for example, the climate is ideal for oranges. On the other hand, in Nebraska, the climate is better for corn.

The variety of food crops grown in the United States farming industry is very important. Without farms to grow different fruits and vegetables, people couldn't get the foods that they need to stay healthy.

A healthy diet is one that includes many different kinds of foods. For instance, oranges provide a great deal of Vitamin C, but do not have much Vitamin D. In order to balance your vitamin intake, you should see which foods have which vitamins and plan your meals accordingly.

▶ Skill Focus

The cause of something is the reason it happens. The effect is what happens as a result of the cause. Think about **causes** and their **effects** as you read "Vitamins

and Other Nutrients." For example, if a person is angry, he or she might slam a door. The cause is anger. The effect is the slamming of a door. Sometimes it is very clear what effect a certain cause will have. Sometimes it is not so clear. Look for words, such as *cause, effect, because, so, result, that is why*. They often signal cause and effect. Read the following sentences.

> Sue got a good grade in English so she was happy.
>
> Sue was happy *because* she got a good grade in English.

In the first sentence, the cause is given first. In the second sentence, the effect is given first.

Sometimes you need to read more than one sentence to find the cause and effect. Read the following sentences.

> Carlos was quite unhappy. He failed his math test.
>
> Carlos failed his math test. As a *result*, he was quite unhappy.

In the first pair of sentences, the effect is given first. In the second, the cause is given first. In both, the effect is that Carlos

was unhappy.

▶ Word Clues

Read the sentences below. Look for context clues that explain the underlined word.

> Nutrients are <u>substances</u> that the body needs to stay healthy. These materials give the body energy and help it to grow and to repair itself.

If you do not know the meaning of the word *substances*, the word *materials* in the next sentence can help you. The words *substances* and *materials* are synonyms. Substances are materials.

Use **synonym** context clues to find the meaning of the three underlined words in the selection.

▶ Strategy Tip

Look for causes and effects as you read "Vitamins and Other Nutrients." Remember that a cause is the reason something happens. An effect is what happens as a result of a cause. Also remember to look for signal words.

Vitamins and Other Nutrients

Nutrients (NOO tree ənts) are substances that the body needs to stay healthy. These materials give the body energy and help it to grow and to repair itself. A balanced diet provides all the nutrients that the body needs. A balanced diet helps a person stay in good health. The food pyramid is shown in Figure 1 below. Eating the number of suggested servings from each of the food groups will provide a balanced diet.

✔ Vitamins, **organic** (or GAN ik) substances found in foods, help control the body's functions. An organic substance is something that is, or once was, part of a plant or an animal. Vitamins are nutrients, but they do not provide energy by themselves. They work with other nutrients to regulate the body's functions. The body cannot work without them.

Scientists have identified 13 vitamins. Vitamins are needed only in tiny amounts, but the lack of some vitamins can cause diseases. A Scottish doctor, James Lind, was one of the first to suggest that the lack of certain nutrients could cause illnesses. The word *vitamine* was first used in 1912 by a Polish scientist named Casimir Funk.

Today scientists put vitamins into two main groups: water-soluble and fat-soluble. Water-soluble vitamins dissolve, or melt, in water. Fat-soluble vitamins dissolve, or melt, in fat. The water-soluble vitamins are B_1, which is also called **thiamin** (THY ə meen); B_2, which is also called **riboflavin** (RY bə flay vin); **niacin** (NY ə sin); B_6, also called **pyridoxine** (pir ə DOK seen); **pantothenic** (pan tə THEN ik) acid; B_{12}, **biotin** (BY ə tin); C, which is also called **ascorbic** (ə SKOR bik) **acid**; and **folic** (FOH lik) **acid**. The fat-soluble vitamins are A, D, E, and K.

The body needs specific amounts of certain vitamins for good health. Scientists have discovered what these certain amounts are. They have figured out a Recommended Dietary Allowance, or RDA, for most vitamins. If a person has a **deficiency** (di FISH ən see), or lack, of these vitamins, the result can be a deficiency disease. Figure 2 shows the effects of certain vitamin deficiencies.

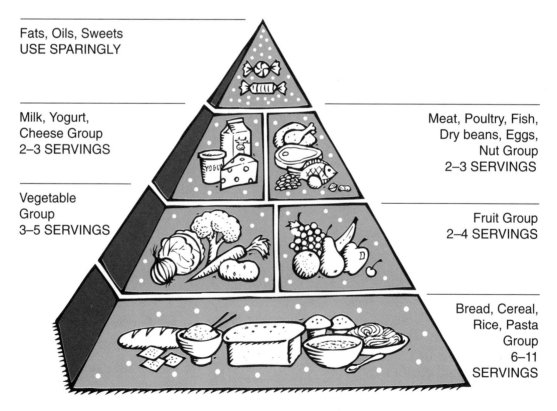

Fats, Oils, Sweets
USE SPARINGLY

Milk, Yogurt,
Cheese Group
2–3 SERVINGS

Meat, Poultry, Fish,
Dry beans, Eggs,
Nut Group
2–3 SERVINGS

Vegetable
Group
3–5 SERVINGS

Fruit Group
2–4 SERVINGS

Bread, Cereal,
Rice, Pasta
Group
6–11
SERVINGS

Figure 1. The suggested number of servings from each of the food groups should be eaten daily.

Vitamin	Disease Caused by Deficiency	Symptoms	Foods Containing Vitamin
B_1 (thiamin)	beriberi	stiffness and pain in legs; weakness	pork, green vegetables, yeast, nuts
niacin	pellagra	nervousness; indigestion	beef, liver, yeast, whole wheat bread
C (ascorbic acid)	scurvy	sore, bleeding gums; bruising	oranges, lemons, grapefruit, melon, raw cabbage, tomatoes
D	rickets	soft, crooked bones in young children	enriched milk, fish oils

Figure 2. Deficiency diseases are caused by a lack of certain vitamins.

The body can make some vitamins. When sunlight shines on the skin, the body produces vitamin D. Some vitamins cannot be made or stored in the body. Vitamin C is an example. If a person doesn't take in any vitamin C over a period of time, a deficiency can develop in the body.

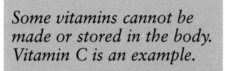

Some vitamins cannot be made or stored in the body. Vitamin C is an example.

Vitamins are now added to many foods so that people take in more vitamins. For example, vitamin D is added to milk. Because of enriched foods, deficiency diseases are not as common today as they once were.

Many people also take vitamin pills. Most vitamin pills contain **synthetic** (sin THET ik) vitamins. Synthetic vitamins are made in laboratories. Natural vitamins are found in foods. The vitamins that are added to enriched foods are also synthetic.

In the future, scientists may discover several new vitamins. New uses may also be discovered for the known vitamins. Scientists are experimenting to find out if vitamins can cure or prevent diseases like cancer and heart disease. It may be that vitamins are even more important than we think.

RECALLING FACTS

Recalling details
1. What are nutrients?
Nutrients are substances that the body needs for energy to help it grow and repair itself.

Recalling details
2. What is an organic substance?
An organic substance is something that is, or once was, part of a plant or an animal.

Identifying cause and effect
3. How do vitamins work in the body?
Vitamins work with other nutrients to regulate the body's functions.

Recalling details
4. Who are two scientists who worked with vitamins?
James Lind and Casimir Funk both worked with vitamins.

Recalling details
5. What is a deficiency?
A deficiency is a lack of something.

Recalling details
6. What are synthetic vitamins?
Synthetic vitamins are vitamins made in laboratories.

Recalling details
7. What are natural vitamins?
Natural vitamins are vitamins found in foods.

8. Reread the paragraph in the selection that has a check mark next to it. Underline the sentence that has the main idea.

9. What are the two main groups into which scientists classify vitamins?

Scientists classify vitamins into water-soluble and

fat-soluble groups.

10. A person who has scurvy might need more foods from which food group?

A person with scurvy might need more food from

the fruit group.

11. A person who has rickets might need more foods from which two groups?

A person with rickets might need food from the milk,

yogurt, and cheese group and the meat, poultry, fish, dry

beans, eggs, and nuts group.

12. A person should have up to 11 servings daily from which food group?

A person should have up to 11 servings of food from the

bread, cereal, rice, and pasta group.

13. Which vitamin can the body make when sunlight shines on the skin?

The body can make vitamin D.

14. If a person is suffering from beriberi, what vitamin does that person need?

A person with beriberi needs the B_1 vitamin.

15. A deficiency of niacin can cause which disease?

A deficiency of niacin can cause pellagra.

16. A child with soft, crooked bones might need which vitamin?

The child might need vitamin D.

17. Underline the word that correctly completes each sentence.

a. Chicken pox and mumps are kinds of childhood _____.

vitamins   **nutrients**   **diseases**

b. Turn the temperature knob to _____ the heater.

regulate   **dissolve**   **melt**

c. Thiamin is a _____ type of water-soluble vitamin.

deficiency   **specific**   **healthy**

INTERPRETING FACTS

1. On the lines next to each food, write the food group to which it belongs.

a. candy — fats, oils, and sweets

b. carrots — vegetable group

c. noodles — bread, cereal, rice, and pasta group

d. hamburger — meat, poultry, fish, dry beans, eggs, and nuts group

e. oranges — fruit group

2. List the foods that you would include for a balanced meal. Be sure to list foods from the food pyramid. _____ Answers will vary.

3. Long ago, English sailors developed scurvy while on long overseas trips. Why do you think they developed this disease?

There was no refrigeration, which made storage of fruits impossible. Because the sailors did not include fruits in their

diets, they were very likely to develop scurvy.

SKILL FOCUS

Draw a line to match each cause with its effect.

Causes	*Effects*
1. sun shining on person's skin	**a.** good health
2. vitamin deficiencies	**b.** important discoveries
3. enriched foods	**c.** vitamin D
4. a balanced diet	**d.** fewer people with deficiency diseases
5. scientists conducting experiments	**e.** deficiency diseases

Write a sentence that states each cause and effect that you matched above. Start the first three sentences with the cause, the remaining two with the effect. Be sure to use signal words. Answers may vary. Possible answers include:

1. The sun shining on a person's skin causes vitamin D to be produced.

2. Vitamin deficiencies can cause deficiency diseases.

3. There are many enriched foods being sold today, so fewer people have deficiency diseases.

4. Good health is the result of a balanced diet.

5. Important discoveries will be made because scientists are conducting experiments.

▶ **Real Life Connections** Based on what you know about the food pyramid, plan a healthful diet for yourself for one day. Be realistic. Be sure to include foods that you would enjoy eating.

Reading a Thermometer

— Reading a Mathematics Selection

▶ Background Information

Temperature, or the amount of heat in a substance, is measured by a thermometer. They are used for measuring both indoor and outdoor air temperatures. They are also used to measure the cooking temperatures of various foods. We rely on thermometers to tell us what kind of clothes are appropriate for any given day. We also use thermometers to measure our body temperature. For instance, if your body temperature is 101° F, or 101 degrees Fahrenheit, you should probably stay home from school.

Today there are three temperature systems in use—**Fahrenheit** (FER ən hyt), **Celsius** (SEL see əs), and **Kelvin** (KEL vən). In "Reading a Thermometer," you will learn more about Fahrenheit and Celsius. Kelvin is the system that scientists use. (If you would like to learn more about the Kelvin system, ask your science teacher.)

Fahrenheit is the system most widely used in the United States. When someone tells you that it is

95° F, they are using the Fahrenheit system.

The Fahrenheit system was developed by Gabriel Daniel Fahrenheit in 1714. Fahrenheit used mercury (the silver liquid that is in thermometers). Until that point, alcohol was used in thermometers.

Most of the rest of the world uses Celsius. Also called Centigrade (SEN tə grayd), this system was developed by Anders Celsius in 1742. While the Celsius system also uses mercury, its readings are vastly different from those of the Fahrenheit system.

In this selection, you will learn how to read both the Fahrenheit and Celsius systems. Knowing the basics of both systems is important because they are still widely used systems for measuring temperatures.

▶ Skill Focus

Learning to read a thermometer is an important skill. It is necessary for people to record a variety of temperatures in many different professions. For example, weather forecasters report the air temperature in their forecasts. Nurses take a

patient's body temperature to measure the person's health.

▶ Word Clues

When reading the following selection, look for these important words: *Fahrenheit, Celsius, centigrade, degrees.* They will help you understand more about temperature and thermometers.

▶ Strategy Tip

When reading about mathematics or science, it is often necessary to refer to the diagrams. Use the text and diagrams until you understand the ideas and concepts being explained. Also look for special words that refer to temperature.

Reading a Thermometer

Look at Figure 1 below. It shows a type of thermometer found in many homes in the United States. Notice that the colored liquid is at the line marked 68. The symbol ° stands for the word *degree*. The letter *F* stands for the word *Fahrenheit*. The temperature shown on the Fahrenheit thermometer in Figure 1 is written as 68°F.

As the air gets warmer, the colored liquid in the thermometer goes up, or rises. This upward movement shows that the temperature is increasing, or rising.

The invention of the thermometer is attributed to Galileo. The first sealed thermometer was produced by the German physicist Daniel Gabriel Fahrenheit in 1714.

As the air becomes cooler, the liquid goes down, or drops. This downward movement shows that the temperature is decreasing, or dropping.

Notice that the degree lines are numbered above and below zero. There are two degree lines numbered 10 and two numbered 20. The numbers below zero are marked with a minus sign. When speaking of a temperature that is less than zero, the following wording is used: *minus* 10 degrees Fahrenheit, or 10 degrees *below zero* on the Fahrenheit scale.

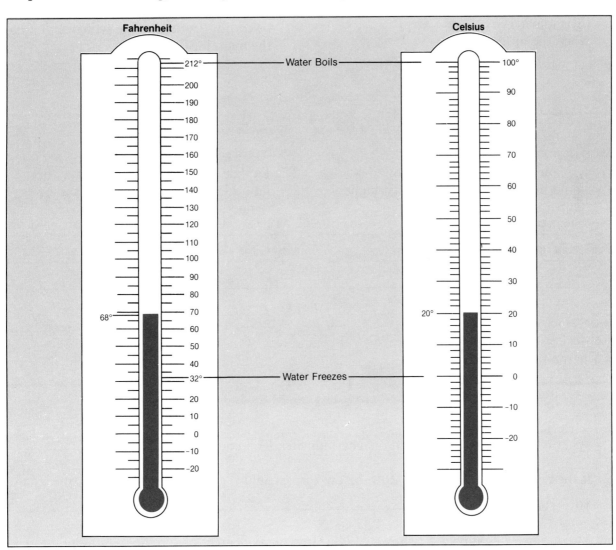

Figure 1. The Fahrenheit thermometer is still used in the United States.

Figure 2. The Celsius thermometer is used in most parts of the world.

The Celsius thermometer works in the same way, but different numbers are used to show the same degree of heat. On the Celsius scale, 0° is used to show the temperature at which water freezes. On the Fahrenheit scale, 32° is used to show the temperature at which water freezes. On the Celsius scale, 100° is used to show the temperature at which water boils. On the Fahrenheit scale, 212° is used to show the temperature at which water boils.

Now look at Figure 2 on page 79. It shows a Celsius, or centigrade, thermometer. The degrees are called Celsius, or centigrade. The letter *C* stands for *Celsius*. Notice that 0°C is the same as 32°F. In Figures 1 and 2, each of the small lines stands for two degrees. The markings on the four thermometers shown on page 81 are also in two degree increments.

RECALLING FACTS

Recalling details
1. Most thermometers are numbered above zero and _____below_____ zero.

Recalling details
2. The liquid in both Fahrenheit and Celsius thermometers _____rises_____ when the air gets warmer.

Recalling details
3. The liquid _____drops_____ when the air gets cooler.

Identifying the main idea
4. Reread the paragraph in "Reading a Thermometer" that has a check mark next to it. Underline the sentence that has the main idea.

INTERPRETING FACTS

Making inferences
1. Explain in your own words how the liquid in a thermometer shows a higher temperature.
As the air gets warmer, the liquid expands and needs more room. It therefore moves up the glass tube.

Making inferences
2. Explain in your own words how the liquid in a thermometer shows a lower temperature.
As the air gets colder, the liquid contracts and needs less room. Therefore, it moves down the glass tube.

SKILL FOCUS

1. What is the temperature shown on Thermometer 1 on page 81? _____0°F_____

2. If the temperature dropped to 20°F below zero, would this be colder than or warmer than 10°F above zero? _____colder_____

3. Thermometer 2 on page 81 shows 212°F. How many degrees above the freezing point of water is its boiling point? _____180°_____

4. In Thermometer 3 below, the temperature is shown as 98°F. This is close to the usual temperature of our bodies. How many degrees above the usual room temperature (70°F) is the usual body temperature? ———— 28° ————

5. If the temperature of the water at the beach in the summer is 67°F, how much cooler is the water than a person's body? ———— 31° ————

6. Thermometer 3 below shows your normal body temperature on a Fahrenheit scale. Thermometer 4 shows it on the Celsius scale. What is the normal body temperature in Celsius degrees? ———— 36°C ————

7. Which is colder, 10°F or 10°C? ———— 10°F ————

8. Which is colder, –25°F or 7°C? ———— –25°F ————

9. What is the freezing point of water on the Celsius scale? ———— 0°C ————

10. What is the boiling point of water on the Celsius scale? ———— 100°C ————

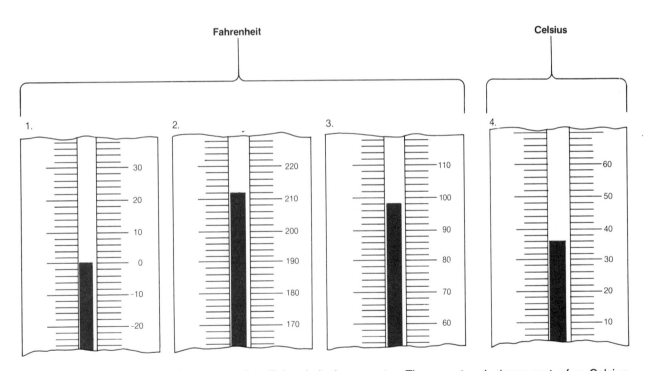

Thermometers 1, 2, and 3 show parts of a Fahrenheit thermometer. Thermometer 4 shows part of a Celsius thermometer.

▶ **Real Life Connections** What is today's temperature outside?

———— on a Fahrenheit scale   ———— on a Celsius scale

What is today's temperature inside your classroom or house?

———— on a Fahrenheit scale   ———— on a Celsius scale

Lesson 28

r-Controlled Vowel Sounds

Vowels can have sounds in addition to their long and short sounds. If the letter *r* comes after a vowel, the *r* controls the sound of the vowel. The sounds of *ar, er, ir, or,* and *ur* are called **r-controlled vowel sounds**.

Say the word pairs below, listening to each vowel sound. Answer the questions that follow.

cap	hem	sit	fog	fun
car	her	sir	for	fur

1. Is the sound of the vowel in the top word of each pair long or short? __short__

2. Does the vowel in the bottom word of each pair have a different sound? __yes__

3. What letter follows the vowel in the bottom word of each pair? __r__

Say the words in the list after each number below. Listen to the vowel sound in each word. Answer each question with *yes* or *no*. Then complete the guide below.

1. bar
   star
   farm
   Does the *a* in these words have a sound that is different from either long *a* or short *a*? __yes__

2. dare
   hare
   share
   Does the *a* in these words have a sound that is different from either long *a* or short *a*? __yes__

3. herd
   term
   stern
   Does the *e* in these words have a sound that is different from either long *e* or short *e*? __yes__

4. shirt
   bird
   third
   Does the *i* in these words have a sound that is different from either long *i* or short *i*? __yes__

5. for
   born
   storm
   Does the *o* in these words have a sound that is different from either long *o* or short *o*? __yes__

6. burn
   hurt
   curve
   Does the *u* in these words have a sound that is different from either long *u* or short *u*? __yes__

Guide 4a: When the vowel in a one-vowel word is followed by __r__, the sound of the vowel is usually changed by the __r__, and the sound of the vowel is neither short nor long.

Listen to the sound of *e, i,* and *u* in the following words. Then complete the guide below.

jerk	term	dirt	mirth	fur	curl
perk	her	fir	shirk	burn	urn

Guide 4b: When the vowels *e, i,* and u are followed by __r__, all three vowels usually have the __same__ sound.

Prefixes, Suffixes, and Root Words

A **prefix** is a word part that is added to the beginning of a root word. A **suffix** is a word part that is added to the end of a root word. Both prefixes and suffixes change the meaning of a root word.

Some common prefixes and suffixes with their meanings are listed below. Study them before doing the exercises that follow.

Prefix	Meaning	Suffix	Meaning
in	in, toward	en	made of, to become
pre	before	er	one who does
re	again, or do over	ful	full of
un	not, or the opposite of	ly	like in appearance or manner
		ness	quality or state of

Choose one of the listed prefixes to add to the beginning of each root word below. Write the prefix on the line to the left of the root word. Make the new word mean the same thing as the phrase to the right of the word.

1. __re__ do — do again
2. __pre__ pay — pay before
3. __un__ happy — not happy
4. __pre__ game — before the game
5. __re__ paint — paint again
6. __un__ tie — not tied

7. __re__ wrap — wrap again
8. __un__ lock — not locked
9. __re__ start — start again
10. __pre__ war — before the war
11. __re__ make — make again
12. __pre__ cook — cook before

Choose one of the listed suffixes above to add to the end of each root word below. Write the suffix on the line to the right of the root word. Make the new word mean the same thing as the phrase to the right of the word.

1. teach __er__ — one who teaches
2. kind __ly__ — in a kind way
3. truth __ful__ — full of truth
4. loud __ness__ — state of being loud
5. polite __ness__ — quality of being polite
6. hope __ful__ — full of hope

8. build __er__ — one who builds
9. dark __en__ — to become dark
10. slow __ly__ — in a slow way
11. paint __er__ — one who paints
12. read __er__ — one who reads
13. joy __ful__ — full of joy

Syllables

A **syllable** is a word or part of a word. Each part of a word in which you can hear a vowel sound is a syllable.

A. Look at the following pictures and say their names. Listen for the number of vowel sounds that you hear in each one. Write 1 or 2 on the line after each picture to show the number of vowel sounds in its name.

 dog
___1___

 monkey
___2___

 fish
___1___

camel
___2___

giraffe
___2___

tiger
___2___

B. Write the number of vowel letters that you see in each word below. Then read each word and write the number of vowel sounds that you hear.

	Vowel Letters	Vowel Sounds			Vowel Letters	Vowel Sounds
skin	1	1		darkness	2	2
jacket	2	2		pencil	2	2
pelt	1	1		trap	1	1

Write the correct word in the sentence below.

The number of vowel sounds that you hear tells you the number of ___syllables___ a word has.

You have learned that *e* is usually silent when it comes at the end of a word that has only one other vowel, such as *mile* or *same*. A final silent *e* is not counted as a vowel sound in deciding how many syllables are in a word.

What about a word in which two vowels are together, such as *boat* or *reach*? Would you count each one of these vowels as a vowel sound?

Write the correct numbers on the lines.

	Vowels	Sounded Vowels	Silent Vowels	Syllables		Vowels	Sounded Vowels	Silent Vowels	Syllables
race	2	1	1	1	wait	2	1	1	1
trade	2	1	1	1	coast	2	1	1	1
wise	2	1	1	1	team	2	1	1	1

Write the correct word in the sentence below.

The only vowel that affects the number of syllables is the one that is ___sounded___.

Lesson 31

Syllables

To help you pronounce compound words that you don't know, divide the words into syllables. Then you can pronounce each syllable until you can say the whole word. There are several ways of deciding how a word should be divided.

Compound Words

One of the easiest guides to use in dividing words is the one that is used with compound words. Since a compound word is made up of two words, it must have at least two syllables. Always divide a compound word into syllables by separating it between the two smaller words first.

rowboat   row boat

Read each of the following compound words. Divide the word into syllables by writing each of the two smaller words separately on the line to the right of the compound word.

1. snowflake — snow flake
2. sunlight — sun light
3. daytime — day time
4. snowshoe — snow shoe

5. flashlight — flash light
6. cupboard — cup board
7. sandstorm — sand storm
8. classroom — class room

9. campfire — camp fire
10. fishhook — fish hook
11. popcorn — pop corn
12. spearhead — spear head

Fill in the words necessary to complete the following guide.

> **Guide 1:** A compound word is divided into ___syllables___ between the ___two___ smaller words.

Words with Double Consonants

Another guide that you may use is for words with double consonants. In such words, divide the word into syllables between the two consonants.

hammer   ham mer

Underline the double consonants in each of the following two-syllable words. Then divide each word into syllables between the double consonants. Write each syllable separately on the line to the right of each word.

1. ga<u>ll</u>on — gal lon
2. ma<u>mm</u>al — mam mal
3. ha<u>pp</u>en — hap pen
4. vi<u>ll</u>age — vil lage
5. le<u>tt</u>er — let ter

6. su<u>mm</u>er — sum mer
7. su<u>pp</u>ose — sup pose
8. a<u>pp</u>ear — ap pear
9. le<u>tt</u>uce — let tuce
10. flu<u>tt</u>er — flut ter

11. bottom — bot tom
12. pu<u>pp</u>y — pup py
13. fellow — fel low
14. parrot — par rot
15. ra<u>bb</u>it — rab bit

Fill in the words necessary to complete the following guide.

> **Guide 2:** A word that has a ___double___ consonant is divided into syllables between the ___two___ consonants.

Comparing Food Labels

When shopping at a supermarket for a product, such as applesauce, you will notice that several brands are available. How do you know which kind to buy? The best thing to do is to compare the **labels** on the jars.

The information on food labels tells you about the products. Every food label identifies the weight of the product in ounces or quarts and in grams or liters. Federal law requires food companies to list ingredients on every food label. The ingredients show exactly what the product is made of. They are generally listed in order from largest amount to the smallest amount. A food label also provides nutrition facts that note how many servings are in the container and the number of calories per serving. The percent daily value is also listed for nutrients most closely related to health, based on a 2,000-calorie diet.

Food labels provide facts about weight, ingredients, and nutrition. Be aware, however, of other information provided on a label to try to convince you to buy the product. Such information represents the opinion of the company that sells the product and may or may not be true.

Study the labels on the jar of Mighty Apple applesauce and Uncle Mort's applesauce.

Use the information on the labels to complete each sentence.

1. The applesauce made in Iowa is __Uncle Mort's applesauce__.

2. Each jar of Uncle Mort's applesauce contains __200__ calories.

3. The larger jar of applesauce is called __Mighty Apple applesauce__.

4. According to the label, you'll love __Mighty Apple applesauce__.

5. Corn syrup and __sugar__ are added to Mighty Apple applesauce to make it sweeter.

6. The two ingredients common to both brands of applesauce are __apples and water__.

7. The applesauce that adds vitamin C to retain color and flavor is __Uncle Mort's__.

8. The most of any one ingredient used in both kinds of applesauce is __apples__.

9. The ingredient used in the least amount in Uncle Mort's applesauce is __vitamin C__.

10. The ingredient used in the least amount in Mighty Apple applesauce is __water__.

11. The nutrient in Uncle Mort's applesauce with the highest percent daily value is __carbohydrates__.

12. Someone on a diet would be better off eating __Uncle Mort's__ applesauce because __it contains fewer calories__.

13. There are __2__ servings in a __$7\frac{1}{2}$__ -ounce jar of Uncle Mort's applesauce.

14. There are __4__ servings in a __15__ -ounce jar of Mighty Apple applesauce.

15. A $7\frac{1}{2}$-ounce jar of Uncle Mort's applesauce costs $.79. A 15-ounce jar of Mighty Apple applesauce costs $1.55. Which applesauce is less expensive per serving? If four servings of Mighty Apple applesauce cost $1.55, then one serving would cost __$38\frac{3}{4}$ cents__ cents. One serving of Uncle Mort's applesauce would cost __$39\frac{1}{2}$ cents__. So __Mighty Apple__ applesauce is less expensive.

16. The applesauce that offers a money-back guarantee is __Mighty Apple applesauce__.

17. The money-back guarantee means that if you are dissatisfied with the product, __Right Off the Tree Foods__ will return the money you paid for the applesauce.

18. You know that no preservatives or artificial colorings are added to Uncle Mort's applesauce because the label states that this applesauce is __natural__.

19. The name Uncle Mort's applesauce may have been created to make the buyer think that __someone's uncle makes the applesauce__.

20. The company that manufactures Uncle Mort's applesauce is __Mort Corp.__.

21. The metric weight of Mighty Apple applesauce is __425 grams__.

22. What is the percent daily value of protein in one serving of Uncle Mort's applesauce? __0%__

23. If you were going to purchase one of these two brands of applesauce, you would buy __answers will vary__ because __answers will vary__.

Lesson 33 _____

Theme

Reading a Literature Selection _____

▶ **Background Information**

Have you ever had something to do that you had to do all by yourself? Was it because of a contest? Was it just because you wanted to be proud of doing something alone?

In "Hopping Mad!" Nancy is rebuilding a car. Her dad and one of her friends are mechanics. How can she resist their help?

▶ **Skill Focus**

Theme is the meaning or message in a story. It also reflects the purpose, or reason, that the author had for writing the story. The theme is usually a message about people or about life in general. The theme in many stories is stated directly. Usually one of the characters will state the theme.

However, most writers do not directly tell the theme of their stories. Instead, the reader has to infer, or figure out, the theme. In stories in which you must figure out the theme, you have to look at the whole story and think about what the author is

trying to tell you.

Often the title of a story tells in very few words what the story is about. Many times, the title is a clue to a story's theme. Always pay attention to the titles of the stories that you read.

The questions below will help you figure out the theme of a story.

1. What does the title of the story mean?
2. What do the people in the story discover about themselves or others by the end of the story?
3. What do the characters in the story discover about life by the end of the story?
4. What is the author's message to the reader?

▶ **Word Clues**

Read the sentences below. Look for the context clues that explain the underlined word.

The figure stood up, gradually stretching out its legs. It moved almost in slow motion, like an old man who had been underlined crouching in one position too long.

If you do not know the meaning of the word *crouching* in the second sentence, read the first sentence. It explains the meaning of *crouching* by giving details about it. The details describe how the figure came out of a crouching position, by standing, and moving gradually, stretching out its legs. A crouching position is one of stooping low, with bent legs.

Use **detail** context clues to find the meaning of the three underlined words in the selection.

▶ **Strategy Tip**

As you read "Hopping Mad!" think about the message that the author is trying to tell the reader. What do you suppose the author wanted you to think by the end of the story? Use the questions about theme to help you figure out the story's theme.

HOPPING MAD!

Fwwwp! The welding torch went out. Nancy Fuentes rocked back onto her heels. She <u>eased</u> the tight-fitting welding mask off her head and wiped the sweat off her face with the back of her glove. The car was taking shape. But her welding was terrible. It was the only thing her dad hadn't taught her at the garage. Maybe the car wouldn't be finished in time for the contest!

There was a sudden, tiny grinding sound in back of her, and Nancy leaped to her feet. Her heart was pounding as she spun around.

"Fernando, don't you ever sneak up on me like that!" she shouted, almost dropping the welding torch.

Fernando grinned. The expression on his face was playful. "Sorry, Nan," he said. "I didn't want to <u>interrupt</u> your welding. And when you stopped, you just stood there. I shifted my weight, and my boot rolled over a pebble. That's what scared you." Fernando had on a clean white T-shirt and clean jeans. He worked in his uncle's garage a few blocks away, but he had obviously had time to clean up before coming to visit Nancy. Only the ground-in grime on his hands marked him as a fellow mechanic.

He looked at the car. It was a 1969 four-door that Nancy had bought a year ago. It was in really bad shape, but Nancy had been working hard to restore it. Now it was running fine, but the body needed a lot of work. In fact, it needed more work than usual because she was converting it into a "low rider."

A low rider is created when the springs are cut to lower the body about four inches. Low riders usually have special paint, body work, and inside decorations. Sometimes special lifting parts are put in so that the car can be raised or lowered on its wheels. The lifters are sometimes powerful enough to make the car hop off the ground. There are low-rider clubs that have contests and award prizes to the best-looking or most unusual cars.

Nancy really wanted to win first prize in the Low-Rider Club's yearly contest. For one thing, she had already worked very hard. For another, no woman had ever won first prize. And finally, she could use the money. Her car had cost a lot to rebuild, and her savings were almost gone.

"You know, you've got some really tricky curves on those fenders. If I were you, I'd simplify the design." Fernando pointed to the welding that troubled Nancy. "Either that, or I could do the welding for you."

"No way," Nancy answered. She swallowed hard. She knew Fernando was one of the best welders in town. "I know you can do it. But then I'd never find out if I could do it. I'll try again tomorrow."

"The deadline is getting close," Fernando reminded her. "Do you even have a color picked out? Or a name?"

"I can't worry about colors or names now," Nancy replied. She walked away. "I have to close up the garage. Dad went home early to fix dinner."

Fernando started to say something more about the contest, but suddenly he had no one to talk to. Nancy had rolled the big door down between them. It didn't lock. The lock had been broken for years, but Fernando didn't try to open it. He just smiled and walked away.

The next morning, Nancy got to the garage just before her dad. She unlocked the pumps, got the cash drawer out of the safe, and opened the big door next to her car.

"Oh, no!" she yelled. "What happened?" Nancy started yelling and stomping around. She pounded the car with her fists. "No, no, no, no!" she yelled. Her father ran over to see what the problem was.

Nancy whirled around and stuck her face in front of his. "Did you do this?" she demanded.

"Do what?" said her father.

"This! This!" Nancy shouted, pointing to her car's fenders. The welding had been done, tricky curves and all.

Nancy saw that her father was looking confused. She backed off and patted him on the shoulder.

"Sorry, Dad," she said. "I just yelled at the first person I saw. Fernando did this. We were talking about it last night. When I get my hands on him . . ." Her voice started to rise again.

"Whoa, slow down," Mr. Fuentes said. "Look, you need a day away from this car, and I need parts from the city. Get the list from the office and take the pickup—some of the parts are heavy."

Nancy looked over her shoulder at the car. "It'll be here when you get back," her father said. "It's not going anywhere. And a day off will do you some good."

Reluctantly, Nancy got the list and drove off in the pickup.

The parts hadn't been ready when Nancy got to the city, and she had to wait for her order. When she got back to the garage, it was nearly dark. As she turned off the highway onto her street, she could see a bright light flickering in the garage. Someone was welding! Nancy gritted her teeth. Fernando was really going to get it now!

She parked the truck and ran toward the garage. A figure was bending over the left rear fender. She could see sparks flying. "Fernando, you get away from that car!" she shouted as loud as she could.

The figure stood up, gradually stretching out its legs. It moved almost in slow motion, like an old man who had been crouching in one position too long. In the middle of her yelling, Nancy noticed how familiar the motion was, and her voice trailed off into silence, as if someone was turning the volume down on a stereo. The figure was her dad.

"You, too?" Nancy said. "Won't anyone let me finish this car by myself?"

Mr. Fuentes put down the welding torch. "Have a look," he said.

Nancy brushed past him. There was the car, looking just as though Fernando had never touched it. "Wow!" she said, understanding at last. She turned and looked at him and then lowered her eyes a little. "Dad, how did you do that?" she asked quietly.

"I just undid everything Fernando did," her father replied. "I want this car to be all yours, too. Maybe I shouldn't have helped you either. But . . ."

Nancy threw her arms around him. "You did just the right thing," she said. "I got mad at you before I had all the facts. I should have known you wouldn't mess up my car."

Her father said, "You know, even Fernando was just trying to help. That doesn't excuse his barging in like that, I know."

"Yes, I shouldn't have pushed myself in like that." Fernando had walked into the garage and stood next to Nancy's father. "Your dad told me all about it—how

> "Won't anyone let me finish this car by myself?"

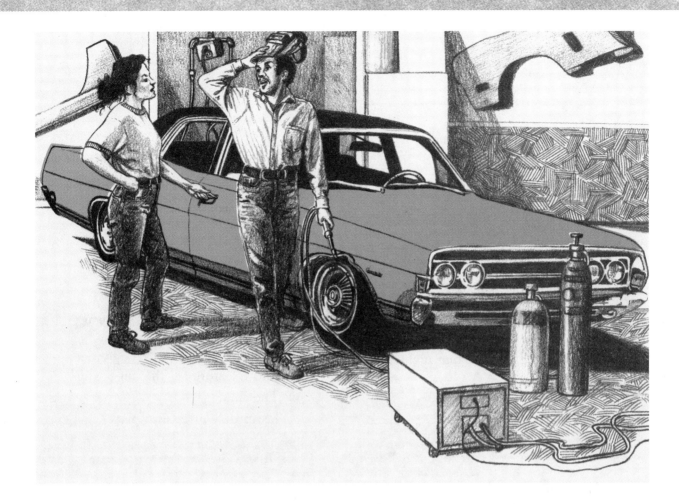

angry you were and everything. I guess I wanted to show off what a great welder I was instead of just being a good friend. What I did wasn't any help at all. I came over to apologize."

"I accept. Anyway, you did help in one way," laughed Nancy.

"How's that?" Fernando asked.

"I'm going to get stronger lifters, paint the car bright red, and call it Hopping Mad."

Recalling details

1. Who are the characters in the story?

Nancy Fuentes, Mr. Fuentes, Fernando, and Fernando's

uncle are the characters in the story.

Recalling details

2. Who is Fernando? Fernando is Nancy's

friend.

Recalling details

3. What kind of car is Nancy preparing?

She is preparing a low rider.

Recalling details

4. What is special about this kind of car?

Possible answers include: The springs are cut to lower

it; the inside is decorated; special lifters allow the car to

be raised or lowered.

Recalling details

5. What part of Nancy's work is she having trouble with? She is having

trouble with the welding.

6. Where does Fernando work?

Fernando works at his uncle's garage.

7. What does Fernando offer to do for Nancy?

He offers to help Nancy with the welding.

8. Why does Nancy refuse the offer?

She wants the work to be her own.

9. What does Fernando do that night?

He does the welding for Nancy.

10. How does Nancy feel about what Fernando did?

She is very angry.

11. What does Nancy's father do while she is gone? He returns the car to the way it was before Fernando helped.

12. Complete each sentence with the correct word from below.

eased   interrupt   barging

a. A rainstorm could ___interrupt___ the World Series.

b. The shoppers were ___barging___ into the store for the huge sale.

c. The child ___eased___ the last puzzle piece into place.

INTERPRETING FACTS

1. Why do you think Nancy is so jumpy at the beginning of the story?

Possible answers include: She is very nervous about getting the car finished in time for the contest, and she isn't doing well with the welding.

2. How does Fernando get into the garage to do the welding? The lock on the door is broken.

3. What sort of person is Nancy?

Possible answers include: Nancy is determined, proud, a skilled mechanic, and hot-tempered.

4. What sort of person is Fernando?

Possible answers include: Fernando is friendly, willing to help, egotistical, pushy, meddling, and one of the best welders.

5. What three reasons does Mr. Fuentes have for sending Nancy to the city? Which is the real reason? He wants to get her away from her car. He needs parts from the city. The real reason is that he wants to work on the car.

6. How do you think Nancy feels after she sees what her father has done?

Possible answers include: She is embarrassed. She is ashamed of herself for yelling at him or for thinking he would do something that would hurt her.

7. What do you think happens after the end of the story? Write a few sentences telling what happens.

Answers will vary.

The following questions will help you figure out the theme of "Hopping Mad!" Thinking about the title of the story and the people in the story will help you find the message behind the story.

1. *Title of the Story*

What is the title of the story? The title of the story is "Hopping Mad!"

Who becomes extremely angry? Nancy becomes extremely angry.

What two events brings on the anger?

Fernando tries to help Nancy by doing the welding for her. Nancy thinks that her father has also helped with the car.

How does this person's anger cause trouble?

Answers may vary. Nancy's anger causes her to accuse her father of something that he didn't do.

Why is the title a good one for this story?

Answers may vary. Nancy's getting "hopping mad" gives her the idea for a name for her car.

2. *People in the Story*

What does Nancy learn about herself in the story?

Answers may vary. She learns that she should get the facts before coming to conclusions.

What does Fernando learn about himself in the story?

Answers may vary. He learns that being helpful can sometimes be a way of showing off.

3. *Theme of the Story*

What is the author's message to the reader?

Answers may vary. The theme is that it is better to be a good friend than to show off how helpful we can be. It is all

right to get angry, but you should also get the facts first.

▶ Real Life Connections Nancy was upset with her dad and Fernando because she wanted to finish the car herself. Have you ever felt like Nancy? Describe an experience.

Reading a Table

Reading a Social Studies Selection

▶ **Background Information**

The history of automobiles is one of the most important and interesting stories in U.S. history. Did you know that in the 1890s cars were so new and so exciting that they were shown in circuses? Now cars are a symbol of the American way of life. America is a nation on wheels.

Cars made more than 20 years ago were very big and heavy, and they had large engines. These cars used a lot of gasoline. Large cars and higher speed limits meant that people had to buy and use a lot of gas. Both of these things contributed to the gas shortage in the 1970s.

Because of advances in technology, car makers are now able to build smaller cars that have been designed to use less gas. Using less gas saves people money. It also helps the environment by cutting down on the amount of pollution released into the air.

▶ **Skill Focus**

When reading textbooks, you will sometimes find **tables.** You should read tables very carefully. They will often give you information that is not found anywhere else in the selection.

Social studies and science selections often present information in the form of tables and charts. Presenting information in this way allows writers to give readers a lot of information in a small amount of space. Readers can learn a great deal of information from tables and charts, provided they know how to read them.

When reading a table, read the title first. Then use your finger to read down the columns and across the rows.

Turn to the first table on page 95. Read the title of the table. Then read down the left column. There you will find the number of miles per gallon that a car might get. Read across the top to find out how much a gallon of gas might cost. Then read across each row to find out how much a person would pay for gas in one year.

Follow the same three steps to read the table on page 96, reading the title first, then the left column, across the top, and finally across each row.

▶ **Word Clues**

Read the sentences below. Look for the context clues that explain the underlined word.

This table shows how much a <u>consumer</u> would pay for gas each year to go 12,000 miles. A consumer is a person who buys and uses goods.

If you do not know the word *consumer* in the first sentence, read on to the next sentence. The words *a person who buys and uses goods* tell the meaning of *consumer.* A word meaning that is stated directly can often be found before or after a new word.

Use **definition** context clues to find the meaning of the three underlined words in the selection.

▶ **Strategy Tip**

As you read, "Gassing Up– or Down?" study the tables carefully. The first table tells how much it costs to buy gas for a car during one year. The second table tells how much gas people use in various countries and how many people usually ride in a car. These tables give readers information that is not found in the selection.

Gassing Up–or Down?

How often does a car need gas? If you have a family car, how often do you visit a gas station? once a week? once a month? every few days? How far does your car go between fill-ups? How far does your car go for each gallon it burns? What does it cost to buy gas for one year?

The table below shows how much a consumer would pay for gas each year to go 12,000 miles. A consumer is a person who buys and uses goods.

Cost of Gasoline at 12,000 Miles per Year					
	Cost per gallon				
	$1.00	1.25	1.50	1.75	2.00
10	$1200.00	1500.00	1800.00	2100.00	2400.00
15	800.00	1000.00	1200.00	1400.00	1600.00
20	600.00	750.00	900.00	1050.00	1200.00
Miles per Gallon 25	480.00	600.00	720.00	840.00	960.00
30	400.00	500.00	600.00	700.00	800.00
35	343.00	429.00	514.00	600.00	686.00
40	300.00	375.00	450.00	525.00	600.00

Buying the Cheap Stuff

Gas used to be very cheap in the United States. Companies bought oil cheaply from overseas and turned it into gasoline. The government encouraged the low prices and did not tax gas much. Americans became used to larger and larger cars that took a lot of gas to run. The amount of gas a car uses depends on the car's size and weight, along with the design of the engine.

Gas in Western Europe and Japan, however, was a different story. Gas was very expensive in these places, partly because governments put high taxes on gas to raise money. Cars built in Western Europe and Japan were generally small and light, and they used much less gasoline.

Then, in 1973, some of the countries that sold oil to the United States stopped selling it. There was a huge gas shortage. The price of oil products, including gasoline, rose sharply. Gas became scarce, and there were long lines at gas stations. There was also gas rationing, in which people could get gas only every other day. The prices stayed high when the oil-producing countries started to sell oil again in 1974. Suddenly, it had become very expensive to run a car. Some changes were needed so that Americans would never experience a gas shortage again.

People started buying smaller cars, mostly those made in Japan. American car makers hurried to design smaller, more <u>efficient</u> cars because the Japanese had cars that didn't waste gas. However, they had been surprised by the sudden rise in gas prices. The American companies had financial problems while they were trying to catch up with Japan. They did not know how to make small cars, and they couldn't make them as cheaply as the Japanese.

Less Is More

Because smaller cars burn less gasoline, we are using less. Cars may become even more efficient in the future. But we may still need to change some habits so that we use even less gas. How can we use less gasoline? We could drive less. That is sometimes difficult. Our cities are farther apart than those in Europe or Japan. Many of our cities are very large. People often live far from where they work. And bus or train transportation is often inconvenient and expensive.

We could still manage to drive less, however. Many people take a car to go very short distances, such as under a mile. They lose out on getting good exercise, and they are hard on their cars and the environment. Short-distance driving can wear out a car quickly. Also, short trips cause more pollution. That is because the engine never gets hot enough to use gas efficiently.

✔ If you live near a street that people use for getting to work, notice how many people are in each car. You're likely to see just one, the driver, or perhaps the driver and one passenger. In fact, the average number of people in a car is just 1.8 in the United States. As you can see in the table, the average number of people in a car in other countries is higher—as high as 4 in Japan. A car's gallons-per-person figure is even better if you add people to the car.

American car makers eventually figured things out. They made smaller cars. They became partners with some of the Japanese companies. Look in any parking lot today. You will see mostly smaller cars. Many of them have Japanese names, such as Nissan, Toyota, Honda, or Mitsubishi. But names can fool you. These cars are not all imports. Imports are goods made in a foreign country. Some cars with Japanese names are now made in the United States. And some cars with American names are now built in Japan. The important fact about these cars, however, is that they use much less gas than their gas-guzzling cousins of the 1970s.

> *If you live near a street that people use for getting to work, notice how many people are in each car.*

Why is it important to use less gas? Here are three reasons. First, people do not want to spend any more money than they have to. As long as gas prices are high, it makes sense to buy less of it. Second, the world's oil supply is not unlimited. The world will someday run out of oil. Since gasoline is one of the most common uses of oil, it make sense not to use it up quickly. Third, burning gas causes pollution. The exhaust of a car has a lot of poison in it. The atmosphere can take only so much. Even the nonpoisonous gas, carbon dioxide, is bad for the atmosphere.

Gasoline Use and Number of Persons per Car		
	Gallons used per person each year	Persons per car
Italy	87	2.4
Netherlands	83	2.8
France	127	2.5
Germany (western)	159	2.1
Belgium	99	3.8
United Kingdom	152	2.9
Japan	94	4.0
United States	432	1.8

The table also shows how many gallons each person uses each year. Clearly, we could do better in not using our cars so much, and in sharing rides.

What to Do?

Using less gasoline may be a good idea, but how can we get people to do it? You can talk to your parents, of course, and ask them to walk more. You can offer to walk on errands, or take your bike. You can talk to people about sharing rides.

Government leaders can help, too. They can <u>legislate</u>; that is, they can pass laws that will make it cheaper and more convenient to take buses and trains. They can make gas more expensive by raising the taxes on it. The United States has a very low tax rate on gas. In 1993, the tax rate was 33 cents a gallon. In Italy, it was $2.37—over seven times as much as the U.S. tax rate. Raising taxes could make the car less attractive. People might be more careful about using their cars. On the other hand, people who must drive a lot, such as

salespeople, taxi drivers, and delivery people, would have a difficult time. How would you balance things? Would you raise taxes a lot right away? Would you raise taxes just a little? Would you leave things the way they are?

RECALLING FACTS

Identifying cause and effect

1. Match each of the following causes with its effect.

Cause	*Effect*
_e_ The people who sold gas to the United States stopped selling it.	a. More gas is used in the United States than anywhere else.
_a_ People in the United States drive almost everywhere, both for long trips and for short trips.	b. People bought smaller cars that were mostly foreign imports. American car makers began to design smaller cars.
_b_ Gas remained expensive after the gas shortage of 1973.	c. Car makers had financial problems because Americans were not buying as many cars.
_d_ Gas was very cheap in the United States.	d. People got used to buying larger and larger cars.
_c_ American car makers were not prepared for the gas shortage.	e. Gasoline became scarce, and prices went up sharply.

Comparing and contrasting

2. What kind of car can go farther on a gallon of gas? <u>A smaller, lighter car can go farther.</u>

Comparing and contrasting

3. What are some advantages to using less gasoline? <u>Using less gas costs less; it uses up the world's oil supply more slowly; and it pollutes less.</u>

Comparing and contrasting

4. What are two ways to use less gasoline? <u>Answers may vary. We could walk or bike for shorter trips; we could share rides.</u>

Comparing and contrasting

5. What would happen if the government raised gas taxes? <u>People might drive less; some people would have a difficult time adjusting, however.</u>

Identifying the main idea

6. Read the paragraph with the check mark next to it. Underline the sentence that tells the main idea of the paragraph.

Using context clues

7. Complete each sentence with the correct word from below.

efficient   imports   legislate

a. A kind of tractor made in Japan is used on many farms in the United States. These tractors are <u>imports</u>.

b. Evan is able to do all his homework, clean his room, and walk the dog before dinnertime. He is very <u>efficient</u>.

c. Congress can pass laws. Its members have the power to <u>legislate</u>.

INTERPRETING FACTS

Distinguishing fact from opinion

1. Write **F** or **O** next to each sentence to tell whether it is a fact or an opinion.

   <u>F</u> **a.** Smaller cars generally use less gasoline than larger cars.

   <u>F</u> **b.** Gas prices were very low before the gas shortage of 1973.

   <u>O</u> **c.** People should be free to drive anywhere and any time they want.

   <u>O</u> **d.** Smaller cars are better in every way than larger cars.

   <u>F</u> **e.** In the United States, there are fewer riders per car than in other countries.

   <u>O</u> **f.** Higher gas taxes will ruin the country.

Distinguishing fact from opinion

2. Find two facts in the selection that support the following opinion.

   It is important for people in the United States to use less gasoline.

a. <u>Burning gas causes pollution; the atmosphere can take only so much pollution.</u>

   _____

b. <u>The supply of oil is limited; oil resources are limited.</u>

   _____

Inferring the unstated main idea

3. Which of the following sentences best tells the main idea of the selection? Circle its letter.

   a. The countries that sell oil to the United States could stop again at any time.

   (b.) Because the price of gasoline has gone up sharply, people are driving smaller, lighter cars and are thinking about ways of using less gasoline.

   c. Smaller cars have become so popular in the past twenty years that American car makers have joined with Japanese car makers to make smaller cars.

Turn to the table on page 95. To understand this table, read down the left column first. There you will find the number of miles per gallon a car might get. Then read across the top of the table to see how much a gallon of gas might cost. Now read across each row to see how much you would have to spend in a year if you drove 12,000 miles.

1. What is the title of the table? <u>Cost of Gasoline at 12,000 Miles per Year</u>

2. What is the best miles-per-gallon number? <u>40</u>

3. What is the lowest cost per gallon in the table? <u>$1.00</u>

4. What is the highest cost per year? What are the miles per gallon and cost per gallon for the highest cost? <u>Highest cost: $2400.00. Miles per gallon: 10. Cost per gallon: $2.00.</u>

5. If gasoline costs $1.75 a gallon, how much would you spend for a car that gets 30 miles per gallon? <u>$700.00</u>

6. Imagine that gasoline costs $1.50 a gallon. You can afford no more than $600.00 a year for gas. What kind of gas mileage must your car get? <u>30 miles per gallon or better</u>

Turn to the table on page 96. To understand this table, read down the left column first. There you will find the names of several countries. Then read the labels at the top. These lables tell the number of gallons of gasoline used by each person every year and the number of persons in each car. Read across the rows to find the numbers.

1. In which country are the most gallons used per person? <u>United States</u>

2. In which countries are three or more people in the car for a typical car ride?
<u>Belgium and Japan</u>

3. In which country are fewer than two people in the car for a typical car ride?
<u>United States</u>

4. Which country uses the least amount of gasoline per person each year?
<u>Netherlands</u>

5. Which countries use more than 100 gallons of gasoline per person each year?
<u>France, Germany, United Kingdom, United States</u>

6. Which country is the closest to the United States in the number of people per car?
<u>Belgium</u>

▶ **Real Life Connections** What advice would you give to the mayor of your city or selectmen in your community to get people to use less gasoline?

Diagrams

━━ Reading a Science Selection ━━━━━━━━━

▶ Background Information

Throughout your life, you will have to read things that contain **diagrams**, or pictures. For example, instructions often have diagrams to help people understand what they are supposed to do. You are probably already familiar with the diagrams in instructions.

Science articles also often have diagrams to help readers understand a topic better. For example, understanding how an automobile engine works can seem very complicated. It will seem much simpler, however, if you understand the different parts and how they work together. The selection that follows explains how a car engine works.

▶ Skill Focus

When reading a selection with diagrams, remember to study each diagram as you read the text. If a diagram has a **caption**, read that first. The caption is like a title. It tells what the diagram is about.

In many diagrams, you will also find **labels**. Labels name the parts of the objects shown in the diagram. Sometimes a paragraph describes something that you have never seen. When you see a

picture of the object labeled in a diagram, you will understand it better. Sometimes you will need to study a diagram and read the paragraph that goes with it several times. In this way, you can work with the words and diagrams together to understand the ideas in the selection.

When you are reading a selection that has diagrams, use the following steps.

1. Read the paragraph before each diagram. Then study the diagram and read the caption that goes with it. If there are labels, read them while studying the diagram. The paragraph below the diagram may explain what is pictured. Read that paragraph, too.

2. Slowly read the rest of the paragraphs. Look back at the diagrams whenever you think they will help.

3. After you have finished reading the paragraphs and studying the diagrams, look away from the reading. Try to picture what you have read and the details in the diagrams. If you are not able to do this, read the paragraphs and study the diagrams again.

4. Work in this way until you understand all the ideas in the selection.

▶ Word Clues

Diagrams can be used as a kind of context clue. If you are unfamiliar with the term *intake stroke*, you would read the text and look at the diagram on page 101. The diagram shows part of an automobile engine. It shows the four steps in the operation of a cylinder. Step 1 of the diagram shows you that the *intake stroke* occurs when the piston moves down, allowing air and gasoline to move into the cylinder.

Use **diagram** context clues to find the meanings of the four underlined terms in the selection.

▶ Strategy Tip

Science selctions often contain diagrams. Diagrams help readers visualize, or see, what the author is writing about. While you read, study the diagrams carefully. You may want to go back and forth from the words in the selection to the diagrams several times.

WHAT MAKES A CAR RUN?

The heart of the automobile is the engine. The first successful American gasoline engine was invented in 1892 by Frank and Henry Duryea. The gas engine became successful very quickly. Blacksmith shops that made horseshoes were soon changed into service stations and garages. The gasoline engine has become more complicated since the early days of the automobile, but the idea is still the same. Gasoline has to be mixed with air and burned. The gasoline and air mixture burns at a high temperature. The following paragraphs explain how and where the mixture burns.

How the Gasoline Engine Works

All the parts of a car engine work together. An important part of the engine is a hollow metal tube called a **cylinder** (SIL ən dər). Tightly fitted inside the cylinder is a solid piece of steel called a **piston** (PIS tən). It is here, in the cylinders, that air and gasoline are mixed and the gasoline is burned. The gasoline burns so fast and at such a high temperature that it produces hot gases. When the gasoline burns, the cylinder is tightly closed. The gases are under great pressure. This rapid burning is called an **explosion** (ik SPLOH zhən). The spark that causes the explosion is made by a spark plug. An automobile engine gets its power from hundreds of small but powerful explosions. The earliest gasoline engines had only one cylinder. Today's gasoline engines have four, six, or eight cylinders.

How the Cylinders Work

✔ Look at the diagrams in Figure 1. <u>Each diagram shows one of the four steps in the operation of a cylinder.</u> Each step is called a stroke. The piston moves down during the <u>intake stroke</u>. At the same time, the air and gasoline mixture moves into the cylinder (step one). As the piston moves upward, the mixture is compressed, or squeezed into a smaller space. This is the <u>compression stroke</u> (step two). Next comes the <u>power stroke</u>. A spark is given off by the spark plug. The air and gasoline mixture explodes. The pressure of the explosion forces the piston down (step three). This is followed by an <u>exhaust stroke</u>, when the gases produced by the explosion are forced out of the cylinder (step four). As the pistons move up and down, they move the piston rods. Look at Figure 1 again.

How the Power is Sent to the Wheels

The up-and-down motion of the pistons produces power. But to move a car forward, the up-and-down motion has to be changed to a turning or spinning motion. Piston rods connect the pistons to the backbone of the engine, the **crankshaft** (KRANK shaft). As the pistons move up and down, they move the piston rods. The piston rods then turn the crankshaft. The crankshaft changes the up-and-down motion to a spinning motion. As the crankshaft turns, it spins the <u>flywheel</u>. In most cars, the spinning power is carried to the rear wheels that move the car. Look at Figure 2.

Figure 1. These diagrams show the four strokes in the operation of a cylinder.

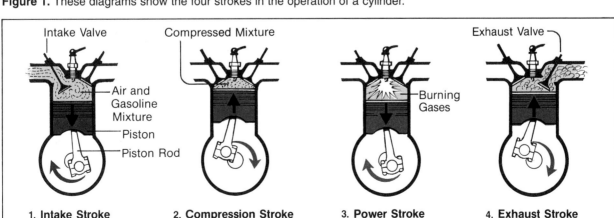

1. **Intake Stroke**   2. **Compression Stroke**   3. **Power Stroke**   4. **Exhaust Stroke**

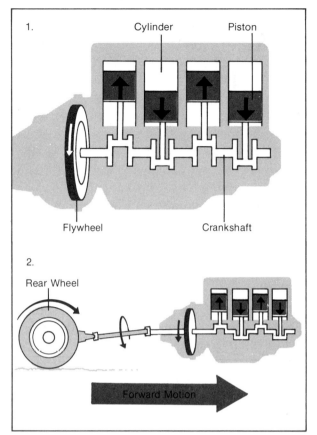

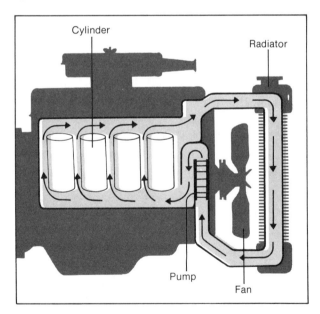

Figure 2. Part 1 shows how the pistons turn the crankshaft and the crankshaft turns the flywheel. Part 2 shows how power is carried to the wheels.

Figure 3. The engine is cooled by water. The water is cooled by air that is blown by the fan.

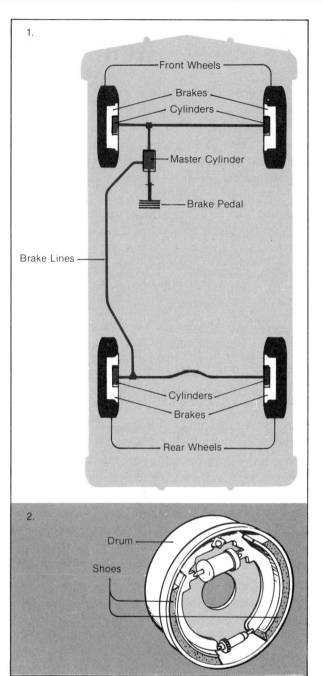

Figure 4. Part 1 shows the whole hydraulic brake system. Part 2 shows a drum brake inside a wheel.

How the Engine is Cooled

When gasoline burns inside the cylinders, the temperature can get as high as 4,500° Fahrenheit, or 2,481° Celsius. This much heat can melt iron and speed up rusting. Because of the heat that can build up, a gasoline engine must have a cooling system. The job of the cooling system is to remove heat from the metal parts. Water stored in the **radiator** (RAY dee ayt ər) does the job. A pump moves the water through the engine and cools the cylinders. In doing this, the water also gets very hot. It has to be cooled. This is the job of the fan. Look at Figure 3. In very cold weather, antifreeze is added to the water. The antifreeze helps keep the water from freezing.

How the Brakes Work

The braking system is used to slow or stop a car. **Hydraulic** (hy DRAW lik) brakes are used in today's cars. Hydraulic brakes use liquid pressure. When the driver presses the brake pedal, liquid is forced from the master cylinder through the brake lines, or tubes, to the wheel cylinders. (Neither the master cylinder nor the wheel cylinders have anything to do with the engine cylinders.) The liquid forces the brake shoes against the brake drums inside the wheels. The drums rub against the wheels and stop them from turning. Disk brakes work differently from drum brakes, but they are also operated by hydraulic pressure. Look at Figure 4.

RECALLING FACTS

Recognizing sequence of events
1. Write the following steps in the order in which they occur in a cylinder: compression stroke, intake stroke, exhaust stroke, power stroke.

   a. intake stroke

   b. compression stroke

   c. power stroke

   d. exhaust stroke

Recalling details
2. Who invented the first successful American automobile engine?

Frank and Henry Duryea invented the first successful

automobile engine.

Recalling details
3. In what part of the engine is the gasoline burned?

Gasoline is burned in the cylinders.

Recognizing cause and effect
4. What provides the spark that causes the gasoline to explode?

The spark plug provides the spark that causes the

gasoline to explode.

Recognizing cause and effect
5. What moves up and down, causing the piston rods to move?

The piston moves up and down, causing the piston

rods to move.

Recalling details
6. What cools the water in the engine?

Air cools the water in the engine.

Recalling details
7. Where are the brake drums?

The brake drums are inside the wheels.

Identifying the main idea
8. Reread the selection paragraph that has a check mark next to it. Underline the sentence that has the main idea.

Using context clues
9. Use Figures 1 and 2 on pages 101 and 102 to answer the following questions.

   a. Does the piston move up or down during the compression stroke?

   The piston moves up during the compression

   stroke.

   b. Does the piston move up or down during the power stroke?

   The piston moves down during the power stroke.

   c. Where do the burning gases go out during the exhaust stroke?

   The burning gases go through the exhaust valve.

   d. What causes the flywheel to spin?

   The crankshaft causes the flywheel to spin.

For questions 1-3, place a check mark in the box next to the word that completes each sentence.

Making inferences
1. An engine with eight cylinders would probably be _____ powerful than an engine with four cylinders.

   ☐ **a.** less   ☐ **b.** equally   ☑ **c.** more

Making inferences
2. When a car is moving along a highway, the pistons move up and down

   ☑ **a.** very quickly.

   ☐ **b.** and from side to side.

   ☐ **c.** very slowly.

Making inferences
3. In cars with front-wheel drive, the power is carried to the _____ wheels.

   ☐ **a.** rear   ☑ **b.** front   ☐ **c.** side

Inferring cause and effect
4. What causes the water in an engine's cooling system to get hot?

   The water picks up heat from the hot engine.

Making inferences
5. Why is the engine referred to as the heart of the automobile?

   The engine is what makes a car run in the same way

   that the heart makes our bodies run.

SKILL FOCUS

Write the answers to the following questions on the lines provided.

1. In Figure 1, what causes the power stroke? A spark from the spark plug causes an explosion. The pressure of the explosion forces the piston down.

2. In Figure 2, what turns the flywheel? The crankshaft turns the flywheel.

3. In Figure 3, what moves the water through the engine? A pump moves the water.

4. In Figure 4, what does the brake fluid move through to get from the master cylinder to the brake cylinder? The brake fluid moves through the brake lines.

5. Explain in your own words the four-stroke operation of a cylinder as shown in Figure 1.
   In the first step, the piston moves down, and the air and gasoline mixture moves into the cylinder. In the second step, the piston moves up, and the mixture is compressed. In the third step, a spark causes the mixture to explode, and the piston is forced down. In the fourth step, the piston moves up, and the burned gases are forced out of the cylinder.

▶ **Real Life Connections** In the future, do you think cars will be powered by electricity or some source other than gasoline? Give reasons for your response.

Large Numbers

Reading a Mathematics Selection

▶ Background Information

Numbers are a very important part of life. The number of friends coming to your house, the amount of money you have in your pocket or purse, or the number of students in a classroom are all described by our number system.

However, the system that we use today is certainly not the first numerical system ever used. After all, there have been many great civilizations, including the Egyptian, Greek, Roman, and Arab civilizations. Early peoples like us, needed numerical systems to help them in their everyday lives.

Believe it or not, as early as 3000 B.C.E., the Egyptians were using a numerical system. This system used hieroglyphics, or picture writing. They based this system on the number 10, just like we do today. This system, however, was difficult to write. There had to be a picture for every number. Because of this, it was difficult to read and write large numbers.

Another interesting fact is that the Egyptian numerical system did not include a symbol for zero. The first system that used a symbol for zero was the Hindu-Arabic numerical system. This system was developed in 200 B.C.E. Of all the ancient systems, the Hindu-Arabic system was the most complete. For this reason, we adopted this system, and it is still used all around the world.

As you read above, even early peoples struggled with reading large numbers. Large numbers can sometimes be intimidating. When you look at a number like 1,334,768,765, you may be overwhelmed. This feeling is natural. But you can overcome this feeling by understanding a few of the key terms needed to read large numbers.

In "Place Value," you will learn new words that are important to understanding some concepts in mathematics and in learning how to read large numbers. As you read the selection, pay attention to the function of zero in large numbers.

▶ Skill Focus

The value of a **digit**, or numeral, in a number depends on the position, or place, of the digit. This position is called **place value.**

For example, the digit 9 in the number 93 has a value different from the digit 9 in the number 39.

▶ Word Clues

When you finish reading the selection, you should understand the meanings of the words *digit, place value,* and *place holder.* The selection has several examples that will help you with the meanings of these words.

▶ Strategy Tip

Knowing the place value of each digit in a numeral will help you to understand large numbers. Learning how commas are used in large numbers will help you read them.

Place Value

When a number has four, five, or six digits, a comma is usually used to separate the three digits, or numbers, at the right from the others. The digits to the left of the comma are read as *thousands*. You first read the digits to the left of the comma. Then add the word *thousands*.

For example, beginning at the left and reading toward the right, the number 487,216 is read as four hundred eighty-seven thousand, two hundred sixteen.

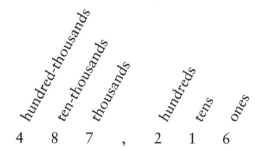

The place value of each digit is shown above each number.

The 4 means 4 hundred-thousands, or ⟶ 400,000
The 8 means 8 ten-thousands, or ⟶ 80,000
The 7 means 7 thousands, or ⟶ 7,000
The 2 means 2 hundreds, or ⟶ 200
The 1 means 1 ten, or ⟶ 10
The 6 means 6 ones, or ⟶ 6
487,216

The number 325,007 is read as three hundred twenty-five thousand, seven.

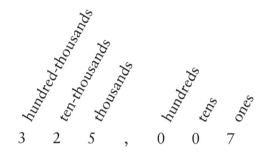

When reading large numbers that have one comma, the comma should signal you to say the word *thousand*.

Also, do not use the word *and* to connect parts of the number. For example:

5,611   five thousand, six hundred eleven

The word *and* is used only when reading dollars and cents. The *and* is used between the dollars and cents.

$8,684.54   eight thousand, six hundred eighty-four dollars *and* fifty-four cents

✔ <u>Zero is used as a place holder.</u> In the number 589,068, the zero holds the place for hundreds. It tells you that there are no hundreds in the number. The number is read as five hundred eighty-nine thousand, sixty-eight.

RECALLING FACTS

Recalling details
1. When there are more than three digits in a number, a comma is used to separate the _____three_____ digits at the right from the other digits.

Recalling details
2. The value of the place to the left of hundreds is _____thousands_____.

Recalling details
3. The value of the place to the left of ten-thousands is _____hundred-thousands_____.

Recalling details
4. _____Zero_____ is used as a place holder.

Identifying the main idea
5. Reread the paragraph with a check mark next to it. Draw a line under the sentence that states the main idea.

Using context clues

6. Write the meaning for each of the
following words.

digit: <u>zero through nine, as 0, 1, 2, 3, 4, 5, 6, 7, 8, 9</u>

_____

place value: <u>the value of a digit in a number based</u>

<u>on its position.</u>

place holder: <u>zero when it is used to show there is</u>

<u>no value for a particular place in a number.</u>

_____

_____

_____

INTERPRETING FACTS

Circle the letter of the word that completes each sentence.

Drawing conclusions

1. The value of the digit in the place that is
on the far _____ affects the total
value of a number most.

   (a.) left   **b.** right

Inferring cause and effect

2. In the number 4,932, raising the value of
the digit 9 would cause the place to the
left of it to _____.

   (a.) increase   **b.** decrease

Inferring cause and effect

3. Zero _____ affect the value of a
number if it is in the first place on the far
left of the number.

   a. does   **(b.)** does not

Inferring cause and effect

4. In the number 9,710, decreasing the value
of the digit 1 would cause the place value
to the right of it to _____.

   (a.) increase   **b.** decrease

SKILL FOCUS

A. Read the number words below. Then rewrite them using numbers. Remember to put in commas and zeros where they are needed.

  1. Six thousand, two hundred fifteen _____6,215_____

  2. Ten thousand, seven hundred eighty-eight _____10,788_____

  3. Nine thousand, four _____9,004_____

  4. Seven hundred sixty-four thousand, two hundred ninety _____764,290_____

  5. Four hundred forty thousand, two hundred six _____440,206_____

  6. Three hundred thousand, five hundred twenty _____300,520_____

  7. Nine hundred forty thousand, five hundred two _____940,502_____

  8. Eighty-six thousand, fifty _____86,050_____

  9. Five hundred twenty-eight thousand, four hundred seventy-nine _____528,479_____

  10. Sixty-three thousand, four hundred seventeen _____63,417_____

B. Rewrite each of the following numbers in words. Include commas where they are needed.

1. 2,008   two thousand, eight

2. $348.22   three hundred forty-eight dollars and twenty-two cents

3. 240,000   two hundred forty thousand

4. 4,682   four thousand, six hundred eighty-two

5. 75,343   seventy-five thousand, three hundred forty-three

6. 279,600   two hundred seventy-nine thousand, six hundred

7. $3,001.18   three thousand, one dollars and eighteen cents

8. $243,078   two hundred forty-three thousand, seventy-eight dollars

9. $89,266.16   eighty-nine thousand, two hundred sixty-six dollars and sixteen cents

C. Rewrite each group of three number words as numbers on the lines at the right. Add up the three numbers and write the sum as a number and then, at the left, as number words.

1. one hundred twenty-seven thousand, four hundred twenty

   sixty thousand, four hundred twenty-eight

   thirty-two

   one hundred eighty-seven thousand, eight hundred eighty

   127,420
   60,428
   +   32
   187,880

2. six hundred thirty-six thousand, forty

   three

   five hundred fifteen

   six hundred thirty-six thousand, five hundred fifty-eight

   636,040
   3
   +   515
   636,558

▶ **Real Life Connections** For what type of job would you need to be able to read large numbers?

Accented Syllable and Schwa

When words contain two syllables, one of the syllables is stressed, or accented, more than the other. In dictionaries, the **accent mark** (') is placed at the end of the syllable that is said with more stress. For example, the first syllable in *funny* is said with more stress than the second syllable.

fun′ ny

Say each of the following words to yourself. Write an accent mark after the syllable that is accented.

mar′ket	sur prise′	plas′ tic	be fore′	pic′ nic
or′chard	bas′ ket	won′ der	no′ tice	al low′
ho tel′	de pend′	proc′ ess	rad′ ish	friend′ ly
farm′ er	poul′ try	or′ der	pro tect′	a mount′
drag′ on	prod′ uct	spark′ ling	chick′ en	

Sometimes the vowels *a, e, i, o,* and *u* all have the same sound. This is a soft sound like a short *u* pronounced very lightly.

Pronounce *balloon.* Did the *a* sound like a soft, short *u*?

Pronounce *children.* Did the *e* sound like a soft, short *u*?

Pronounce *easily.* Did the *i* sound like a soft, short *u*?

Pronounce *confuse.* Did the *o* sound like a soft, short *u*?

Pronounce *support.* Did the *u* sound like a soft, short *u*?

When any one of the five vowels has this sound, it is called the **schwa** sound.

Place an accent mark where it belongs in each of the words below. Then underline the letter that stands for the schwa sound in each word. The first word is marked for you.

a̲ bout′	o′ pe̲n	jew′ e̲l	a̲ loud′	wool′ e̲n
cab′ in	cen′ tra̲l	suc̲ cess′	sof′ te̲n	par′ e̲nt
pi′ lo̲t	A′ pri̲l	meth′ o̲d	kitch′ e̲n	so′ da̲
wal′ ru̲s	su̲p pose′	post′ e̲r	po̲ lice′	cir′ cu̲s
prob′ le̲m	pur′ po̲se	sev′ e̲n	wag′ o̲n	

Look back at the words in the list above. Does the **schwa** sound come in the accented syllable or the unaccented syllable? Write the correct word in the sentence below.

The schwa sound always falls in an _____unaccented_____ syllable of a word.

In most dictionaries, the schwa sound is shown by the symbol ə. When you see this symbol in a dictionary respelling, you now know that it stands for the schwa sound and that it is pronounced like a soft, short *u*.

Syllables

You have learned guides for dividing two-syllable compound words and words with double consonants into syllables. A third guide shows you how to divide into syllables words that have a prefix or a suffix.

Words with a Prefix or Suffix

A **prefix** is a word part that is added to the beginning of a root word to change its meaning. The prefixes *re* and *un* have one vowel sound. When added to a word, they form their own syllable.

unwrap   un wrap

A **suffix** is a word part that is added to the end of a root word. The suffixes *er* and *ness* have one vowel sound. When added to a word, they form their own syllable.

painter   paint er

When a two-syllable word has a prefix or suffix, you divide it into syllables between the prefix or suffix and the root word.

Divide each word below into two syllables by writing each syllable separately on the line to the right of the word.

Dividing Words with Prefixes

1. unsafe ____un safe____
2. refill ____re fill____
3. subway ____sub way____

3. preview ____pre view____
5. dislike ____dis like____
6. refund ____re fund____

7. exchange ____ex change____
8. untrue ____un true____
9. disband ____dis band____

Dividing Words with Suffixes

1. farmer ____farm er____
2. rarely ____rare ly____

3. useful ____use ful____
4. fewer ____few er____

5. careful ____care ful____
6. treeless ____tree less____

Fill in the words necessary to complete the following guide.

Guide 3: A word that has a prefix or ____suffix____ is divided into syllables between the prefix or suffix and the ____root____ word.

Dividing Compound Words

1. sidewalk ____side walk____
2. barefoot ____bare foot____
3. rainfall ____rain fall____

4. wishbone ____wish bone____
5. football ____foot ball____
6. textbook ____text book____

7. snapshot ____snap shot____
8. sundown ____sun down____
9. spaceship ____space ship____

Dividing Words with Double Consonants

1. trapper ____trap per____
2. correct ____cor rect____

3. cabbage ____cab bage____
4. button ____but ton____

5. ladder ____lad der____
6. barren ____bar ren____

Fact and Opinion

How many advertisements do you hear or read each day? You hear them on radio and television, and you read them in magazines and newspapers.

Most advertisements contain both **fact and opinion**. The writer of the ad hopes that the reader or listener will believe the whole ad. A good reader is able to sort out facts and opinions and decide how much to believe. How do you tell the difference? Look at these two statements:

a. Flakies are good for you.

b. A cup of Flakies gives you 60 grams of protein, all the protein needed in a day.

Which sentence states a fact and which states an opinion? A fact can always be checked. You can find out if it's true or not. Therefore, *b* is a statement of fact. You still don't know if it's true, but at least it can be checked. Statement *a* is an opinion. What does "good for you" mean? Perhaps you agree with the opinion, but you cannot check it. When you see words, such as *good, better, terrible, pretty,* or *ugly,* you are reading someone's opinion. There is nothing wrong with opinions, but a careful listener or reader should be able to tell the difference between opinion and fact.

The following statements might be found in an ad. Some contain facts and some contain opinions. If the statement contains a fact, fill in the circle before the word **fact**. If the statement contains an opinion, fill in the circle before the word **opinion**.

1. Everyone thinks that the Zippy is the car of the future.

   ○ fact   ● opinion

2. Road tests show that the Zippy gets 45 miles per gallon in highway driving.

   ● fact   ○ opinion

3. Zippy carries a warranty on 50,000 miles or 12 months, whichever comes first.

   ● fact   ○ opinion

4. Famous race car driver, Hotrod Harry, says, "Buy a Zippy! It's the best car on the road."

   ○ fact   ● opinion

5. The Zippy has an air-cooled engine.

   ● fact   ○ opinion

6. All the Zippy dealers are good people.

   ○ fact   ● opinion

7. We offer more attractive rates for longer leases.

   ○ fact   ● opinion

8. All Zippy cars come with air conditioning.

   ● fact   ○ opinion

9. Zippy dealers go wild on convertible prices.

   ○ fact   ● opinion

10. Pound for pound, dollar for dollar, Zippy is the best car in the world.

    ○ fact   ● opinion

11. Now through April 1, all new Zippy cars have a $300 rebate.

    ● fact   ○ opinion

12. Zippy model T14 comes with a CD player at no extra charge.

    ● fact   ○ opinion

Main Idea and Supporting Details

Many times in reading, you will look for the **main idea and supporting details**. Details give more information about the main idea. They are called supporting details because they support the main idea.

Below is a paragraph about how the brakes work in a car. After the paragraph, its main idea and the supporting details are listed.

Braking a car is an interesting process. In most cars, a liquid called brake fluid begins the steps that stop the moving automobile. When the brakes are not being used, the fluid rests in the master cylinder and the brake tubes. When the driver steps on the brake pedal, the fluid is pushed toward the brake shoe. The brake shoe presses against the brake drum, stopping the wheel. Each wheel has its own braking system.

Main Idea   Braking a car is an interesting process.

Supporting Details

a. In most cars, a liquid called brake fluid begins the steps that stop the moving automobile.

b. When the brakes are not being used, the fluid rests in the master cylinder and the brake tubes.

c. When the driver steps on the brake pedal, the fluid is pushed toward the brake shoe.

d. The brake shoe presses against the brake drum, stopping the wheel.

e. Each wheel has its own braking system.

On the next page, write the main idea and three supporting details for each paragraph.

1. In the United States, almost everyone's life is linked to the auto industry. Most people depend on a car, bus, or truck for transportation. More than 12 million people earn their living in some part of the car industry by building, shipping, servicing, or selling cars, buses, or trucks. These people account for about one tenth of the labor force. In fact, there are 500,000 automobile-related businesses in the United States.

2. Several steps go into designing a new car model. Automobile designers create hundreds of sketches on computers. Final ideas for the new model come from these sketches. Then a full-sized clay model is made. Further improvements are made in the design. A fiberglass model is made. Finally, when every part has been approved, blueprints of the car are drawn so that the car can be cut out of steel and built.

3. Most of the early automobile builders were mechanics or knew about machines before they built cars. Ransom E. Olds made gasoline engines for farm equipment. Henry Ford was an engineer in a power house. Alexander Winton repaired bicycles. Elwood Haynes was in charge of a gas company.

4. When cars were first made, most drivers did not go past the city limits in case the "horseless buggy" broke down. Drivers had to wear goggles because there were no windshields to keep dust and dirt from their eyes. Women had to tie their hats on their heads with scarves to keep the hats from blowing off. Everyone wore linen dusters to protect clothes against the clouds of dust from the dirt roads. The early days of cars were an adventure.

5. Today the manufacture of cars is aided by technology. Computer-aided manufacturing (CAM) directs computers to make car parts. It also directs robots in performing assembly tasks. To insure quality in all stages of the assembly, cars are inspected by lasers.

Paragraph 1

Main Idea   In the United States, almost everyone's life is linked to the auto industry.

Supporting Details   Answers may vary.

a.   Most people depend on a car, bus, or truck for transportation.

b.   More than 12 million people earn their living in some part of the car industry by building, shipping, servicing, or selling cars, buses, or trucks.

c.   In fact, there are 500,000 automobile-related businesses in the United States.

Paragraph 2

Main Idea   Several steps go into designing a new car model.

Supporting Details   Answers may vary.

a.   Automobile designers create hundreds of sketches on computers.

b.   Then a full-sized clay model is made. Further improvements are made in the design.

c.   Finally, when every part has been approved, blueprints of the car are drawn so that the car can be cut out of steel and built.

Paragraph 3

Main Idea   Most of the early automobile builders were mechanics or knew about machines before they built cars.

Supporting Details   Answers may vary.

a.   Ransom E. Olds made gasoline engines for farm equipment.

b.   Henry Ford was an engineer in a power house.

c.   Alexander Winton repaired bicycles.

Paragraph 4

Main Idea   The early days of motoring were an adventure.

Supporting Details   Answers may vary.

a.   When cars were first made, most drivers did not go past the city limits in case the "horseless buggy" broke down.

b.   Drivers had to wear goggles because there were no windshields to keep dust and dirt from their eyes.

c.   Women had to tie their hats on their heads with scarves to keep the hats from blowing off.

Paragraph 5

Main Idea   Today the manufacture of cars is aided by technology.

Supporting Details   Answers may vary.

a.   Computer-aided manufacturing (CAM) directs computers to make car parts.

b.   It also directs robots in performing assembly tasks.

c.   To insure quality at all stages of the assembly, cars are inspected by lasers.

Table of Contents

Sometimes you may need to find information about a certain subject in several books. To locate the information that you need, you should use the **table of contents** in each book.

The table of contents is found at the beginning of a book. A table of contents lists the titles of the chapters and gives the page on which each chapter begins. Sometimes a table of contents gives the most important topics included in each chapter. It may also give the page on which each topic begins.

To use a table of contents, glance through the title and topics until you find one that has to do with your subject. Then turn to the page number given next to the chapter title or topic and read until you find the information. In this way, you don't have to "leaf through" the whole book. You can locate the information that you want quickly.

Below is a table of contents from a book about automobiles. To answer the questions that follow it, use two steps.

1. Look at the chapter titles to find out in which chapter you might find the information asked for.

2. Read through the topics under that title to find out on which page the topic in the question begins.

Contents

1. Suppose you wish to find information about the auto industry at the present time.
   a. Under which chapter title would you look? _____ The Automobile Today _____
   b. On which page would you start to read? _____ 97 _____

2. Suppose you wish to find information about the drive train in a car.
   a. Under which chapter title would you look? _____ Major Systems of an Automobile _____
   b. On which page would you start to read? _____ 160 _____

3. Suppose you wish to find information about different kinds of early cars.
   a. Under which chapter title would you look? _____ The First Automobiles _____
   b. On which page would you start to read? _____ 2 _____

4. Suppose you wish to find out the kinds of materials used in building a car.
   a. Under which chapter title would you look? _____ Building an Automobile _____
   b. On which page would you start to read? _____ 217 _____

5. Suppose you wish to find information about the problems of pollution and auto safety.
   a. Under which chapter title would you look? _____ The Automobile Today _____
   b. On which page would you start to read? _____ 115 _____

6. Suppose you wish to find information about a career as an auto salesperson.
   a. Under which chapter title would you look? _____ Careers in the Auto Industry _____
   b. On which page would you start to read? _____ 232 _____

7. Suppose you wish to find information about Henry Ford.
   a. Under which chapter title would you look? _____ Growth of the Auto Industry _____
   b. On which page would you start to read? _____ 53 _____

8. Suppose you wish to find information about research and testing of cars.
   a. Under which chapter title would you look? _____ Building an Automobile _____
   b. On which page would you start to read? _____ 192 _____

9. Suppose you wish to find information about car production in Japan.
   a. Under which chapter title would you look? _____ Growth of the Auto Industry _____
   b. On which page would you start to read? _____ 81 _____

10. Suppose you wish to find information about the brake system.
    a. Under which chapter title would you look? _____ Major Systems of an Automobile _____
    b. On which page would you start to read? _____ 175 _____

Comparing Car Ads

If you are interested in buying a new car, reading ads in newspapers and magazines should start you in the right direction. The details in ads can help you decide what kind of car will suit your needs and your budget. After you decide on the best car for your needs, you shop around for the best price.

Carefully read the following ads to compare the two cars.

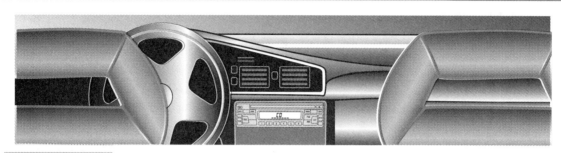

PASHUBI: WE DESIGNED OUR CAR FOR ■ *YOU* ■ *THE* DRIVER

At Pashubi, we think you are very important. So we created the 630-X, a fully equipped luxury sports car. The 630-X surrounds the driver with more window than other sports cars. The 630-X has a steering wheel and instrument panel that can be moved up or down.

The roomy bucket seats can be easily moved and can tilt back as far as you like. And the large storage area in back lifts up to become two additional seats.

There are 30 standard equipment features, including power disc brakes, power windows, electrically heated outside rearview mirror, two-tone paint, and CD player.

At $20,025, the 630-X offers more than other imported cars. And you'll save on gas—an exceptional 43 EST HWY MPG, 28 EST MPG. Use MPG for comparison. Mileage may differ depending on conditions. Highway mileage may be less.

The 630-X. By Pashubi. It's *not* for everyone—but it is for *you*.

TILTON:
The American way to get more for your money.

You get more for your money with our cars. Take the Star, for example. This compact car uses 3,000 computer-assisted robot welds, more than any other car. This helps to create an easy-to-maintain car which will give you more for your money for years to come.

The Star gives you more for your money because it's sensibly priced. It starts as low as $16,999*. The Star gives you more for your money with front-wheel drive. With the engine pulling in front and rack-and-pinion steering, you get the real feel of the road.

The six-passenger Star gives you more for your money with comfort.

And the Star gives you more for your money when you study the mileage figures:

41 EST HWY, 26 EST MPG.+

The Star's standard equipment includes power disc brakes, CD player, and 5-speed transmission (3-speed automatic is extra). Among the other extras are two-tone paint, luggage rack, leather steering wheel, power windows, and more.

Last year's Star was the best-selling compact car. See the Star today—and learn how to get more for your money the American way.

* $19,698 as shown in photograph

+ Use EST MPG for comparison. Mileage may vary depending on speed, trip length, and weather. Actual highway mileage lower.

A. Circle the letter in front of the phrase that correctly completes each sentence.

1. The Pashubi ad stresses that
   a. the gas mileage of the 630-X is comparable to that of other cars.
   (b.) the 630-X is designed with the driver in mind.
   c. you get more for your money when you buy the Pashubi.

2. The Tilton ad stresses that
   a. much of the Star's standard equipment is considered extra on other cars.
   b. the Star uses fewer robot welds than any other compact car.
   (c.) you get more for your money when you buy a Star.

3. All car ads must state the estimated miles per gallon (EST MPG) of gas that a car needs for highway (HWY) and for city driving. So a car boasting 43 EST HWY MPG, 28 EST MPG means that
   (a.) its estimated mileage is 43 miles per gallon for highway driving and 28 for city driving.
   b. its estimated mileage is 28 miles per gallon for highway driving and 43 for city driving.
   c. its actual mileage is 43 miles per gallon for highway driving and 28 for city driving.

4. Both ads advise that the gas mileage may vary from the estimates because
   a. the gas mileage the cars get probably has never been tested.
   b. the cars probably get much better mileage than the ad states.
   (c.) the cars may get lower gas mileage than the ad states.

5. The ad states that the Star is sold for as low as $16,999, but the car pictured in the ad costs $19,698. The price of the car in the picture is probably higher because
   (a.) it has many of the extra features, such as two-tone paint and a luggage rack.
   b. it is not really a Star but another kind of car made by Tilton.
   c. $16,999 is the sale price.

6. The standard equipment common to both the 630-X and the Star includes
   a. a leather-covered steering wheel and two-tone paint.
   (b.) power disc brakes and CD player.
   c. an electrically heated outside rearview mirror and power windows.

B. Complete the chart comparing the 630-X and the Star. If no information is given for a particular item, write NI. Then answer each question.

	630-X	STAR
Price	$20,025	$16,999
Number of passengers	4	6
City gas mileage	28 EST MPG	26 EST MPG
Number of standard equipment features	30	3
Country where the car is made	NI	U.S.

1. Which car do you think is made in Japan? _____630-X_____

2. Which car comes with more standard equipment? _____630-X_____

3. Which car holds more people? _____Star_____

Lesson 43

Character

Reading a Literature Selection

▶ **Background Information**

Long ago, many Native American boys tested and proved their bravery in battle and by counting coup. To count coup, a warrior would approach his enemy and touch him with a coup stick. He would not kill him. Those days, are now gone. And Native American boys must show their bravery in other ways.

In "Test of Fire," Tom Swift Eagle, a young Lakota Sioux, grew up in a city where he had to find a way to prove his bravery. In this story, Tom faces a test as difficult as any that his ancestors ever faced.

▶ **Skill Focus**

The people in a story are called **characters**. Some stories have many characters. Others have only one or two. A story usually has only one **main character**. The other characters are not as important as the main character.

The main character usually wants to reach a goal or solve a problem. Look for the main character's actions and the reasons for them. These actions and their causes tell you the kind of person the main character is.

When you read a story, keep in mind the questions below. They will help you understand the main character.

1. Who is the main character?
2. What goal does the main character want to reach? Why is it important for the main character to reach this goal?
3. What problem does the main character want to solve? Why is it important for the main character to solve this problem?
4. What kind of person is the main character at the beginning of the story?
5. How does the main character change by the end of the story?
6. What has the main character learned by the end of the story?

▶ **Word Clues**

Read the sentences that follow. Look for context clues that explain the underlined word.

Some of the Native Americans Tom grew up with no longer followed the old traditions. In Tom's family, however, these old customs were not forgotten.

If you do not know the meaning of the word *traditions,* the word *customs* in the next sentence can help you. The words *traditions* and *customs* are synonyms. Traditions are customs.

Use **synonym** context clues to find the meaning of the three underlined words in the selection.

▶ **Strategy Tip**

Tom is the main character in "Test of Fire." As you read, think about what Tom wants to do. His actions tell you a lot about the kind of person he is. Does he pass his "test of fire"? Does he change by the end of the story?

Test of Fire

Excitement ran through Tom Swift Eagle as he looked out the plane window. This would be his training unit's first jump with other firefighters.

These firefighters belonged to a special group called smoke jumpers. They were trained to jump from planes to fight fires in parts of a forest that could not be reached by firefighters on the ground. Tom thought smoke jumpers were the bravest men alive. Today he would have the chance to use all that John Dull Knife had taught him. He would show himself to be as brave as the bravest smoke jumper.

Long ago, every Lakota boy learned how to become a warrior. He learned the arts of shooting arrows, throwing spears, tracking animals, and fighting enemies. To become a man, a boy had to go through several sacred ceremonies. Once he became a man and received his adult name, he was expected to prove his bravery by counting coup and going on his first buffalo hunt.

Those days are gone now. Many Native Americans, like Tom and his family, live in cities. Some of the Native Americans Tom grew up with no longer followed the old traditions. In Tom's family, however, the old customs were not forgotten.

But Tom lived in the 1990s. He couldn't prove his bravery as his ancestors had done in the past. Instead of proving himself with a bow and arrow, he would show his bravery by fighting a forest fire.

Tom pressed his face to the plane window and watched the green woods below him. Then he saw it. Great clouds of thick, black smoke were foaming up into the sky. His heart beat faster and faster.

Others in the plane had fought fierce fires like this one many times before. They were talking together as they got their <u>gear</u> ready. Their equipment included hard hats, gloves, shovels, and axes.

"This fire is a bad one," Rita Connelly said gravely.

Bill Williams nodded. "Soon Pineville will be nothing but ashes unless we can stop the fire," he said.

The test that Tom faced today was far more important than any test at school. He had to pass this test. It was a test of life or death.

Tom wanted nothing more than the respect of these brave firefighters. He reached inside his shirt to be sure that he was wearing his sacred medicine bag. The medicine bag contained sacred objects that would protect him. It was important to Tom to have his sacred medicine with him when he made his first jump.

It was almost time to jump. Jumping at the right instant was important. Smoke jumpers have to land near the fire without falling into the hungry flames.

At John's signal, Tom leaped out of the plane. He slowly dropped through the smoky air—down, down, toward the raging fire. He guided his parachute to an open spot between the trees. He had learned how to keep his parachute from getting hung up in tree branches.

As Tom hit the ground, the sharp smell of burning wood surrounded him. He heard the great fire roaring in the distance like a huge waterfall.

The firefighters quickly put on their hard hats and protective gloves. Armed with shovels and axes, they set to work making a firebreak. They cut down trees and cleared away brush on a wide strip of land in front of the racing flames. Then they scraped away some of the soil till bare ground showed. When the fire reached this bare ground, it would have nothing to feed on and would stop.

If they could finish in time.

The fire was moving fast, pushed by the wind and by its own heat. The air was full of flying sparks, ash, and falling branches.

Tom swung his ax as fast as he could. He could hardly breathe the hot, smoke-filled air. He had never felt anything like this heat. The thick smoke stung his eyes and burned his throat.

A <u>crackling</u> sound was all around them. The popping noises from dry, burning wood grew louder. Worst of all were the echoing booms as trees crashed down. Tom worked as he had never worked before.

Over the roar of the fire, Tom heard John shout, "Hurry! The fire is almost on us!"

Tom's arms were sore and tired, but he swung his ax even faster. He didn't even stop to wipe the tears from his stinging eyes. The <u>greedy</u> fire kept coming. The more the fire destroyed, the more it wanted. Tom worked shoulder to shoulder with the other smoke jumpers. His only thought was to stop the flaming monster that was raging through the forest.

At last the the smoke jumpers finished the firebreak. If the fire was powerful enough, it would jump over the firebreak that they had worked so hard to make. Then they would have to start all over again.

A man is brave only when he forgets about himself.

Tom stood motionless, his face black with ash, his shirt wet with sweat. He was too exhausted to move. He had given all of himself to fighting the fire. He turned his head and noticed John watching him. John nodded.

Suddenly all that John had taught Tom about proving his bravery was clear. A man was not brave if he did something just to prove his courage. He was brave only when he forgot about himself. Today Tom had showed that he cared very much about the others with whom he was working. Like John, Bill, Rita, and the others, he wanted most of all to stop the fire.

"Look!" Rita yelled.

The fire was burning down. It was not going to jump the firebreak.

"Pineville is saved!" Tom cried. He felt more tired than he ever had in his life. Yet a feeling of joy rose in Tom. He had proved that, like the other brave smoke jumpers, he could make a contribution. He had helped his friends save Pineville.

John put his hand on Tom's shoulder, as the others looked on. "Good work, Tom," he said. "Glad you're with us." Tom knew that he had passed his test and proven his bravery.

120 **Lesson 43** *Understanding character*

Recalling details

1. Why did the firefighters jump from planes instead of going to the fire in trucks?

The fire could not be reached by land.

Recalling details

2. Why is it important that the firefighters jump at just the right time?

Timing is important because the firefighters don't want

their parachutes to get caught in the trees. They want

to land near the fire but not fall into the flames.

Recalling details

3. What is in danger if the fire isn't stopped?

The forest and the town of Pineville are in danger.

Identifying setting

4. a. Where did Tom grow up?

Tom grew up in a city.

b. Where does Tom fight the fire?

He fights the fire in a forest.

Recalling details

5. Who prepared Tom for his "test of fire"?

John Dull Knife prepared him.

Recalling details

6. What does Tom wear on his first jump?

He wore his sacred medicine bag.

Identifying cause and effect

7. Why does the fire stop when it reaches the firebreak?

Because the ground is bare and the fire has nothing to

feed on, it stops.

Identifying plot

8. What is the most exciting moment in the story's plot?

The most exciting part occurs when the smoke

jumpers finish the firebreak, and all they can do is wait

to see if it will stop the fire.

Using context clues

9. Draw a line to match each word to its correct meaning.

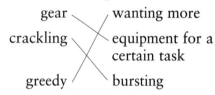

gear — wanting more

crackling — equipment for a certain task

greedy — bursting

Inferring comparisons and contrasts

1. At the beginning of the story, why does the test of fire mean more to Tom than any test at school?

The test of fire was so important to Tom because it would prove that he was brave; no school test could prove that.

Inferring sequence of events

2. What would the firefighters have to do if the fire jumped over the firebreak?

They would have to start all over again and make another firebreak.

Drawing conclusions

3. Do you think that Swift Eagle is an appropriate adult name for Tom? Tell why.

Although answers may vary, students should show an awareness that (a) the eagle's powerful wings and sharp

vision make it strong, fierce, and brave. These qualities are important to a Native American boy wishing to prove

that he is brave; (b) the eagle is a bird and flies. Tom Swift Eagle is part of a special group of firefighters who are

dropped from planes to fight fires.

Making inferences

4. How does Tom Swift Eagle pass his "test of fire"?

Tom passes his test by working with brave people and being as courageous as they are. Like them, he thinks only

about the general good (stopping the fire), not about himself.

Making inferences

5. Why does John say to Tom, "Glad you're with us"?

Tom has successfully passed his "test of fire"; he has shown himself to be brave and courageous like the other

firefighters.

Making inferences

6. There is a message in "Test of Fire." What do you think the author is trying to tell you?

Answers may vary. The author's message is that it is important to prove one's bravery by working with others rather

than working alone.

S KILL FOCUS

Understanding the main character's actions will help you appreciate the story.

1. Who is the main character?

Tom Swift Eagle is the main character.

2. a. What goal does he want to reach?

Tom's goal is to pass a test of fire.

b. Why is it important for him to reach this goal?

Reaching this goal is important because it will prove that he is brave.

3. What kind of person is Tom at the beginning of the story?

Tom is a very determined person. He joins the firefighting unit because he wants to show his bravery and courage in

fighting fires. If he passes this "test of fire," he will have proved that he is brave.

4. How has Tom changed by the end of the story?

By the end of the story, Tom is more concerned about others than about himself. Stopping the fire has become more

important to him than proving his bravery.

5. What has Tom learned by the end of the story?

Tom has learned that a person is brave only when he or she forgets about himself or herself and works instead for

the common or general good.

▶ **Real Life Connections** Describe someone who you think is brave.

Primary Source

Reading a Social Studies Selection

▶ Background Information

The Nez Percé lived in the plateau country, an area that is now where the states of Washington, Oregon, and Idaho meet. The Nez Percé originally called themselves Nee Me Poo, which means "the Real People." French-Canadian fur trappers called them Nez Percé and the people adopted the name, pronouncing it *nez purse*.

The most famous chief of the Nez Percé was Chief Joseph, whose Indian name was Thunder Traveling to Loftier Mountain Heights. Joseph was 31 years old when he became chief after the death of his father.

In this lesson, you will read about Chief Joseph. You will also read the stirring speech that he delivered to President Hayes in Washington, D.C.

▶ Skill Focus

Using a **primary source** will help you learn about past events. A primary source is a firsthand account. It is usually written by a person who took part in the event being described. Primary sources give facts about events. They also give insight into the thoughts and feelings of the people in the events. Letters, speeches, and newspaper articles are primary sources.

Often textbooks, magazines, encyclopedias, and so on, will contain excerpts, or pieces, of primary source materials. These excerpts are usually set apart in some way from the rest of the text.

When reading a primary source, use the following two steps.

1. **Find out all you can about the primary source.** Ask yourself the following questions.
   a. What type of document is it? Is it a letter, a report, an article, or a speech?
   b. Who wrote it? Was the author part of the event?
   c. When was it written?
2. **Study the primary source to learn about a past event.** Try to distinguish facts from opinions. A fact can be proven. An opinion is a judgment that reflects a person's feelings or beliefs.
   a. What facts can I learn from this document?
   b. What was the author's opinion about what was reported?

▶ Word Clues

Read the sentences below. Look for context clues that explain the underlined word.

As the early underlined settlers moved west, they came into conflict with the Indians who lived there. The settlers had left their homes to find new land. They wanted land for farming and for raising cattle.

If you do not know the word *settlers* in the first sentence, read the next two sentences. They give details about the settlers. The details tell more about the word so that you understand it.

Use **detail** context clues to find the meaning of the three underlined words in the selection.

▶ Strategy Tip

As you read Chief Joseph's words, keep in mind the two steps for using a primary source. Reading this speech will give you insight into the thoughts and feelings of Chief Joseph and his people.

A Great and Honorable Leader

The Gold Rush

The Nez Percé lived peacefully in their country for hundreds of years. They had experienced good relations with the white trappers and explorers. But in 1860, white prospectors illegally entered Nez Percé territory and found gold. During the gold rush, thousands of miners settled on Nez Percé reservation lands, disobeying an earlier treaty. For the first time, friction developed between whites and the Nez Percé.

In 1863, under pressure from the gold miners to remove the Nez Percé from valuable mineral sources, the U.S. government demanded that the Nez Percé cede, or give up, about 6 million acres of reservation land. The majority of Nez Percé refused. A government commissioner bribed several chiefs who sold the land and signed the treaty. The government official reported to the U.S. government that he had secured all lands demanded "at a cost not exceeding 8 cents per acre."

As a result of the land sale, the Nez Percé divided into "treaty" and "nontreaty" bands. Among those who were angry about the selling of Indian land was Tuekakas, also known as Old Joseph. By 1871, thousands of settlers had moved onto reservation land, as was allowed by the new treaty. Near his death, Old Joseph spoke to his son Young Joseph about their homeland:

> My son, my body is returning to my mother earth, and my spirit is going very soon to see the Great Spirit Chief. When I am gone, think of your country. You are the chief of these people. They look to you to guide them. Always remember that your father never sold his country. You must stop your ears whenever you are asked to sign a treaty selling your home.
>
> . . . My son, never forget my dying words. This country holds your father's body. Never sell the bones of your father and your mother.

Chief of Peace

Upon his father's death, Joseph became the civil, or peace, chief of his father's band. Joseph held many councils, or meetings, with civil and military officials. In 1873, Joseph convinced the government that it had not legally secured title to the reservation lands. The government ordered the whites to move out of the territory. However, the government then reversed its decision under pressure from Oregon politicians and settlers.

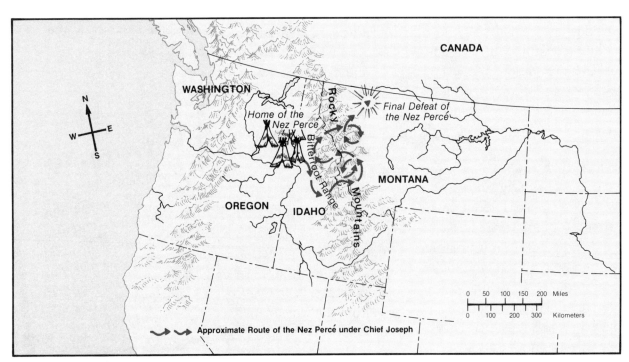

This map shows the retreat of the Nez Percé.

Understanding the dilemma of the U.S. government, Joseph continued to strive for a peaceful solution to the land problem. In 1877, General Oliver O. Howard concluded that the only solution was to force all the Nez Percé off their land and onto a reservation in Washington.

Many of the "nontreaty" Nez Percé wanted to fight for their land. Chief Joseph didn't want to fight. He knew that fighting would only bring death and sadness to his people. Joseph believed that he had no other choice but to lead his people to the reservation. So in the spring of 1877, Joseph agreed to the demands of the U.S. government. Several other nontreaty bands joined Joseph's for one last gathering on their land. While there, several men decided to seek revenge on white settlers for the death of one's father and for other grievances. They killed four white settlers.

Knowing that General Howard would send troops after them, the bands withdrew to Whitebird Canyon. Thus began a remarkable <u>retreat</u>, in which the Nez Percé fought, alluded, and outwitted one military force after another for four months. With about 750 people, including sick and elderly people, women, and children, the Nez Percé circled over a thousand miles trying to reach safety in Canada.

The soldiers who fought Chief Joseph thought that he was a great and honorable man. The soldiers knew that the Nez Percé never killed without reason. They could have burned and destroyed the property of many settlers, but they did not. Joseph and his people fought only to defend themselves and their land. The white soldiers were also impressed with their ability to allude the army for so many months and over so many miles.

"I Will Fight No More, Forever"
But the end finally came. Unaware that the army under Colonel Nelson A. Miles was in close <u>pursuit</u>, the Nez Percé camped less than 40 miles south of the Canadian border. At the end of a five-day siege, Chief Joseph decided to <u>surrender</u> to Miles on October 5, 1877. He rode into the army camp alone and handed his rifle to the soldiers. He said:

I am tired of fighting. My people ask me for food and I have none to give. It is cold and we have no blankets, no wood. My people are starving. . . . Hear me, my chiefs. I have fought, but from where the

sun now stands, Joseph will fight no more, forever.

After Joseph's surrender, the U.S. government ordered them onto a reservation in Kansas, then to a disease-ridden reservation in Oklahoma. Many of the Nez Percé died of malaria and other sicknesses.

Chief Joseph pleaded on behalf of his people to gain permission to return to a reservation in the Northwest. In 1879, Chief Joseph traveled to Washington to plead his case to President Hayes.

Chief Joseph's Speech
If the white man wants to live in peace with the Indian, he can live in peace. There need be no trouble. Treat all men alike. Give them the same laws. Give them all an even chance to live and grow.

All men are made by the same Great Spirit Chief. They are all brothers. The earth is the mother of all people, and all people should have equal rights upon it. You might as well expect all rivers to run backward as that any man born a free man should be contented penned up and denied liberty to go where he pleases. If you tie a horse to a stake, do you expect he will grow fat? If you pen an Indian

Chief Joseph of the Nez Percé Indians.

up on a small spot of earth and compel him to stay there, he will not be contented, nor will he grow and prosper.

I have asked some of the Great White Chiefs where they get their authority to say to the Indian that he shall stay in one place, while he sees white men going where they please. They cannot tell me.

I only ask of the government to be treated as all other men are treated. If I cannot go to my own home, let me have a home in a country where my people will not die so fast. I would like to go to Bitterroot Valley. There my people would be healthy; where they are now, they are dying. . . . Three have died since I left my camp to come to Washington. When I think of our condition, my heart is heavy. I see men of my own race treated as outlaws and driven from country to country, or shot down like animals.

Whenever the white man treats the Indian as they treat each other, then we shall have no more wars. We shall all be alike—brothers of one father and mother, with one sky above us and one country around us and one government for all. Then the Great Spirit Chief who rules above will smile upon this land and send rain to wash out the bloody spots made by brothers' hands upon the face of the earth. For this time, the Indian race are waiting and praying. I hope no more groans of wounded men and women will ever go to the ear of the Great Spirit Chief above, and that all people may be one people.

In 1885, after eight years of campaigning on behalf of his people, Joseph and the other Nez Percé were allowed to return to the Northwest. Unable to join the treaty bands on the Idaho reservation, Joseph and the others were escorted to the Colville Reservation in Washington Territory. It was there that Joseph died in 1904, reportedly from a broken heart.

RECALLING FACTS

Recalling details
1. Where did the Nez Percé originally live?

They lived where the states of Washington, Oregon,

and Idaho meet.

Recalling details
2. Why did the settlers want the Nez Percé land?

They were searching for gold.

Identifying cause and effect
3. What event divided the Nez Percé into two groups

Several chiefs sold reservation land and signed a

treaty, thereby dividing the Nez Percé into "treaty" and

"nontreaty" groups.

Recalling details
4. Why did Chief Joseph lead his people to the reservation in 1877?

He knew that fighting the settlers would bring only

death and sadness to his people.

Comparing and contrasting
5. Why did the soldiers think that Chief Joseph was a great leader?

His people never killed without a reason, did not burn

or destroy the property of settlers, and fought only to

defend themselves and their land.

Recalling details
6. After living on a reservation, where did Chief Joseph say he wanted to take his people? Why?

Chief Joseph wanted to take his people to Canada,

where they would not have to live on a reservation.

Using context clues
7. Write the letter of the correct meaning in front of each word.

c	retreat	**a.**	following in order to capture
a	pursuit	**b.**	to give up
b	surrender	**c.**	to go to a safe place

Identifying point of view

1. For each pair of sentences, circle the letter next to the statement that expresses Chief Joseph's thoughts and opinions in his speech.

    (a.) The white man can live in peace with the Indian if all men are treated alike under the same law.

    b. Because so many promises have been broken, there can never be peace between the white man and the Indian.

    a. There will be no more wars when the settlers sign a peace treaty with the Indians.

    (b.) There will be no more wars when the settlers treat the Indians as they treat each other.

Drawing conclusions

2. Decide whether Chief Joseph is a great and honorable leader. To reach a conclusion, you must look carefully at Chief Joseph's actions and the reasons for them. His major actions are listed in order below. For each action Chief Joseph takes, give the reasons.

    a. Chief Joseph first agrees to lead his people to the reservation without a fight.
    He knows that the small number of Nez Percé cannot win against the army.

    b. Chief Joseph decides to lead his people to Canada.
    He wants to escape the army's punishment for some of his warriors' actions. Also, in Canada, they would not be
    put on reservations.

    c. Chief Joseph will fight the army only if they try to stop him.
    He knows that the battle will end only in defeat because of the greater number of army soldiers.

    d. Chief Joseph leads his people on a twisting trail through the mountains for four months.
    He is trying to avoid battle and being captured by the soliders who are pursuing him and his people.

    e. During this time, Chief Joseph tries not to get into battles with the army.
    He knows that the skills of his warriors will not allow them to win against the army in direct battle.

    f. Chief Joseph says that he will "fight no more, forever" and leads his people to the reservation.
    The army has trapped them. His people have suffered great losses. They are cold and hungry.
    They must either surrender or die.

    g. Two years later, Chief Joseph speaks out against being "penned up" on a reservation even though he led his people there.
    He believes that taking away a people's freedom is another kind of death. People, like animals, were not meant to
    live "penned up." Yet, he has given his word.

Now answer this question: Do you think that Chief Joseph was a great and honorable leader? In your answer, first tell what you mean by the words *great* and by *honorable*. Then tell why you think Chief Joseph was or was not a great and honorable leader.

Conclusions will vary, but all answers should include the following: (a) Student's definition of *great* and *honorable* and

(b) student's conclusion about Chief Joseph should be consistent with their definitions of *great* and *honorable* and

should cite facts in the selection and speech that led to the conclusion.

SKILL FOCUS

Reread Chief Joseph's speech. Pay special attention to what it tells you about Chief Joseph's feelings and motives. Then answer the questions below.

1. *Find out all you can about the primary source.*

What type of document is this? _____a speech_____

Who wrote it? _____Chief Joseph_____

Was the author involved in the event? _____yes_____

When was it written? _____1879_____

2. *Study the primary source to learn about a past event.*

What facts can you learn from this document? Indian lands were being overrun by white men; many Indians were dying and being treated as outlaws.

What was the author's opinion about what was reported? Chief Joseph believed that the Indians and white men could live in peace if all were subject to the same laws. He thought that his people would prosper if they could be moved back to the Pacific Northwest (Oregon).

▶ **Real Life Connections** Write an interesting fact or story about the history of your community. List your primary sources.

Main Idea and Supporting Details

Reading a Science Selection

▶ **Background Information**

National parks and wilderness areas are areas set aside by the federal government for everyone to enjoy. Many of these areas remain undeveloped so that their natural beauty is unspoiled. However, because of lack of funding the future of these parks and wilderness areas is now threatened. In this selection, you will read about the ways in which some people are destroying these areas.

▶ **Skill Focus**

When reading textbooks, it is helpful to look for **main ideas and supporting details**. As you know, the main idea is the most important idea in a paragraph. The supporting details tell more about the main idea. They help to prove that the main idea is true.

Read the paragraph below.

Sandra loves to ride horses. She saved the money that she earned after school to buy a horse. Now she rides her horse every day. She also goes roller-blading three times a week.

The first sentence has the main idea. It says that Sandra loves to ride horses. The second sentence says that she saved her money to buy a horse. This sentence supports the main idea because a person who does not love to ride horses probably wouldn't buy one. The third sentence also supports the main idea. However, the last sentence does not support the main idea. The fact that Sandra roller-blades three times a week has nothing to do with her love of horses. This sentence does not belong in the paragraph.

When you read a selection that is packed with information, use the following steps:

1. Find the main idea in each paragraph.
2. Find the supporting details that tell about this main idea.
3. Reread the supporting details carefully and decide whether they support the main idea.

▶ **Word Clues**

Read the following sentences. Look for detail clues that explain the underlined word.

Today's national parks are the result of work done long ago. Beautiful trees and ponds have been handed down to us by people who cared about nature. The efforts to save some of our natural <u>heritage</u> began more than one hundred years ago.

The word *heritage* in the last sentence is explained by the sentences before it. These sentences give details about our natural heritage. They help you understand the meaning of the word *heritage.*

Use **detail** context clues to find the meaning of the three underlined words in the selection.

▶ **Strategy Tip**

As you read each paragraph in the following selection, try to find the supporting details for each main idea. Remember that each paragraph has one main idea, which can be stated in any sentence in the paragraph.

Preserving Park and Wilderness Areas

1. For years, people have been changing the earth, but the changes have not always been for the better. Suddenly, we discover that the best scenery and wilderness areas are disappearing. Every summer, millions of people take outdoor vacations in hope of enjoying nature. Too often they find parks crowded with people, fast food restaurants, and gift shops.

2. Today's national parks are the result of work done long ago. Beautiful trees and ponds have been handed down to us by people who cared about nature. The efforts to save our natural heritage began more than one hundred years ago. In 1872, the U.S. Congress passed a law setting up Yellowstone National Park for public use. Since then, about two hundred other national park areas have been set up. They are run by the National Park Service. Hundreds of state parks have also been set up. Many parks are overcrowded in the summer. Over the years, more and more people are visiting national parks

3. Because of <u>vandalism</u>, federal and state governments are finding it difficult to keep up the parks. It is difficult to believe that there are people who like to destroy or spoil beautiful things. Unfortunately, some people ruin things and places that everyone could enjoy. Some people damage museum <u>exhibits</u>. Objects, such as valuable paintings, jewels, or old books and clothing, are displayed in museums. There is always the chance that these artifacts will be damaged. Some people throw all kinds of litter in park areas. Others spoil what is left of very old buildings by writing on them. They use paint or lipstick that makes cleaning and repairing difficult to do. The <u>defacement</u> of historic buildings and monuments has become a big problem. Millions of dollars are spent each year to repair damage caused by vandals.

4. Not everybody understands how important **sanctuaries** (SANK chew wer eez) and wilderness areas are. Sanctuaries are places where it is illegal to hunt birds and animals. Many people do not seem to understand why roads should not be built through these areas. They don't see why homes and businesses are not allowed in them. If these places were built up with homes and roads, they couldn't be used for **habitat** (HAB ə tat) studies. A habitat is an area where a certain type of animal is usually found.

5. Some ranchers would like to raise more cattle. Some mining companies would like to dig for minerals. Some real estate developers would like to build houses and sell land in "undeveloped" areas. Some people who are very eager to make more money don't want more public parks.

Recalling details

1. When did Congress set up Yellowstone National Park as a public park?

_____1872_____

Identifying cause and effect

2. Why are national and state governments finding it difficult to keep up the parks?

Vandalism is the primary cause of this problem.

Recalling details

3. What is a wildlife sanctuary?

A wildlife sanctuary is a place where it is illegal to hunt

birds and animals.

Recalling details

4. What do some mining companies want to do in undeveloped areas?

They want to dig for minerals.

INTERPRETING FACTS

Making inferences

1. Why might the building of roads and homes in wildlife sanctuaries ruin habitat studies?

It might change the way in which the animals live.

_____

Inferring cause and effect

2. How do wilderness areas disappear?

People cut down trees, drain swamps, and build

roads and homes.

_____

_____

Making connections

3. Decide if each of the following statements is true or false. Write *true* or *false* on the lines.

a. Picking up trash on the sidewalk would be considered vandalism.

_____false_____

b. A display of movie costumes and a showcase of puppets are both exhibits.

_____true_____

c. Sticking chewing gum on the seat of a bus is an example of defacement.

_____true_____

SKILL FOCUS

The main idea of each numbered paragraph is given below. Write the supporting details on the lines below each main idea. Use your own words. Leave out any details that do not support the main idea. The first one is done for you.

Paragraph 1

Main Idea   For many years, people have been changing the earth, but the changes have not always been for the better.

Supporting Details

a. Much of the best wilderness land is disappearing.

b. Millions of people take outdoor vacations in the hope of enjoying nature.

c. Parks and wilderness areas are crowded with people, restaurants, and shops.

Paragraph 2

Main Idea   The efforts to save our natural heritage began more than one hundred years ago.

Supporting Details

a. In 1872, Yellowstone National Park was set up for public use.

b. About two hundred other national parks have been set up.

c. They are run by the National Park Service.

d. Hundreds of state parks have been set up.

Paragraph 3

Main Idea   Because of vandalism, federal and state governments are finding it difficult to keep up the parks.

Supporting Details

a. Some people damage museum exhibits.

b. Some people throw litter in park areas.

c. Some people destroy what is left of very old buildings by writing on them.

d. They use paint or lipstick that makes cleaning or repairing difficult to do.

e. The defacement of historic buildings and monuments is a big problem.

f. Repairing the effects of vandalism costs millions of dollars each year.

Paragraph 4

Main Idea   Not everybody understands that sanctuaries and wilderness areas are important.

Supporting Details

a. Many people don't understand why roads shouldn't be built through these areas.

b. They don't understand why houses and businesses aren't allowed.

c. If these areas were built up, they couldn't be used for habitat studies.

Paragraph 5

Main Idea   Some people who are very eager to make more money don't want more public parks.

Supporting Details

a. Ranchers want land for raising cattle.

b. Mining companies want land for digging minerals.

c. Real estate developers want land for building houses and selling lots.

▶ **Real Life Connections** What could you do to beautify or preserve a park or wilderness area in your city or town?

Reading a Table

Reading a Mathematics Selection

▶ **Background Information**

As you probably already know, organization is an important skill to learn. When you are organized, you will usually succeed at whatever task you are doing.

When you look at a table, think about what is really happening. The numbers are *organized* so that the person looking at the table can gather the information that he or she needs in a short period of time.

In this way, tables are really nothing more than tools for your convenience. Just like a calculator or a ruler, tables are there to assist you.

Imagine for a moment that you live in a world without tables. Because there are no tables, you would probably use lists to present most information. One of the drawbacks with lists is that the information is not as readily available. It would probably take you twice as long to find the information that you need.

In the following lesson, you will learn about the growth in population as settlers moved west from 1790 to 1830. In addition, you will learn how easy it is to use and read tables, as well as how to set up a table from information presented in a paragraph.

When reading the following selection, remember to read the table carefully. Read across the rows and then down the columns. Notice the headings.

▶ **Skill Focus**

Information can be presented in a variety of ways, such as tables, charts, and diagrams. It is a valuable skill to be able to read and interpret information that is presented in these ways.

Tables that show number facts appear in many books, including textbooks, encyclopedias magazines, and newspapers.

You read tables to find certain facts, as well as to compare facts. It is often easier to find and use number facts presented in a table than number facts given in a paragraph. When reading a table, first read the title and the headings. They will tell you what the numbers in the table stand for.

▶ **Word Clues**

Look for the following words in the selection: *population, data, asterisk.* Be sure that you understand their meanings.

Use **synonym** context clues to find the meaning of these words if you are unfamiliar with the words. Remember that synonym clues use familiar words to restate and, therefore, define the unfamiliar words. Synonym clues can often be found in the same sentence. They can also be found in the sentence before or the sentence after the sentence in which the unfamiliar word appears.

▶ **Strategy Tip**

When reading a mathematics selection, you must learn how to read information that is presented in tables, charts, and diagrams.

In order to get all the information from a table, remember to read both across the rows and down the columns.

Reading a Table

Shortly after Europeans came to the New World, they established 13 colonies in what are now Maine, New Hampshire, Rhode Island, Massachusetts, Connecticut, New York, New Jersey, Pennsylvania, Maryland, Virginia, North Carolina, South Carolina, and Georgia. Over time, though, people began to look toward the West. Slowly at first, brave individuals and families loaded everything that they owned into wagons and moved West. When gold was discovered in California in 1849, the westward migration increased rapidly. Populations in other areas increased again during the gold rushes of 1860 and 1874.

The table below presents information on the populations of several states during the years 1790–1830. Population means "the number of people living in an area." These states were among the first ones to be colonized in the West after the first 13 colonies in the East. Information, or data, about population is often shown in a table.

The title of the table tells what the table shows. Always read the title before studying a table. In the chart below, the states are listed in the column on the far left. The years are printed across the top. The population figures are listed in columns under each year.

✔ When reading a table, you may wish to use a sheet of paper or ruler to make sure that you are looking at the correct row. Place a sheet of paper under the word *Indiana* in the chart. Now look across until you find the number in the column labeled 1830. The number is 343,000. This number means that there were 343,000 people living in Indiana in 1830.

Read across from *Ohio*. You can see that in the year 1790, there were 73,600 people living in Ohio. In the year 1800, 145,300 people were living there. Keep reading across and find Ohio's population in 1810, 1820, and 1830. As you can see, the number of people living in Ohio increased over the years.

Now look down the column on the far left until you find Illinois. Did the number of people living in Illinois also increase over the years?

Look for Michigan's population in 1800. The star, or asterisk, in that column tells you to look at the bottom of the table. In the lower left corner of the table, find the words *no data available*. In other words, there is no record of the population of Michigan in the year 1800.

Population Growth in the West 1790–1830					
	1790	1800	1810	1820	1830
Alabama	*	*	*	127,900	309,500
Arkansas	*	*	1,060	14,200	30,300
Illinois	*	*	12,200	55,200	157,400
Indiana	*	5,600	24,500	148,100	343,000
Kentucky	35,690	220,900	406,500	564,300	687,400
Louisiana	*	*	76,500	153,400	215,700
Michigan	*	*	4,760	8,900	31,600
Mississippi	*	8,800	40,300	75,400	136,600
Missouri	*	*	19,700	66,500	140,400
Ohio	73,600	145,300	230,700	581,400	937,900
Tennessee	*	105,600	261,700	422,800	681,900

*no data available

Use the table on page 134 to answer the following questions.

Reading a table
1. Which state had the largest population in 1820? _____ Ohio _____

Reading a table
2. Which state had the smallest population in 1800? _____ Indiana _____

Reading a table
3. For Tennessee, what does the asterisk mean under 1790? _No record of population is available._

Reading a table
4. From 1810 to 1820, did the population of Ohio or Kentucky increase more? _____ Ohio _____

Reading a table
5. Which state had the lowest population in 1830? _____ Arkansas _____

Recalling details
6. What should you read first before studying a table? _____ the title _____

Recalling details
7. When reading a table, what should you use to make sure that you are looking at the correct

row? _____ a sheet of paper or ruler _____

Identifying the main idea
8. Reread the paragraph that has a check mark next to it. Draw a line under the sentence that has the main idea.

INTERPRETING FACTS

Use the table on page 134 to answer the following questions.

Making inferences
1. Why are the states listed in the table in alphabetical order?
Listing the states in alphabetical order makes it easier to find a particular state.

Making inferences
2. Why do you think there is more information available in later years than in early years?
The government probably counted the people in later years.

Making inferences
3. Why might the population of the western states have increased faster than the population in northeastern states?
People from the northeast moved west, where more land was available.

A. Use the table below to answer the questions that follow.

Native American Population by Selected Regions, 1990	
Region	**Population**
Northeastern States	33,000
Mountain States	481,000
Pacific States	362,000
South Atlantic States	156,000

1. What is the title of the table?

Native American Population by Selected Regions, 1990

2. What is the Native American population of the Mountain States region?

481,000

3. Which region has a Native American population of 362,000?

Pacific States

4. Which region has the largest Native American population?

Mountain States

5. What is the total Native American population in the Northeastern States and Mountain States?

514,000

6. What is the difference between the population of Native Americans in the Pacific States region and those in the South Atlantic States region?

206,000

B. Use the information in the following paragraph to complete the table below. The paragraph gives information about some federal and state reservations for Native Americans.

Arizona has 23 reservations where 203,500 Native Americans live. Massachusetts has only 1 reservation, with 12,200 people living there. New York has 8 reservations for 62,700 people. Wyoming has 1 reservation where 9,500 people live.

Some Federal and State Reservations for Native Americans		
State	**Number of Reservations**	**Population**
Arizona	23	203,500
Massachusetts	1	12,200
New York	8	62,700
Wyoming	1	9,500

C. Make your own table using the following information. Then write three questions about your table. Use another sheet of paper for your table and questions.

In 1990, there were 203,500 Native Americans in Arizona. Oklahoma had about 252,400 Native Americans, and South Dakota had 50,600. Washington state had 81,500 Native Americans. Minnesota had 50,000.

▶ **Real Life Connections** Create a table showing the population growth of your community or state over the last 10 years.

Syllables

You have used three guides for dividing words into **syllables**: Guide 1, dividing between the two smaller words in a compound word; Guide 2, dividing between double consonants; and Guide 3, dividing between a prefix or suffix and a root word. Now you will have practice in using another guide.

Words with Two Consonants Between Two Sounded Vowels

The words in the list below have been divided into syllables. Write an answer to each of the questions in the headings below.

	How many sounded vowels?	*How many consonants between the vowels?*	*Where is the word divided?*
dan ger	2	2	between the two consonants
bas ket	2	2	between the two consonants
mar ket	2	2	between the two consonants
har bor	2	2	between the two consonants
don key	2	2	between the two consonants
pic ture	2	2	between the two consonants

Fill in the words necessary to complete the following guide.

Guide 4: A word that has two _____consonants_____ between two sounded _____vowels_____ is usually divided into syllables between the two _____consonants_____.

Divide each word below into two syllables by writing each syllable separately on the line to the right of the word.

1. winter ___win ter___
2. turban ___tur ban___
3. number ___num ber___
4. shelter ___shel ter___
5. jersey ___jer sey___
6. larva ___lar va___

7. magnet ___mag net___
8. seldom ___sel dom___
9. practice ___prac tice___
10. circus ___cir cus___
11. hemlock ___hem lock___
12. surface ___sur face___

13. sentence ___sen tence___
14. monkey ___mon key___
15. furnace ___fur nace___
16. service ___ser vice___
17. entire ___en tire___
18. compare ___com pare___

Syllables

Words with One Consonant Between Two Sounded Vowels

Here is a guide that will help you divide words into **syllables**. It shows you how to divide words that have one consonant between two sounded vowels. The guide has two parts.

The words in the list below are divided into syllables. Write an answer to each of the questions in the headings.

	How many sounded vowels?	How many consonants between the vowels?	Is the first vowel long or short?	Is the word divided before or after the consonant?
spi der	2	1	long	before
me ter	2	1	long	before
to tal	2	1	long	before

Fill in the words necessary to complete the first guide.

> **Guide 5a:** A word that has one ___consonant___ between two sounded ___vowels___,
>
> with the first vowel long, is usually divided into syllables before the ___consonant___.

Divide each of the words below into two syllables by writing each syllable separately on the line to the right of the word.

1. tiger ___ti ger___   **3.** pilot ___pi lot___   **5.** silent ___si lent___

2. local ___lo cal___   **4.** moment ___mo ment___   **6.** minus ___mi nus___

To complete the second part of the guide, write an answer to each of the questions in the headings below.

	How many sounded vowels?	How many consonants between the vowels?	Is the first vowel long or short?	Is the word divided before or after the consonant?
cab in	2	1	short	after
top ic	2	1	short	after
riv er	2	1	short	after

Fill in the words necessary to complete the second guide.

> **Guide 5b:** A word that has one ___consonant___ between two sounded vowels, with the first
>
> ___vowel___ ___short___, is usually divided into syllables ___after___ the ___consonant___.

Words with Blends

The word *betray* has two consonants between the two sounded vowels, but you do not divide the word between the two consonants.

bet ray

Since *tr* is a consonant blend, it is considered in the same way that one consonant would be considered. So Guide 5a applies, and the word is divided before the blend.

be tray

If three consonants are in the middle of a word, it is possible that two of those consonants are a blend. You treat the blend as one consonant. For example, *compress* has a *pr* blend. You divide the word between the consonant and the consonant blend.

com press

In words ending with a consonant and -*le,* these letter groups are treated as one syllable.

tum ble

Circle the blend or consonant and -*le,* in each word below. Then divide the word into syllables by writing each syllable separately on the line to the right of the word.

1. replied _____ re plied _____
2. congress _____ con gress _____
3. declare _____ de clare _____
4. children _____ chil dren _____
5. explain _____ ex plain _____
6. control _____ con trol _____
7. increase _____ in crease _____
8. complain _____ com plain _____
9. purple _____ pur ple _____
10. subtract _____ sub tract _____

11. cradle _____ cra dle _____
12. matron _____ ma tron _____
13. central _____ cen tral _____
14. reply _____ re ply _____
15. secret _____ se cret _____
16. supply _____ sup ply _____
17. curdle _____ cur dle _____
18. substance _____ sub stance _____
19. complete _____ com plete _____
20. stable _____ sta ble _____

21. Pilgrim _____ Pil grim _____
22. microbe _____ mi crobe _____
23. muscle _____ mus cle _____
24. hustle _____ hus tle _____
25. tremble _____ trem ble _____
26. between _____ be tween _____
27. circle _____ cir cle _____
28. emblem _____ em blem _____
29. comprise _____ com prise _____
30. paddle _____ pad dle _____

Fill in the words necessary to complete the following guide.

Guide 6: Do not split a consonant _____ blend _____ or a consonant and _____ -*le* _____.
Treat a consonant blend or _____ consonant _____ and -*le* as if it were one consonant.

Making Inferences

In many of the paragraphs that you read, information is given about a subject. You can use this information to **infer** other information. When you infer, you put together what you read in the selection with what you already know about a topic to figure out something new.

Read the following selection about Ada Deer. Answer the questions by making inferences about what you read.

Ada E. Deer was born and raised in a one-room log cabin on the Menominee Indian Reservation in Wisconsin. All during her childhood, Ada Deer believed that education was very important. When she was ready for college, her tribe gave her a scholarship. She became the first Menominee to graduate from the University of Wisconsin. Later, she was the first Native American to obtain a master's degree in social work from Columbia University in New York City.

Deer's education included law school, but in the 1970s she dropped out to help her people. The Menominee were

struggling for survival. Their land, once held in trust for them by the government, had lost its trust status. She wrote: "As a teenager, I saw the poverty of the people—poor housing, poor education, poor health. I thought, this isn't the way it should be. . . . I wanted to help the tribe in some way. . . . "

Ada Deer became a tribal chief and a social worker. In helping Native Americans, she has kept her vow to repay her tribe for giving her a chance for a higher education. As of 1995, she was working for the U.S. government at the Bureau of Indian Affairs as its assistant secretary.

1. Why do you think that Ada Deer's tribe gave her a scholarship?

The tribe knew that she valued education; the tribe believed that a member with a higher education could help the

Menominee.

2. How do you know Ada Deer works hard?

She has two college degrees; she helped save the Menominee people and their lands; she became a tribal chief.

3. How did Ada Deer repay her tribe for making higher education possible?

She became a tribal chief and social worker and now works at the Bureau of Indian Affairs.

4. How do you think Ada Deer feels about Native Americans?

She respects and honors them; she wants to improve conditions for them.

5. How do you think Ada Deer would feel about the ability of people to change things?

She would be very positive and optimistic because she helped change conditions for her tribe.

Lesson 50

Alphabetical Order

Below are some words that you might find in a science textbook. These words are not in **alphabetical order.** On the numbered lines, write the words in alphabetical order according to the first letter in each word. Cross out each word in the list after you write it.

kerosene	tide	1. ant		13. moon	
nectar	lake	2. bees		14. nectar	
underground	jet	3. cell		15. ocean	
equator	bees	4. dew		16. planet	
planet	ocean	5. equator		17. quartz	
Venus	star	6. fish		18. root	
quartz	wind	7. germ		19. star	
fish	cell	8. hail		20. tide	
hail	moon	9. insect		21. underground	
dew	X-ray	10. jet		22. Venus	
insect	ant	11. kerosene		23. wind	
root	germ	12. lake		24. X-ray	

In a dictionary, you see many pages of words that begin with the same letter. What if you are looking up a word that begins with letter *p*? To find the word, turn to the *p* section of the dictionary, and use the second letter of the word as a guide. For example, the word *pattern* is listed before the word *platter* because *a* comes before *l* in the alphabet. When several words begin with the same letter, they are arranged in alphabetical order according to the second letter in the word.

Below are some words that you might find in a social studies textbook. On the numbered lines, write the words in alphabetical order according to the first two letters in each word. Cross out each word in the list after you write it.

arctic	atlas	1. adobe		8. arctic	
age	aviation	2. Africa		9. Asia	
Asia	Africa	3. age		10. atlas	
axis	automobile	4. airplanes		11. automobile	
alfalfa	Andes	5. alfalfa		12. aviation	
airplanes	Aztec	6. Amazon		13. axis	
adobe	Amazon	7. Andes		14. Aztec	

Lesson 51

Guide Words

At the top of each dictionary page are two words by themselves. These words are called **guide words**. Guide words help you find entry words easily and quickly. They tell you the first entry word on the page and the last entry word on the page. All the other entry words on that page come between these two words in alphabetical order.

Below are two pairs of guide words that might appear on two dictionary pages. Following each pair is a list of entry words. If an entry word would be on the same page as the guide words, write *yes* next to the word. If an entry word would appear on an earlier page, write *before*. If an entry word would appear on a later page, write *after*. Some of the entry words in each list begin with the same first two letters. You will need to look at the third letters to complete this activity.

pencil/polite

1. percent_____yes_____
2. pouch_____after_____
3. pepper _____yes_____
4. pay _____before_____
5. pearl_____before_____
6. power_____after_____
7. permit _____yes_____
8. pigeon _____yes_____

9. pool _____after_____
10. pebble _____before_____
11. petunia _____yes_____
12. pocket _____yes_____
13. pelican_____before_____
14. point _____yes_____
15. pony_____after_____
16. poet _____yes_____

17. pedal _____before_____
18. porcupine _____after_____
19. pester_____yes_____
20. play _____yes_____
21. patient _____before_____
22. perch _____yes_____
23. polish_____yes_____
24. poodle_____after_____

gem/goose

1. gear _____before_____
2. geography _____yes_____
3. graduate_____after_____
4. giant_____yes_____
5. gown _____after_____
6. golf_____yes_____
7. gather_____before_____
8. gelatin _____before_____

9. general_____yes_____
10. goggle _____yes_____
11. got _____after_____
12. geranium_____yes_____
13. geese _____before_____
14. goat _____yes_____
15. gently_____yes_____
16. govern _____after_____

17. gone_____yes_____
18. gourd_____after_____
19. gaze _____before_____
20. gift _____yes_____
21. good _____yes_____
22. genius _____yes_____
23. gate _____before_____
24. gorilla _____after_____

Lesson 52

Dictionary Entry

In a dictionary, the entry word and all the information about it is the **entry**. The entry word always appears in boldface type. If the word has more than one syllable, it is divided into syllables to show where the word can be divided at the end of a line of writing.

The entry word is followed by a **respelling** of the word in parentheses. The respelling shows you how to pronounce the word.

The part-of-speech label follows the respelling. The labels are usually abbreviated as follows: *adj.* for adjective, *adv.* for adverb, *conj.* for conjunction, *interj.* for interjection, *n.* for noun, *prep.* for preposition, *pron.* for pronoun, and *v.* for verb.

The meanings are arranged according to parts of speech. For example, if an entry has noun meanings, they are grouped together and numbered following the *n.* label. Any meanings the word may have for other parts of speech are numbered and placed after the appropriate labels. When an entry has only one meaning for any part of speech, the definition is not numbered.

At the end of some entries are phrases or idioms. An **idiom** is a group of words that has a meaning different from the meaning the words have by themselves. In some dictionaries, idioms have a dash in front of them and appear in boldface type.

Use the dictionary entry below to answer the questions that follow it.

wear (wer) *v.* **1** to have or carry on the body [*Wear* your coat. Do you *wear* glasses?] **2** to have or show in the way one appears [She *wore* a frown. He *wears* his hair long.] **3** to make or become damaged, used up, etc., by use or friction [She *wore* her jeans to rags. The water is *wearing* away the river bank.] **4** to make by use or friction [He *wore* a hole in his sock.] **5** to last in use [This cloth *wears* well.] **6** to pass gradually [The year *wore* on.]—**wore, worn, wear′ ing** ◆*n.* **1** the act of wearing or the condition of being worn [a dress for holiday *wear*.] **2** clothes; clothing [men's *wear*]. **3** the damage or loss from use or friction [These shoes show a little *wear*.] **4** the ability to last in use [There's a lot of *wear* left in that tire.]—**wear down**, **1** to become less in height or thickness by use or friction. **2** to overcome by continuing to try [to *wear down* an enemy].—**wear off**, to pass away gradually [The effects of the medicine *wore off*.]—**wear out**, **1** to make or become useless from much use or friction. **2** to tire out; exhaust.

1. What is the entry word? _____wear_____

2. Write the respelling. _____(wer)_____

3. How many verb meanings follow the part-of-speech label *v.*? _____6_____

4. How many noun meanings follow the part-of-speech label *n.*? _____4_____

5. Write the first noun meaning. the act of wearing or the condition of being worn

6. What is the fifth verb meaning? to last in use

7. Write the idiom with the same meaning as the underlined words below.

Jane overcame by continuous effort her dad's resistance to buying her a car. wore down

A full day at the amusement park was enough to tire out Jill. wear out

Library Catalog

To locate a book in the library quickly and easily, use the **library catalog.** In most cases, the catalog will be a computer database. You find the information that you want by choosing items from a menu or list. On the main, or first menu, one of the numbered items will be the library catalog. When you choose that item, a second menu will appear. Now you can choose to search for a book by the title, author's name, or subject that it is about. If you don't have exact information about the book, you may be able to choose an item called **key words.** The computer will search its database using only one or two important words that you give it.

The catalog gives more information than just the author, title, and subject of a book. Usually each entry gives a summary and describes the book (size, number of pages, kinds of illustrations). It also gives the publisher, the date of publication, and a list of related subjects. It may also tell how many copies there are, which libraries have the book, and whether it is available.

Suppose you want a book about space flight. First, you choose "Subject" from the catalog menu to do a **subject search.** Then you enter the words *space flight.* (You could also enter words such as *space exploration, outer space,* or *astronauts.*) A list of subjects will appear. Choose your subject to see a list of books about that topic. Then you can choose a particular book to find out more about it.

If you want to find a list of books written by a particular author that are in the library, you can do an **author search.** Choose "Author" from the catalog menu and enter the author's name, last name first (for example: Vogt, Gregory). A list of authors will appear. Choose your author to see a list of his or her books. You can then choose a particular book to find out more about it.

If you already know what book you want, you can do a **title search.** Choose "Title" from the catalog menu and enter the exact title. An alphabetical list of titles will appear, including the one you entered. If the title begins with *A, An,* or *The,* the book will be listed by the second word in the title. You can then select the title of the book that you want.

In each kind of search, the last step is to choose a particular book. When you do, a screen like this one will appear:

```
Call Number        Children's Nonfiction        Status: in
J629.4  VOGT 1991

AUTHOR             Vogt, Gregory
TITLE              Voyager
SERIES             Missions in space
PUBLISHER          Brookfield, Connecticut: Millbrook Press,
                   c. 1991
DESCRIPTION        111 pages; color ill.; 24 cm.
SUMMARY            Important new scientific data was collected on the planets
                   Jupiter, Saturn, Neptune, and Pluto by the telescopes aboard
                   the Voyager spacecrafts. For the first time, scientists
                   were able to collect information by studying the giant
                   planets at close range.

SUBJECTS           Space flight; Interplanetary voyages; Planets;
                   Outer space — Exploration
```

Notice the call number at the top of the screen on page 144. This number appears on the spine, or narrow back edge, of the book. Every nonfiction book has its own call number that tells where it is shelved in the library. Nonfiction books are kept in numerical order. The *J* stands for *juvenile*. It tells you that this book is for young readers. Across from the call number is the word *status*. This tells you whether the book is on the shelf or is checked out.

A. Now use the screen to do the following.

1. This book is one of several books in a series. Underline the name of the series.

2. How new is the information in this book? Circle the year that the book was published.

3. What kind of pictures does this book have? Put two lines under the information that tells you.

4. The subject used for this search was *space flight*. Draw a box around other subjects that you could use in your search.

B. Circle the kind of search that you would do to answer each question.

1. Who wrote the book *Animals in Orbit: Monkeynauts and Other Pioneers in Space?*

    author search   (title search)   subject search

2. Does the library have any books about smoke jumpers?

    author search   title search   (subject search)

3. What books by Roberto Terpilauskas are in the library?

    (author search)   title search   subject search

C. Use the information on the screen below to answer each question.

```
Call Number          Children's Nonfiction       Status: checked in
J629.45409 RIDE

AUTHOR               Ride, Sally
TITLE                To space and back
PUBLISHER            New York: Lothrop, Lee & Shepard, c. 1986
DESCRIPTION          96 pages; color ill.; 29 cm.
SUMMARY              Describes in text and photographs what it is like to
                     be an astronaut on the space shuttle Challenger.
                     Includes a glossary of terms.
SUBJECTS             Space flight; Space shuttles
```

1. Suppose you want to find other books by this author. What name would you look under?

    _____ Ride, Sally _____

2. Will this book most likely tell you all about how astronauts are trained? _____ no _____

3. Suppose you want to know more about the space shuttle program. What subject could you

    search under? _____ space shuttles _____

4. What is the call number of this book? _____ J629.45409 RIDE _____

Using a Bus Route Map

Suppose you want to visit a friend who is in the hospital. It is too far from your home to walk, so you decide to take a bus. But it is the first time that you have had to take a bus, and you have no idea which bus to take. What should you do? Your local bus company, perhaps called the Transit Authority, prints a map showing bus routes. Bus routes are the ways different buses travel in your city. Using a **route map,** you can find the best way to travel by bus from place to place.

Examine the bus route map below. The map shows some of the main streets in a city. Different bus routes are indicated on the map. The key below the map will help you read and understand the bus route.

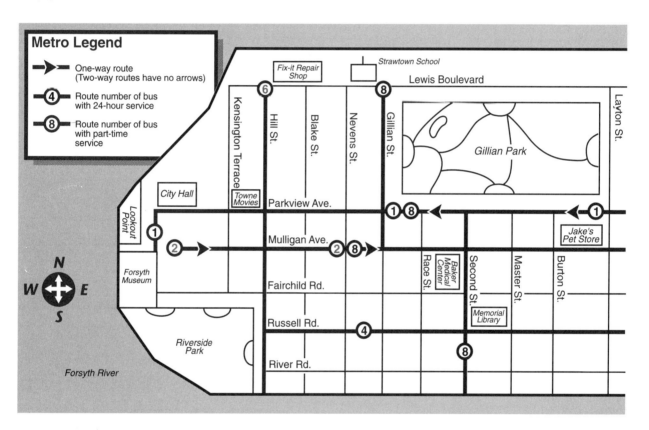

A. Read each statement about the bus route map. Fill in the circle before **true** or **false.**

1. Six bus routes are shown on the map.

    ○ true   ● false

2. Buses on route 6 travel on Hill Street.

    ● true   ○ false

3. Buses on route 6 run north and south.

    ● true   ○ false

4. Buses on route 2 travel in two directions.

    ○ true   ● false

5. Buses on route 8 run north and south on Second Street and west on Parkview Avenue.

● true   ○ false

6. Buses on route 6 travel 24 hours a day.

○ true   ● false

7. Buses on routes 6 and 8 travel past Gillian Park.

○ true   ● false

8. Buses on route 2 travel east on Mulligan Avenue.

● true   ○ false

9. Going south, bus route 8 runs south on Gillian Street, east on Mulligan Avenue, and south again on Second Street.

● true   ○ false

10. Buses on routes 8 travel on four different streets.

● true   ○ false

11. Buses on routes 6 and 8 travel past Riverside Park.

○ true   ● false

12. You can travel from Gillian Park to City Hall without changing buses.

● true   ○ false

13. To go from the corner of Hill Street and River Road to the corner of Mulligan Avenue and Layton Street, you must take three buses.

○ true   ● false

14. You cannot go on one bus from the corner of Gillian Street and Russell Road to the corner of Mulligan Avenue and Hill Street.

● true   ○ false

B. Use the route map to answer each question.

1. Rachel lives at the corner of Kensington Terrace and Mulligan Avenue. She wants to go to the library. Which bus routes should she use?

She should take route 2 to Second Street then take route 8 south to Russell Road.

2. Timothy and his sisters are at the movie theater on the corner of Parkview Avenue and Hill Street. Which bus route can they take to go to Riverside Park? _____6_____

3. How can Dr. Chin get to City Hall from the Medical Center?

Dr. Chin must take route 8 to Gillian Street and Parkview Avenue then take route 1 west on Parkview Avenue

to City Hall.

4. Marvin wants to go from Nevens Street and Parkview to the Forsyth Museum. What is the closest bus route? ____1____ What route can he use to return home? ____2____

5. What two ways could Rosa travel from Strawtown School to Jake's Pet Store?

She could take an 8 bus and get off when it reaches Mulligan Avenue, changing to a 2 bus to Burton Street. Or she

could take an 8 bus to Second Street, changing to a 2 bus.

6. How can Mr. Goldman get from Master Street near River Road to the Fix-it Repair Shop?

He can walk to Second Street and ride an 8 bus to Parkview Avenue and Gillian Street, then take a 1 bus to Hill

Street and change to a 6 bus north to Lewis Boulevard.

Lesson 55

Scene, Dialogue, Stage Directions

Reading a Literature Selection

▶ Background Information

This play is based on a folktale set in ancient Ghana, in western Africa. It is about a trickster named Anansi. A trickster is a humorous character who uses pranks to outwit others. Anansi meets his match, however, when he thinks that he has "tricked" Anene into helping him set his fish traps.

▶ Skill Focus

Like a short story, a play can have characters, plot, conflict, setting, and theme. A play, however, is different in form from a short story.

A play often has many parts. Each part is called a **scene**. When the time or place changes, the scene changes. The time and place are called the **setting** of the play. Information about the setting is usually found at the beginning of each scene. Sometimes much time has passed between one scene and another. The playwright, or author, may tell you at the beginning of the new scene what took place in between.

The characters in the play speak their lines. Their speeches are called **dialogue**. The name of the character who is speaking appears before the lines to be spoken.

When you read a play, you will often find instructions about how the actors are to use their voices or act out their roles. These notes from the author are called **stage directions**. They appear in italic type and are usually in parentheses.

As you read a play, follow these steps.

1. At the beginning of each **scene**, read any notes that describe the play's setting.
2. Note who is speaking each line of **dialogue**.
3. Read all the **stage directions.**

▶ Word Clues

When you read a selection, you may find words that you don't know. Read the following stage direction.

Anene walks to the left, toward Osansa, who is standing near the wing.

You can tell from the context clues that the *wings* are in a theater. However, there are no context clues to tell you where in a theater the wings are located. You will need to use a dictionary.

When you read an unknown word and there are not enough context clues to explain it, use a dictionary to find the word's meaning. You may find it more convenient to finish what you are reading first and then look up the word.

Use a **dictionary** to find the meaning of the three underlined words in the play.

▶ Strategy Tip

As you read "Anansi's Fishing Expedition," notice who is speaking in each scene and how the setting changes. Pay attention to the notes at the beginning of each scene. Also, read the stage directions carefully.

Anansi's Fishing Expedition

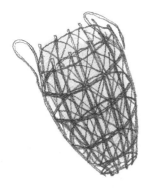

Cast

Anansi, a clever trickster
Osansa
Anene } friends tired of Anansi's tricks
Village Chief
Villagers

Scene One

The setting of this play is a west African village in a long-ago time. The action takes place along the banks of a river near the village. The river bank is at stage left, toward the rear of the stage. A grove of palm trees is at the far right rear of the stage. The village street runs along the front of the stage from left to right.

The action begins at center stage, where Anansi is sitting on the ground. Osansa approaches along the street.

Anansi: Hello there, friend Osansa. I have an idea. Why don't we go set our fish traps together? Then we shall sell our fish and be quite rich!

Osansa: No, Anansi. I have as much food as I can eat or sell. I am rich enough. Why don't you set your fish traps by yourself?

Anansi: Ha! Fish alone? Then I'd have to do all the work! What I need is a fool for a partner!

Osansa *(walks off to the left):* Well, I won't be your fool, but perhaps you'll find someone else.

Anene *(approaches from the right):* Good day, Anansi. What clever plans have you today?

Anansi: I am looking for someone to set fish traps with me tomorrow. We shall sell the fish and be quite rich.

Anene: That sounds like a fine idea. Two people can catch more fish than one. Yes, I'll do it.

Anansi: Good. Meet me in the palm grove at dawn.

Anene walks to the left, toward Osansa, who is standing near the wings.

Osansa: Don't you know he is trying to make a fool of you? He says he needs a fool to go fishing with him. He just wants someone to set the fish traps and do all the work while he gets all the money for the fish!

Anene: Don't worry, friend. I won't be Anansi's fool!

Scene Two

Early the next morning, Anene and Anansi meet in the palm grove near the village.

Anene: Give me the knife, Anansi. I shall cut the branches for the traps. We are partners. We share everything. My part of the work will be to cut the branches. Your part will be to get tired for me.

Anansi: Just a minute. Let me think. Why should I be the one to get tired?

Anene: Well, when there's work to be done, someone must get tired. So if I cut the branches, the least you can do is get tired for me.

Anansi: Ha! You take me for a fool? Give me the knife. I shall cut the branches, and you shall get tired for me!

Anansi takes the knife and begins the hard work of cutting branches. As he cuts, Anene, who is relaxing on the ground, groans loudly with weariness. When all the wood is cut, Anansi ties it in bundles.

Anene: Anansi, let me carry the wood, and you get tired for me.

Anansi: Oh no, my friend. I am not that simple-minded. I'll carry the wood myself, and you can take the weariness for me.

Anansi <u>hoists</u> the bundle to the top of his head, and the two set off toward the village,

walking center stage, then right, toward the wings.

Anene *(arrives at the village):* Let me make the fish traps, Anansi, and you sit down and get tired for me.

Anansi: Oh no. You just keep on as you are.

Anansi makes the traps while Anene sits under a tree and groans with weariness.

Anansi *(to himself):* Look at him there, moaning with weariness, practically dying from tiredness. All I have to do is the work! How silly he is!

Anene: Now that the traps are finished, Anansi, let me carry them to the water. Surely you won't mind getting a little tired for me.

Anansi: Oh no. You just come along and do your share. I'll carry the traps, and you get tired.

Anansi and Anene go to the river bank.

Anene *(at the water's edge):* Now wait a minute, Anansi. Let's think a minute here.

There are sharks in the water. Someone is apt to get hurt. So let me go in and set the traps, and should a shark bite me, you can die for me.

Anansi: What do you take me for? I'll go in the water and set the traps. If I am bitten, you can die for me!

After the traps are set, Anansi and Anene walk back to the village.

Scene Three

The next morning, Anene and Anansi meet at the river's edge.

Anene: Anansi, there are only four fish in the traps. You take them. Tomorrow there will probably be more, and I'll take my turn.

Anansi: Now what do you take me for? Do you think I am that simple? Oh no, Anene. You take the four fish, and I'll take my turn tomorrow.

Anene takes the four fish to the village and sells them.

Scene Four

The next morning, Anene and Anansi meet again at the river's edge.

Anene: Anansi, take these sixteen fish. Little ones, too. I'll take my turn tomorrow.

Anansi: Of course you'll take your turn tomorrow, it's my turn today. *(stops to think)* Well now, you are trying to make a fool of me again! You want me to take these sixteen miserable little fish so that you can get the big catch tomorrow, don't you? Well, it's a good thing I'm alert! You take the sixteen today, and I'll take the big catch tomorrow.

Anene carries the sixteen fish to the market and sells them. The next day he again tricks Anansi into waiting one more day for a bigger catch.

Scene Five

On the sixth day, Anansi and Anene come to the traps and find them rotten, although they hold a very fine catch.

Anene: Well, it's certainly your turn today. I'm very glad of that. Look, the fish traps are rotten and worn out. We can't use them anymore. I'll tell you what; you take the fish to town and sell them. I'll take the rotten fish traps and sell them. The fish traps will bring an excellent price. What a wonderful idea!

Anansi: Just a moment. Don't be in such a hurry. I'll take the fish traps and sell them myself. If there's such a good price to be had, why shouldn't I get it? Oh no, you take the fish, my friend!

Anansi hoists the rotten fish traps on his head, and Anene carries the fish. They go to the village.

Anene *(walking through the streets and shouting):* Fresh fish for sale! Fresh fish!

Villagers *(gather around Anene):* Fresh fish! Wonderful! We'll buy some!

Anansi: Rotten fish traps! I have rotten fish traps for sale!

The villagers avoid Anansi.

Village Chief *(approaches Anansi):* Now what do you take us for? Do you think we are <u>ignorant</u> people? Your friend Anene came and sold good fish, which the people want. But you come trying to sell something that isn't good for anything. You are smelling up the village with your rotten fish traps. You insult us. For this you must clean the homes of the people of the village. *(to the villagers)* Take him away.

Anansi is hauled offstage. Soon his moans are heard. He stumbles back onstage.

Anene: Anansi, this should be a lesson to you. You wanted a fool to take fishing. You didn't have far to look to find one. The fool you took fishing was you!

Anansi *(rubs his back and legs, which are tired from all the work he has done):* Yes. But what kind of partner are you? *(looks <u>reproachfully</u> at Anene)* At least you could have taken the pain while I did all the cleaning!

RECALLING FACTS

Recalling details

1. Why doesn't Anansi want to set his own fish traps?

He doesn't want to do all the work by himself.

Recalling details

2. Is Osansa fooled by Anansi's trick?

No, Osansa is not fooled by Anansi's tricks.

Recalling details

3. Whom does Anansi think he's tricked into setting his fish traps?

He thinks that he has tricked Anene.

Recognizing sequence of events

4. What four tasks must be performed to trap fish?

First, branches must be cut. Second, traps must be

made. Third, the traps must be set in the water.

Finally, the traps must be checked each day for fish.

Recalling details

5. While Anansi is making the fish traps, what is Anene doing?

Anene gets tired for Anansi and groans with weariness

for him.

Recalling details

6. What tasks does Anene trick Anansi into doing?

Anene tricks Anansi into waiting for a bigger catch and

trying to sell the rotten fish traps.

Identifying cause and effect

7. Why is the village chief angry with Anansi for trying to sell the rotten fish traps?

He is angry because Anansi was insulting the villagers

by trying to sell them something that isn't good for

anything.

Identifying cause and effect

8. Why does Anansi have to clean the homes of the villagers?

Anansi has to clean the homes of the villagers because

he tried to fool the people.

Recalling details

9. Whom does Anansi really fool?

He fools himself.

Using context clues

10. Write the letter of the correct meaning in front of each word.

_b_ hoists	**a.**	finding fault with
_c_ ignorant	**b.**	lifts up
_a_ reproachfully	**c.**	having little knowledge

INTERPRETING FACTS

Analyzing character

1. Why do you think Osansa was not fooled by Anansi?

Anansi had used the same trick too many times. Osansa was wise to his "clever tricks."

Drawing conclusions

2. Do you think that Anene would have been fooled by Anansi if Osansa had not warned him? Explain.

Answers will vary. However, students might conclude that because Anansi was known to be a trickster, it is possible

that Anansi would not have fooled Anene.

Drawing conclusions

3. Who do you think is the cleverest character in the play? Explain.

Anansi, because he fooled many people in the past; other possible answers include Osansa, because he had nothing

to do with Anansi; Anene, because he fooled Anansi.

Making inferences

4. Was Anansi trying to trick people by selling rotten fish traps? Explain.

No. He believed that the fish traps were salable and would bring a good price.

Drawing conclusions

5. Do you think Anansi deserved his punishment? Explain.

Answers will vary. However, most students may conclude that Anansi fooled and tricked people so often that his

punishment was long overdue.

Making inferences

6. Are Anansi and Anene true-to-life characters? Explain.

No. They are exaggerated and humorous characters who illustrate the theme of the play.

Inferring theme

7. What is the message of this play? Put a check mark in front of the correct statement of theme.

_____ Tricking one's friends can be fun.

__✔__ Tricksters can fool people only for so long; eventually the tricksters themselves will be fooled.

_____ Trickery means fooling people into doing your work for you.

SKILL FOCUS

Scenes, dialogue, and stage directions make a play different from a short story. Recognizing and understanding this difference in form will make it easier for you to read a play. To answer these questions, go back to the play.

1. Scene

There are several events in the plot of this play. Briefly tell about the setting and the important events in each scene.

Scene One

Setting: west African village street, day one

Event: Osansa refuses to set fish traps with Anansi; Anene agrees to go fishing with Anansi despite Osansa's

warning.

Scene Two

Setting: early the next morning in a palm grove

Event: Anansi falls for Anene's trick; Anansi does the work while Anene gets tired for him.

Scene Three

Setting: _the next morning, at the river's edge_

Event: _After seeing how many fish they have caught, Anene tricks Anansi into waiting one more day for a bigger catch._

Scene Four

Setting: _the next morning at the river's edge_

Event: _Anene again tricks Anansi into waiting one more day for a bigger catch._

Scene Five

Setting: _the sixth day, at the river's edge and in the village_

Event: _Anansi, tricked into selling rotten fish traps to the villagers, is punished but has not yet learned that he has been tricked by Anene._

2. Dialogue

Reread the dialogue between Anansi and Anene in Scene Five after Anansi cleaned the villagers' homes. From what Anansi says to Anene, what lesson has Anansi learned?

Anansi doesn't seem to have learned anything. His remark indicates that he still believes in Anene's trickery.

3. Stage Directions

Stage directions are notes from the playwright that appear at the beginning of a scene. Sometimes directions appear within or after lines of dialogue. Answer these questions from the information given in the stage directions.

a. What is the setting of the play?

The setting is a west African village in a long-ago time.

b. If Scene One occurs on day one, on what day does Scene Three occur?

Scene Three occurs on day three.

c. On what day do Anansi and Anene discover that their traps are rotten?

They discover that their traps are rotten on day six.

d. How do the villagers respond to Anansi when he tries to sell his rotten fish traps?

The villagers avoid him.

e. In his last speech, why does Anansi look reproachfully at Anene?

Anansi looks at Anene accusingly because Anene did not offer to take the pain while Anansi was cleaning the villagers' homes.

▶ **Real Life Connections** How is the moral of the play applicable to life today?

Reading a Map

Reading a Social Studies Selection

▶ Background Information

The Congo River in Africa is one of the world's longest rivers. It flows through many different regions of Africa. Many other rivers flow into the Congo River on its dramatic journey across Zaire to the Atlantic Ocean.

The Congo River, like many of the other great rivers (the Nile, Amazon, and Mississippi rivers) is very important to the people who live in the region. These people are often called river people. This name is given to these people because of their dependence on the river. Without the river, many of these people couldn't survive.

Almost all of these people fish. It is difficult to fish at times because of the fast-flowing waters of the Congo. People also farm the regions closest to the river. They grow crops, such as cassava, yams, bananas, and other fruits and vegetables. Farming is also often very difficult because of constant flooding, which can sometimes destroy entire crops.

In the following selection, you will learn more about the history and importance of the Congo River.

▶ Skill Focus

Two types of maps— physical maps and political maps— are often found in textbooks. A **physical map** shows surface features, such as plains, plateaus, mountains, lakes, and rivers. These features are often shown by different colors or shades of one color. For example, blue may be used to show bodies of water. A **political map** shows the location and boundaries of a country or state, a capital city, and other important cities. When a map combines features of both types of maps, it is called a **physical/ political map.**

Most maps have a scale of distance. This scale is helpful in measuring distances between two points on the map. One inch on a map can stand for one mile or several hundred miles. Most map scales also show distance in meters. One centimeter can stand for one kilometer or several hundred kilometers.

Remember to read the map key very carefully. The key or legend explains the colors, symbols, and scale of distance on a particular map. Reading a map along with the text will give you more information than either one could provide alone.

▶ Word Clues

Read the sentence below. Look for context clues that explain the underlined word.

From its underline source, or starting point, the river flows north across gently sloping country.

If you do not know the meaning of the word *source*, the phrase *starting point* can help you. A source is a starting point. The term *starting point* is an appositive phrase. An appositive phrase explains a word coming before it and is set off from the word by commas or dashes.

Use **appositive phrases** to find the meaning of the three underlined words in the selection.

▶ Strategy Tip

As you read "The Congo River," look at the physical/political maps. The first map shows the location of Zaire. The second map shows the path of the Congo River. Before you begin to read, study the map key.

The Congo River

The Congo River, the world's sixth longest river, is in west central Africa in the country named Zaire (zah IR). The Congo River is 2,716 miles (4,370 kilometers) long. It is Zaire's most important waterway.

The Course of the Congo River

The Congo begins in the southeastern corner of Zaire, more than 1,000 miles (1,600 kilometers) south of the equator. From its source, or starting point, it flows north across this gently sloping country. The Congo River grows stronger and wider as tributaries—smaller rivers—feed into it. At this point, it is called the Lualaba (loo a LAH ba) River.

The river soon crosses the equator, and at Stanley Falls it becomes the Congo River. It then plunges down a group of cataracts, or large waterfalls, curving west across northern Zaire. The river's long westerly arc takes it south across the equator again to Kinshasa (keen SHAH sah), the capital of Zaire. At Kinshasa, the Congo widens to form Stanley Pool. Then, for 215 miles (346 kilometers), the river

The Congo River crosses the equator not once, but twice.

rushes over seven cataracts below Kinshasa. At this point, the river is a roaring mass, throwing up waves five and ten feet high. At Kinshasa, all Congo River freight must be changed from boat to rail. This is done to bypass the miles of cataracts that make the river unnavigable below Kinshasa. By the time the river reaches Matadi (mah TAH dee), it has dropped hundreds of feet in elevation. Located about 90 miles upriver from the coast, Matadi is Zaire's only port that ocean ships can reach.

The stretch of difficult water between Kinshasa and Matadi prevents boats from sailing from the coast to inland cities. This difficulty was a major factor in preventing the exploration of the heart of Africa in the nineteenth century.

Finally, the mighty Congo River empties into the Atlantic Ocean. Every other African river has a delta—a triangle of sand and soil left at the mouth of a river—but the Congo has none. Its muddy waters rush far out into the South Atlantic. Over the years, the powerful river has cut an underwater canyon in the ocean's floor. This canyon is 4,000 feet (1,200 meters) deep and goes 100 miles (160 kilometers) out into the sea.

A Unique River

The Congo pours 1.5 million cubic feet (.042 million cubic meters) of water into the Atlantic Ocean every second. It carries more water than any other river except the Amazon in South America. No other major river crosses the equator once, let alone twice. No other major river flows in both the Northern and Southern hemispheres.

The Congo River Basin

The basin of the Congo River is more than 1,000 feet (300 meters) above the level of the sea. A river basin is the area drained by a river and its tributaries. The Congo River basin can be thought of as a large plateau. It is flat, open country that makes up more than one-tenth of the land surface of the African

This map shows where Zaire is located on the African continent.

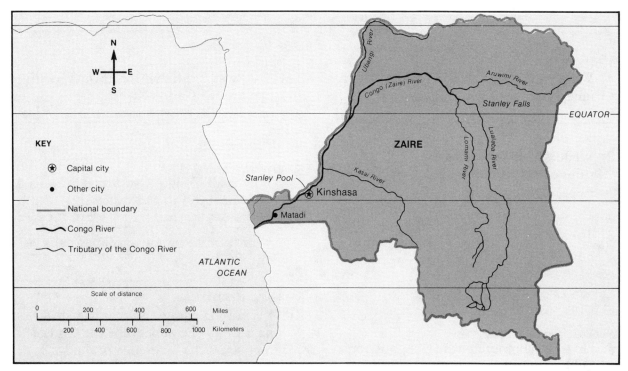

This map of Zaire shows the course of the Congo River and its four major tributaries.

continent. The Congo River basin includes all of Zaire and Congo, most of the Central African Republic, and parts of Zambia, Angola, Tanzania, Cameroon, and Gabon. The area of the river basin is 1.5 million square miles (3.9 million square kilometers).

Tributaries of the Congo River

Many other rivers feed into the Congo River. The Congo has four major tributaries:

Even in the twentieth century, people and cargo are still transported along the Congo River in small dugout canoes.

the Ubangi (oo BAHN gee) and Aruwimi (ah roo WEE mee), two rivers that come into the Congo from the north; the Lomami (loh MAH mee) and Kasai (kah SY), both rivers from the south. These tributaries, together with the Congo, form a network of thousands of miles of navigable rivers throughout the Congo River basin.

The Discovery of the Congo River

Portuguese navigators were the first to locate the mouth of the Congo River. They found it ten years before Columbus landed in America. The Portuguese thought that the river would cut across Africa from the Atlantic Ocean to what they thought was the Indian Ocean. The cataracts a hundred miles upriver, however, kept them from further exploration. Nevertheless, they did find that the river was called *Nzadi*, or "big water," by the people. The Portuguese changed Nzadi to Zaire, which was easier for them to say. Years later, the river was given an African name, Congo. This name comes from the ancient Kingdom of Kongo that the Portuguese found when they arrived in 1482. After the Belgian Congo gained its independence in the 1960s, the country was renamed Zaire, and its mighty river became the Zaire River.

Recalling details
1. What was Zaire called before its independence in the 1960s?

Zaire was called the Belgian Congo.

Recalling details
2. What is Zaire's only port that ocean ships can reach?

The only port is Matadi.

Recalling details
3. The Congo River is the ____sixth____ longest river in the world.

Recalling details
4. How long is the Congo River?

The Congo River is 2,716 miles long.

Comparing and contrasting
5. How is the mouth of the Congo River unlike other African rivers?

The Congo River has no delta.

Comparing and contrasting
6. Name two ways in which the Congo River is different from any other river.

No other major river crosses the equator once, let

alone twice. No other river flows in both the Northern

and Southern hemispheres.

Recalling details
7. What are the four major rivers that feed the Congo?

The Ubangi, Aruwimi, Lomami, and Kasai rivers feed

the Congo.

Recalling details
8. Why was it difficult for navigators to explore the Congo River?

Cataracts prevented vessels from sailing to inland cities

from the coast.

Identifying cause and effect
9. Why is all Congo River freight changed from boat to rail at Kinshasa?

Freight is changed from boat to rail to bypass the miles

of cataracts that make the river unnavigable below the

city.

Identifying the main idea
10. Reread the paragraph that has an **X** next to it. Then underline the sentence that states the main idea of the paragraph.

Using context clues
11. Underline the word that correctly completes each sentence.

a. A triangle of sand and soil left at the mouth of a river is a _____.
source   delta   course

b. Smaller rivers that feed into a larger one are _____.
waterways   cataracts   tributaries

c. Large waterfalls are called _____.
cataracts   tributaries   flows

Making inferences
1. What might be one reason that Kinshasa and not Matadi is the capital of Zaire?

Answers may vary. Matadi is downriver of the rapids and is cut off from river travel to the interior. Kinshasa can be

reached by boat along the Congo River.

Making inferences
2. Why do you think that the Belgian Congo was renamed Zaire after its independence?

Answers may vary. Zaireans were proud of their newly independent country and wanted a name different from the

one used when it was a colony.

Making inferences

3. Look at the photograph on page 157. How are people and goods transported on the Congo River?

One way that people and goods are transported is by dugout canoes.

Is this an efficient means of transportation? Explain.

Answers may vary. Because people still use canoes, despite the availability of more modern methods of transportation,

people must think canoes are an efficient method.

Identifying the unstated main idea and supporting details

4. You have already learned that the main idea is the most important idea in a paragraph. Sometimes you will be asked to figure out the main idea of a group of paragraphs or an entire selection. You can be sure that there will always be supporting details to tell about the main idea.

Only one of the following statements expresses the unstated main idea of the selection you just read. Circle the letter next to the statement that identifies the unstated main idea.

a. Four major tributaries feed into the Congo River.

b. The journey of the mighty Congo River makes it one of the world's most unusual rivers.

c. The Congo River is Zaire's most important waterway.

d. The Congo River is the sixth longest river in the world.

Identifying the unstated main idea and supporting details

5. On the lines below, write at least five supporting details that tell about the main idea. You can go back to the selection to find the supporting details.

a. In its journey, the Congo crosses the equator twice.

b. The Congo's unnavigable cataracts prevented the exploration of central Africa.

c. Matadi, the Congo's only port that ocean ships can reach, is 90 miles upriver from the coast.

d. The Congo River, unlike other African rivers, has no delta.

e. The Congo River flows in both the Northern and Southern hemispheres.

SKILL FOCUS

Use the maps on pages 156 and 157 to answer the following questions. Be sure to reread the map key before you begin.

1. In what part of Africa is Zaire located?

Zaire is located in west central Africa.

2. What is Zaire's capital city? How do you know?

Kinshasa is the capital of Zaire. It has a ✹ next to its name.

3. Name another important city in Zaire. How do you know it is a city?

Matadi is another city in Zaire. It has a ● next to its name.

4. Locate the source of the Congo River. Circle it. Use it as the starting point to answer questions 5, 6, and 7.

5. Is the source of the Congo River north or south of the equator?
The source of the Congo River is south of the equator.

6. From its source, in what direction does the Congo flow?
The Congo River flows north from its source.

7. Name the first tributary that flows into the Congo River.
The first tributary is the Lomami River.

8. The Congo River basin is made up of the Congo River and all its tributaries. What color is this area on the first map?
The area is purple.

9. Put a check mark on the spot where the Congo River turns westward.

10. After the Ubangi River has joined the Congo River, in which direction does the Congo flow?
The Congo River flows south after the Ubangi River joins it.

11. Locate Stanley Pool. At this point, the Congo River has crossed the equator twice. Put an X on the map to mark each place.

12. Locate the mouth of the Congo River. Circle it. Into what body of water does the Congo River empty?
The Congo River empties into the Atlantic Ocean.

13. Why would it be difficult to measure the length of the Congo River using the scale of miles?

The Congo River twists, turns, and drops in elevation. Because its course is not always straight, it would be difficult

to measure its length.

14. Based on the scale of distance, how far south of the equator is Matadi?
Matadi is approximately 400 miles (650 kilometers) south of the equator.

15. Why is it more helpful to have two maps?
One map shows the whole African continent; the other shows the country of Zaire and its major waterways in detail.

▶ **Real Life Connections** Use an encyclopedia or an atlas to find information about the longest river in the United States — the Mississippi. Compare information about the Mississippi River with what you have read about the Congo River.

Inferences

__ Reading a Science Selection

▶ Background Information

Many different kinds of hoofed animals live in Africa. Most of these graze on the open plains. Other kinds of animals hunt them for food.

▶ Skill Focus

Sometimes you can **infer**, or figure out, information that is not stated directly in a selection.

Read the following paragraph. Try to infer the color of the bear's fur.

> A polar bear will slowly crawl toward a sleeping seal. If the seal wakes up and raises its head to look around, the bear will stop moving and put its paw over its black nose. Then it is very difficult for the seal to see the bear against the snow.

The following clues can help you infer the color of the polar bear's fur: the bear covers its black nose with its paw; the bear is then difficult to see against the snow. So the bear becomes difficult to see only when its black nose is covered. You can infer that the bear is the same color as the snow—white.

You could infer several other facts from this

paragraph. You could infer that the bear doesn't want the seal to know that it is approaching. The following clues could help you figure this out: the seal is sleeping and when the seal looks around, the bear stops moving. You know that a sleeping animal would not see the bear coming toward it. The bear would be difficult to see when it is not moving. It would look like part of the snow. That is why the bear stops moving when the seal wakes up and looks around.

You could also infer that polar bears eat seals. You have already inferred that the polar bear doesn't want the seal to know that it is approaching. You know that some animals sneak up on other animals to kill them. If the seal saw the bear, the seal would jump into the water and escape.

If you go through the following steps, you will find it easier to infer information.

1. Read the selection carefully.
2. Think about what you've read. Be sure you understand the information that is stated in the selection.
3. Read again and look for clues to information not stated in the selection.

4. Put together the information stated in the selection with information that you already know. Use clues to help you make inferences.

▶ Word Clues

Read the sentences below. Look for context clues that explain the underlined word.

> Some antelopes have <u>spiral</u> horns. *Spiral* means "turned or twisted."

If you do not know the meaning of the word *spiral*, read on. The second sentence states what the word *spiral* means. A word meaning that is stated directly can often be found before or after the new word.

Use **definition** context clues to find the meanings of the three underlined words in the selection.

▶ Strategy Tip

As you read the following selection on antelopes, pay close attention to all the facts. Use the facts to infer information that is not directly stated in the selection.

Antelopes

1. Antelopes are deerlike animals that live in the grassy plains of eastern and southern Africa and in parts of Asia. Like deer, antelopes are **herbivorous** (h ə r BIV ə r ə s) animals. They eat only grass, leaves, and fruit. All antelopes have two-toed hoofs and hollow horns. Some antelopes have spiral horns. *Spiral* means "turned or twisted." Others have straight horns. Antelope horns are different from a deer's antlers. A deer sheds its antlers every year and grows new ones. Antelopes have <u>permanent</u> horns. *Permanent* means "lasting for a long time."

> Q.: *How is a deer different from an antelope?*
> A.: *An antelope never sheds its horns.*

✔ 2. There are over 150 different kinds of antelopes. Most of them live in Africa. Antelopes range in size from the large eland to the tiny dik-dik. The eland may stand up to 6 feet (1.8 meters) tall at the shoulder. It may weigh up to 1,500 pounds (680 kilograms). The dik-dik is about 2 feet long (61 centimeters), roughly the size of a jack rabbit.

3. All antelopes are built for running. They use speed to get away from their enemies. They can usually outrun wild dogs, cheetahs, leopards, and lions. Antelopes can run at high speeds for a longer time than the big cats.

4. Gazelles and impalas are two of the fastest and most graceful of antelopes.

Gazelles are 2 to 3 feet (60 to 90 centimeters) tall at the shoulder. They can run as fast as 60 miles (96 kilometers) per hour for short distances. Impalas are about 3 feet (90 centimeters) tall at the shoulder. Impalas can cover 30 feet (9 meters) in one leap.

5. Antelopes are in the group called **ruminants** (ROO mə nənts). Ruminants include cattle, goats, deer, and giraffes. Most of these animals have horns and split hoofs. What makes ruminants different from other hoofed animals is that their stomachs have four <u>chambers</u>. A chamber is a closed space.

6. When a ruminant eats grass or leaves, it swallows without much chewing. The grass or leaves are then stored in the first chamber of the stomach. This chamber is called the **rumen** (ROO min). The grass or leaves slowly move to the second chamber. The second chamber is called the **reticulum** (re TIK yə ləm). In the reticulum, the grass or leaves are changed to a sticky substance called **cud**. When the animal is relaxed, the muscles of the reticulum send the cud back up to the mouth. The animal chews its cud thoroughly and swallows a second time. The cud passes through the rumen and the reticulum again and moves into a third chamber. The third chamber is called the **omasum** (oh MAY səm). From the omasum, the cud goes into the fourth chamber. This chamber is called the

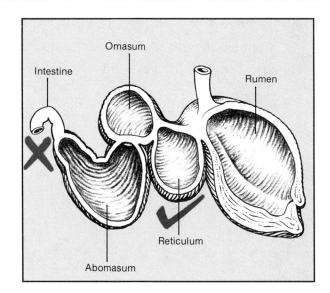

abomasum (ab ə MAY səm). In the abomasum, the cud mixes with <u>digestive</u> fluids and is completely broken down. *Digestion* means "helping to break down food so that it can be used by the body." The food then enters the small intestine, where it is sent into the animal's bloodstream.

7. Certain types of antelopes are now in danger of being wiped out. Cattle are grazed on more and more land that was once used by wild animals. Hunters kill antelopes for meat. However, laws are being passed to prevent antelopes from becoming extinct.

RECALLING FACTS

Recalling details

1. What do herbivorous animals eat?
Herbivores eat grass, leaves, and fruit.

Recalling details

2. What is the difference between a deer's antlers and an antelope's horns?
A deer's antlers are shed every year. An antelope's

horns are permanent.

Recalling details

3. What is the largest type of antelope?
The eland is the largest type of antelope.

Identifying cause and effect

4. Why are all antelopes built for running?
Antelopes are built for running because they must be

fast to escape their enemies.

Reading text with diagrams

5. On the diagram of a ruminant's stomach, put a check mark next to the chamber where the food is changed to cud. Put an **X** next to the chamber where the cud mixes with digestive fluids.

Identifying the main idea

6. Reread the paragraph with a check mark next to it. Underline the sentence that has the main idea.

7. Underline the word or words that correctly complete each sentence.

    a. A closed-off area is a ——————.
       <u>chamber</u>   digestive   tube

    b. Something that is permanent ————.
       changes often   <u>lasts a long time</u>   breaks easily

    c. Digestive juices help to ——————.
       dissolve metal   <u>break down food</u>   burn oxygen

INTERPRETING FACTS

Circle the letter next to each correct answer.

Making inferences

1. Antelopes use their horns for ——————————.

    a. digging

    (b.) fighting

    c. running

Inferring cause and effect

2. A cheetah probably wouldn't hunt an eland because ————————————.

    (a.) elands are too strong for them

    b. elands are too fast for them

    c. elands are too difficult to see

Inferring the unstated main idea

3. Which of the following sentences states the main idea of Paragraph 6?

    a. Ruminants often have digestive problems because their stomachs have four chambers.

    b. Ruminants eat many different types of food.

    (c.) The digestive process of ruminants is quite complicated.

SKILL FOCUS

For each of the following statements, decide which of the items can be inferred from the paragraph listed. Put a check mark next to the statement or statements. On the lines that follow the three items, write the phrase or sentence that contains the clue that you found. Then explain how you inferred the information.

Paragraph 1 (check two)

    ✔   Most antelopes live in a warm climate.

    ✔   Most antelopes have long, slim legs.

    ————   Most antelopes have pointed teeth.

Clue: _Antelopes live in Asia and in the dry, grassy plains of eastern and southern Africa._

Explanation: _These areas have a warm climate._

Clue: _Antelopes are deerlike animals._

Explanation: _Deer have long, slim legs._

Paragraph 3 (check two)

_____ Some antelopes hide from their enemies.

__✔__ Antelopes must be very alert because they have many enemies.

__✔__ If a cheetah can't catch an antelope in the first few minutes of a chase, the antelope will escape.

Clue: _They can usually outrun wild dogs, cheetahs, leopards, and lions._

Explanation: _Because at least four types of animals hunt antelopes, they must constantly be on guard._

Clue: _Antelopes can run at high speeds for a longer time than the big cats._

Explanation: _A cheetah is a big cat. Because an antelope can keep up a high speed for a longer time, it would escape if the cheetah didn't quickly catch it._

Paragraph 6 (check one)

__✔__ Ruminants must often eat quickly. They can't always take the time to chew their food because enemies might be nearby.

_____ Ruminants are larger than other hoofed animals.

_____ Ruminants prefer grass to leaves.

Clue: _When a ruminant eats grass or leaves, it swallows its food without chewing._

Explanation: _An antelope eats quickly and then chews its cud when it knows that it is safe._

Paragraph 7 (check one)

_____ Cattle do not like antelopes.

__✔__ Africa is becoming more developed.

_____ Grazing cattle is against the law in Africa.

Clue: _Cattle are grazed on more and more land that was once used by wild animals._

Explanation: _More cattle ranches are being set up._

▶ **Real Life Connections** Investigate the current status of the antelope. Is it becoming an endangered animal? Support your response with facts.

Reading Fractions

Reading a Mathematics Selection

► **Background Information**

Like other mathematical concepts, you use fractions everyday, probably without even realizing it. There are only just so many instances in which everything can be depicted by whole numbers. Once you have an understanding of fractions, you will be able to do many more types of math problems.

You may recall reading about word problems in Unit 1. (See page 22.) You learned that you use word problems every day. The same can be said for fractions. In fact, you may even use fractions more than word problems. Let's look at a few examples in which you are thinking in terms of fractions without even realizing it.

In sports, statistics, or facts about a game, are recorded in terms of fractions. To determine whether a baseball player is a good batter, his or her batting average is recorded in terms of fractions. If a player gets a base hit seven out of every ten times that he or she is up to bat, then his or her batting average for that game is $\frac{7}{10}$ or seven-tenths.

Scores on tests are also figured out in terms of fractions. If you get 7 questions right out of a possible 12 questions, then your score is $\frac{7}{12}$, or seven-twelfths.

Cooking is perhaps the most common way in which you use fractions. Many ingredients are measured in terms of $\frac{1}{2}$, $\frac{1}{4}$, or $\frac{1}{3}$ cups. These measurements are fractions of a whole cup in the same way that $\frac{1}{2}$ and $\frac{1}{4}$ teaspoons are fractions of a whole teaspoon.

As you read the following selection on fractions, try to picture what is being described. Look carefully at the diagrams. They show what the fractions stand for.

► **Skill Focus**

You use fractions every day. If an apple is cut into four equal parts and you eat three of them, you are eating a fraction of an apple. In a fraction, one number is written above a line and one is written below, like this:

$$\frac{3}{4}$$

You read these numbers together as *three-fourths*.

► **Word Clues**

When you read a selection, you may find words that you don't understand. In this selection, there are two words that are important for you to learn and understand: *numerator* and *denominator*. Both of these words are defined in the selection. Be sure that you understand the meaning of both of these words.

► **Strategy Tip**

When reading a mathematics selection, it is important to read the text and look at the diagrams. Examine the diagrams carefully. They illustrate, or show, what the text is saying. Read the text and look at the diagrams several times, if necessary, until you understand what is being explained in the selection.

Reading Fractions

✔ A fraction shows a part of a whole. Suppose that you broke a stick into three equal parts. The fraction $\frac{1}{3}$ describes each part. You read this as *one-third*. If you have two of the parts, you have $\frac{2}{3}$ (two-thirds) of the whole stick. The fraction $\frac{2}{3}$ is larger than $\frac{1}{3}$. If you have $\frac{2}{3}$ of the stick, you have more parts of the whole than someone with $\frac{1}{3}$.

In the fraction $\frac{2}{3}$, the bottom number shows the number of parts into which the whole has been divided. It is called the **denominator**. The top number shows the number of parts that you have. It is called the **numerator**.

Figure 1

In Figure 1, the whole has been divided into three equal parts. Two of these parts are shaded. The fraction $\frac{2}{3}$ (two-thirds) can stand for the shaded parts of the whole.

Remember that in order to show fractions, the whole must first be divided into *equal* parts. Look at the diagrams in Figure 2. Into how many parts has each whole been divided?

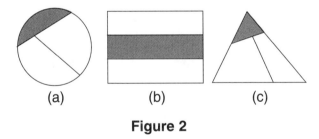

Figure 2

Only one diagram, is divided into three *equal* parts. Only Figure 2(b) shows the fraction $\frac{1}{3}$ (one-third).

Look at Figure 3. The whole has been divided into how many equal parts? How many parts are shaded? What fraction shows how many of the parts are shaded?

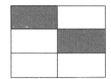

Figure 3

The fraction $\frac{2}{6}$ (two-sixths) is correct.

Below are three more fractions. Study the diagrams and labels carefully.

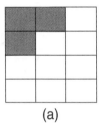

(a)

$\frac{3}{12}$ (three-twelfths)

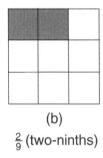

(b)

$\frac{2}{9}$ (two-ninths)

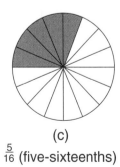

(c)

$\frac{5}{16}$ (five-sixteenths)

Figure 4

RECALLING FACTS

RECALLING FACTS

Recalling details
1. A fraction shows a ___part___ of a whole.

Recalling details
2. The bottom number in a fraction is called the ___denominator___.

Recalling details
3. The top number in a fraction is called the ___numerator___.

Recalling details
4. A fraction shows a whole divided into ___equal___ parts.

Recalling details
5. The denominator shows ___how many equal parts there are in the whole___.

Recalling details
6. The numerator shows ___how many of these parts you have___.

Identifying the main idea
7. Reread the paragraph that has a check mark next to it. Underline the sentence that has the main idea.

INTERPRETING FACTS

Making inferences
1. Put a check mark on the line next to the two situations in which you would have to use fractions.

_____ a. when you go through the check-out counter at a grocery store

__✔__ b. when you want to share a pie equally among several people

_____ c. when you keep track of weekly attendance

__✔__ d. when you are dividing property equally among four people

_____ e. when you use public transportation

Using fractions
2. Tell about two recent situations in which you used fractions.
Answers will vary; however, be sure students have used fractions in the proper context.

SKILL FOCUS

1. Look at the three diagrams below. In each diagram, a whole has been divided into equal parts. Write the fraction that stands for the shaded parts of the whole. Write your answer in the space next to each diagram.

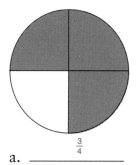

a. $\frac{3}{4}$

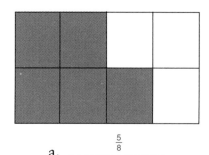

a. $\frac{5}{8}$

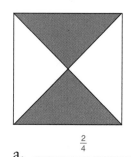

a. $\frac{2}{4}$

2. A whole may be a single thing, or it may be a group of things. The following diagrams show two examples of a whole group divided into smaller, equal groups. Fill out the three columns for each example. In the last column, write the fraction that shows how many of the equal groups have been shaded. The first one has been done for you.

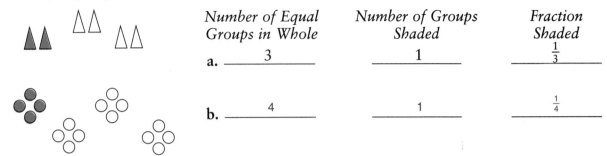

	Number of Equal Groups in Whole	Number of Groups Shaded	Fraction Shaded
a.	3	1	$\frac{1}{3}$
b.	4	1	$\frac{1}{4}$

3. Shade in each diagram below to show the fraction next to it.

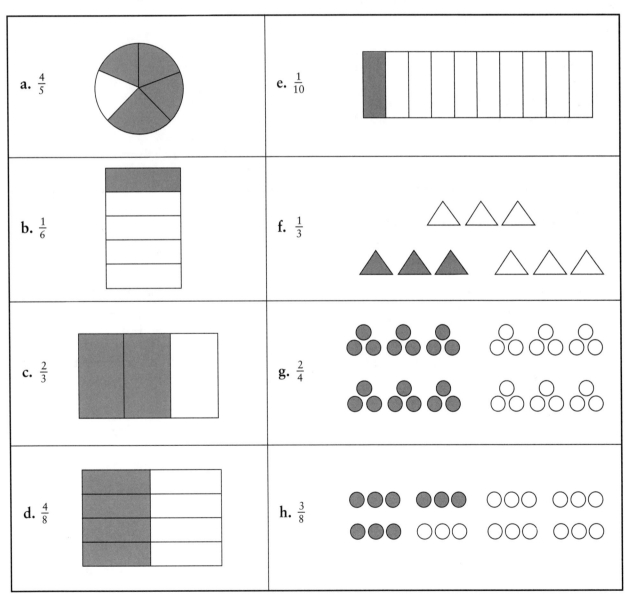

a. $\frac{4}{5}$

b. $\frac{1}{6}$

c. $\frac{2}{3}$

d. $\frac{4}{8}$

e. $\frac{1}{10}$

f. $\frac{1}{3}$

g. $\frac{2}{4}$

h. $\frac{3}{8}$

▶ **Real Life Connections** Tell about two recent situations in which you used fractions.

Multiple Meanings

Sometimes words that we use every day have entirely different meanings when used in the context of science, geography, history, or mathematics. Some words with multiple meanings are listed below.

bank	cape	date	scale
bark	check	mouth	school
bed	crop	pole	yard

Read the two definitions for number 1. Choose a word from the list that goes with those two definitions. Write the word on the line. Do the rest of the lesson the same way.

1. _____mouth_____
   Common use: the opening in the head through which food is taken in
   Geography: the place where a river empties into a larger body of water

2. _____check_____
   Common use: a written order to the bank to pay money to someone
   Mathematics: to test the answers to problems to make sure that they are right

3. _____pole_____
   Common use: a tall, slender piece of wood
   Geography: the point farthest north or farthest south on the earth

4. _____date_____
   Common use: the fruit of one type of palm tree
   History: the exact point in time at which an event takes place

5. _____bed_____
   Common use: a piece of furniture on which to sleep
   Geography: the bottom of a river

6. _____bark_____
   Common use: the short, sharp noise made by dogs
   Science: the outer covering of a tree

7. _____yard_____
   Common use: the ground around or next to a house or other building
   Mathematics: a measure of length

8. _____cape_____
   Common use: a sleeveless garment worn around the shoulders
   Geography: a piece of land extending into the water

9. _____bank_____
   Common use: a place where money is deposited
   Geography: land along the edge of a river

10. _____school_____
    Common use: a place for learning
    Science: a large number of fish traveling in a group

11. _____scale_____
    Common use: a weighing machine
    Science: a small, flat, hard plate forming part of the covering of fishes and reptiles

12. _____crop_____
    Common use: the yield of grain, fruit, or vegetables grown during one season
    Science: a pouch in the throat of some birds

Prefixes

In your reading, you will frequently find a word that has a **prefix** added to the beginning of it. A prefix is a word part that changes the meaning of a word. Look at the following four prefixes and their meanings.

Prefix	Meaning
un	not
in	in, toward
re	back, again
pre	before

Write one of the listed prefixes on the line to the left of each word below. Make the new word mean the same thing as the phrase to the right of the word.

1. _un_ fastened   not fastened   6. _re_ call   to call back

2. _re_ check   to check again   7. _un_ covered   not covered

3. _pre_ view   to view before   8. _re_ view   to view again

4. _in_ land   toward the land   9. _pre_ test   before the test

5. _re_ appear   to appear again   10. _un_ pleasant   not pleasant

Below are some words to which prefixes have been added. Think about the meaning of the prefix before each word. Then write the meaning of the word.

1. uneven   not even   12. prejudge   to judge before

2. remove   to move again   13. input   to put in

3. unable   not able   14. unbend   to not bend

4. unusual   not usual   15. reread   to read again

5. income   come in (money)   16. prearrange   to arrange before

6. repaint   to paint again   17. reclaim   to claim again

7. preheat   to heat before   18. rearrange   to arrange again

8. redraw   to draw again   19. inshore   toward the shore

9. unsafe   not safe   20. rejoin   to join again

10. infield   in the field   21. unselfish   not selfish

11. preschool   before school   22. regain   to gain again

Lesson 61

Suffixes

Many words have **suffixes** added to the ends of them. A suffix changes the meaning of the word. The meanings of five suffixes are given below. Suffixes often have several meanings. The most common meanings are given here.

Suffix	Meaning
er	one who does
en	made of, to become
ful	full of
ly	like in appearance or manner
ness	quality or state of

Write one of the listed suffixes on the line to the right of each root word below. Make the new word mean the same thing as the phrase to the right of the word.

1. wonder ___ful___ full of wonder

2. hard ___en___ to become hard

3. quick ___ly___ in a quick manner

4. dark ___ness___ state of being dark

5. sing ___er___ one who sings

6. spoon ___ful___ a full spoon

7. buy ___er___ one who buys

8. earth ___en___ made of earth

9. brother ___ly___ like a brother

10. own ___er___ one who owns

Below are some root words to which suffixes have been added. Think about the meaning of the suffix at the end of each word. Then write the meaning of the word.

1. worker ___one who works___

2. queenly ___like a queen___

3. thickness ___quality of being thick___

4. sisterly ___like a sister___

5. teacher ___one who teaches___

6. powerful ___full of power___

7. wooden ___made of wood___

8. planter ___one who plants___

9. fatherly ___like a father___

10. fighter ___one who fights___

11. kindness ___quality of being kind___

12. rancher ___one who owns a ranch___

13. leader ___one who leads___

14. friendly ___like a friend___

15. darkness ___quality of being dark___

16. strengthen ___to become strong___

17. joyful ___full of joy___

18. painter ___one who paints___

19. quietly ___quietlike___

20. loudness ___state of being loud___

Lesson 62

Encyclopedia

As you study science, social studies, and mathematics, you will frequently want to look up more information about a topic. Your best source for additional information is a set of books called an **encyclopedia.**

Look at the picture of an encyclopedia. The volumes are numbered in alphabetical order. Each volume has a letter or letters on its spine showing that topics beginning with that letter or letters are in that volume. Words beginning with *a* would be found in Volume 1; words beginning with *t, u,* and *v* would be found in Volume 14.

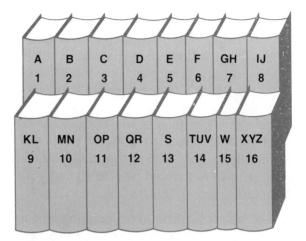

Use the picture of the encyclopedia to answer the following questions. Fill in the space between the lines to the left of the answer.

1. Ken looked at Volume 5. What do you think he was looking up?

   || butterflies

   || hippopotamus

   ▮ elephants

2. Felipe wanted to look up reptiles. Which volume did he need?

   || 5 || 9   ▮ 12

3. After he read about reptiles, Nick decided to look up crocodiles and snakes. Which two volumes did he use?

   ▮ 3 and 13 || 3 and 10 || 14 and 3

4. Shannon had Volume 10. What might she have looked up?

   || parrots and plants

   || seals and snakes

   ▮ mammals and moss

5. Tom wanted to find out all about dogs. What might he have looked up?

   || dogs, cats, and birds

   ▮ dogs, pets, and mammals

   || dogs, reptiles, and snakes

6. Yuan had to do a report on salmon. Which volume did he need?

   || 6 || 11   ▮ 13

7. At the end of the article on salmon, Jim found a note that read "*See fish.*" Which volume did he need next?

   || 3   ▮ 6 || 8

8. Sue looked at Volume 14. What might she have looked up?

   || airplanes   ▮ tunnels || canals

9. Carla had to write a report on Meriwether Lewis and William Clark for social studies. Which two volumes did she need?

   || 4 and 9   ▮ 9 and 3 || 3 and 12

10. Safar chose the explorer Robert LaSalle for his report. Which volume did he use?

    || 12 || 15   ▮ 9

11. If Safar was using the volume that he needed for his report, would Carla have been able to do all her research?

    || yes   ▮ no

    Why? _____ Both need Volume 9.

Using a Mall Floor Plan

You probably have visited a shopping center or mall. Some malls are quite large, with many stores. How can you find one particular store? Most malls have a **floor plan** that shows the location of all the stores in the mall. If you use the floor plan, you don't have to waste time walking up and down the mall looking for a certain store.

Examine the floor plan below. It shows where each store in the Randolph Road Shopping Mall is located. Look for the arrow (⬆) on the floor plan. If you were looking at the floor plan in this mall, you would be standing at the place marked by the arrow. You would be able to find your way around the mall by using the floor plan.

The key below lists the stores in alphabetical order and indicates the number of the store on the floor plan. The key also explains what the symbols represent. Notice the numbers and the symbols on the floor plan. The numbers identify the stores in the mall. The symbols indicate other important places in the mall.

To locate a store, first find the name of the store in the alphabetical listing. Notice the numeral assigned to the store. Find that numeral on the floor plan.

Randolph Road Shopping Mall

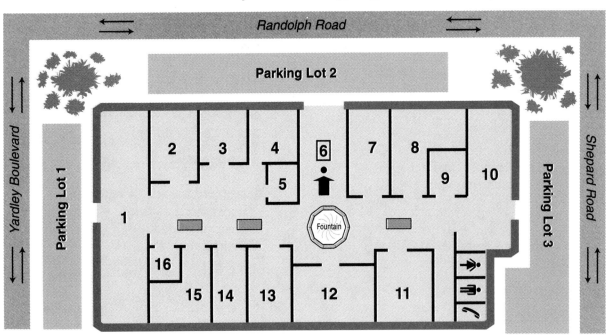

10 Big 30 Bowling Lanes	**9** Flowers by Kim	**15** World of Beauty
14 Bon Voyage Travel Agency	**11** Healthy Life Natural Foods	**6** Ye Olde Popcorn Wagon
2 Books to Grow On	**8** Holly Housewares	▭ Bench
5 Cardon Computers	**12** Nile Furniture Company	
13 Clothes Closet	**7** Pretty Pets, Inc.	✆ Public telephones
16 Dilly's Donuts	**1** Rupert's Department Store	🚻 Restrooms
4 Fancy Feet Shoes	**3** Sports Scene	

A. Use the floor plan to complete each sentence.

1. The store labeled 8 is __Holly Housewares__.

2. The number ___7___ on the floor plan stands for Pretty Pets, Inc.

3. There are ___2___ public restrooms in the mall.

4. The store closest to the Big 30 Bowling Lanes is called __Flowers by Kim__.

5. If you park in Parking Lot 1, you would have to walk through __Rupert's Department Store__ to get to Books to Grow On.

6. To go to the Big 30 Bowling Lanes, it is best to park in __Parking Lot 3__.

7. If you wanted to go to Cardon Computers, park in __Parking Lot 2__.

8. If you are tired of walking, you can sit down and rest on one of the ___3___ benches in the mall.

9. Between World of Beauty and Clothes Closet is __Bon Voyage Travel Agency__.

10. The three ways to enter the mall include going through Rupert's Department Store, going through __Big 30 Bowling Lanes__, and coming in the __Randolph__ Road entrance.

11. Walking from Books to Grow On to Cardon Computers, you pass __Sports Scene__ and __Fancy Feet Shoes__.

12. The only restrooms in the mall are located next to __Big 30 Bowling Lanes__.

B. Decide if each of the following questions can be answered using the mall's floor plan. Write *yes* or *no* on the lines.

1. Where can I get something to eat? __yes__

2. Does the pet shop sell parakeets? __no__

3. On which side of the mall is the shoe store? __yes__

4. Is the mall open on Sundays? __no__

5. Is the furniture store having a sale? __no__

6. Where is the closest public telephone? __yes__

7. Where is the travel agency? __yes__

8. Is a jewelry store in the mall? __yes__

C. Use the floor plan to answer the following questions.

1. If you were leaving the mall through the Randolph Road exit and wanted to eat a snack on the way out, where would you stop?
   Ye Olde Popcorn Wagon

2. If you were shopping at World of Beauty and Books to Grow On, what would be the closest exit?
   through Rupert's Department Store

3. What is the name of one store located between Pretty Pets, Inc., and the Big 30 Bowling Lanes?
   Holly Housewares (or Flowers by Kim)

4. Which two stores are on either side of the Clothes Closet?
   Bon Voyage Travel Agency and Nile Furniture Company

5. The restrooms are closest to which store?
   Healthy Life Natural Foods

Context Clue Words

The following words are treated as context clue words in the lessons indicated. Lessons that provide instruction in a particular context clue type include an activity requiring students to use context clues to derive word meanings. Context clue words appear in the literature, social studies, and science selections and are underlined for ease of location.

Word	Lesson						
ambergris	2	density	15	harpoons	2	regulate	26
asterisk	46	digestive	57	helium	15	reproachfully	55
ballast	15	dirigible	15	heritage	45	retreat	44
barging	33	diseases	26	hoists	55	rotated	14
blubber	2	dock	14	ignorant	55	scallops	3
bustle	24	dunes	13	imports	34	settlers	44
cataracts	56	eased	33	intake stroke	35	source	56
chambers	57	efficient	34	interrupt	33	specific	26
charts	1	embarrassed	24	jolt	13	spermaceti	2
compression stroke	35	equine	25	joystick	14	spiral	57
consumer	34	exhaust stroke	35	legislate	34	substances	26
course	1	exhibits	45	livestock	25	surrender	44
crackling	43	flare	1	lobsters	3	traditions	43
crisp	24	flywheel	35	offerings	14	tributaries	56
crouching	33	galley	1	permanent	57	trudged	13
data	46	gear	43	population	46	urban	25
defacement	45	glared	13	portable	25	vandalism	45
delta	56	greedy	43	power stroke	35	vendors	24
		haddock	3	pursuit	44	wing	55

Concept Words

In lessons that feature social studies, science, or mathematics selections, words that are unique to the content and whose meanings are essential to the selection are treated as concept words. Many of these words appear in boldface type and are often followed by a phonetic respelling and a definition.

Word	Lesson						
abomasum	57	deci-	16	hydraulic	35	piston	35
airships	15	deciliter	16	kilo-	16	place holder	36
ascorbic acid	26	deficiency	26	kilogram	16	place value	36
bag	15	degrees	27	liter	16	pyridoxine	26
basket	15	denominator	58	meter	16	radiator	35
biotin	26	digit	36	milli-	16	reticulum	57
Celsius	27	explosion	35	milliliter	16	riboflavin	26
centi-	16	Fahrenheit	27	mollusks	3	rumen	57
centigrade	27	folic acid	26	neck	15	ruminants	57
crankshaft	35	gondola	15	niacin	26	sanctuaries	45
crustaceans	3	gram	16	numerator	58	synthetic	26
cud	57	habitat	45	nutrients	26	thiamin	26
cylinder	35	hecto-	16	omasum	57	valve	15
deca-	16	hectometer	16	organic	26	vertebrates	3
		herbivorous	57	pantothenic	26		

Read the following selection. Then choose the best answer for each question. Mark your answer on the answer sheet.

The Captive

1. From the day that she learned to walk, Katie's parents had warned her not to wander past the wire fence. The fence divided the Cavanaughs' farm from the open prairie that stretched for miles like a dusty, green sea. A child could get lost in the high, waving grass. Katie's mother would remind her about her sister Hannah. "Hannah was no older than you the day that she disappeared," Mama would say. Then for a week or two, Katie would stay close to home. She couldn't think of anything worse than to be separated from her mother and father.

2. Katie had never seen her sister. Hannah had been lost before Katie was ever born. Katie often thought about the fun that they might have had together. She liked to imagine that one day a beautiful stranger would come driving up the road in a buggy, and it would be Hannah. Katie's mother told her that it was foolish to hope for the impossible. Yet, Katie thought that sometimes even her mother hoped that Hannah was not lost forever.

3. Now, more than twelve years after her disappearance, Hannah was coming home! Major Hawkins rode out from Sioux Falls with the wonderful news. His calvary unit had found Hannah at a Sioux village many miles away. A Lakota woman told them how she had found the lost child many years ago. She had carried her home and raised Hannah like one of her own children.

4. Katie's father and Major Hawkins would bring Hannah back the next day, but the major warned them about Hannah's return. "Hannah might not be able to settle down easily," he said. "She probably has no memory of her childhood before she disappeared. Remember, this is not her real home." Katie found that difficult to believe. How could Hannah not want to live with her real family?

5. Katie and her mother kept busy all day. They dusted and polished the spare bedroom. They set the white china pitcher and the best towels on the washstand. Katie put her own silver-backed mirror and brush on the dresser. She made the big bed with fresh, clean sheets. She also laid out her newest nightgown for Hannah. Then she and her mother dug up a small wild rosebush that was growing on the other side of the fence. They put the plant in a clay pot on the mantelpiece in Hannah's room. The lovely marble mantelpiece had been bare. Now, centered above the fireplace, the roses made the room look pretty.

6. The next day Hannah arrived with her father, Major Hawkins, and an interpreter. Katie flung open the front door and raced out into the yard, her arms open wide. As she came closer to the tall, young woman, her arms dropped. The cry of welcome died in her throat. Hannah had sun-browned skin and her pale hair hung in a long braid. She had a blanket pulled around her shoulders and beaded moccasins on her feet. She stood staring, looking helpless, as Katie's mother moved forward to embrace her.

7. At that moment, Katie remembered the rabbit that she had caught in her trap last winter. It was still alive when she found it. Katie had carried it home gently. She had built a sturdy pen and filled it with fresh wood shavings. The next morning the rabbit was gone. "It was used to freedom," her mother had explained. Katie wondered if her mother remembered that now.

8. Hannah stayed at her new home for almost a month. She never slept in the soft bed or wore the nightgown or used the silver hairbrush. She seldom came out of her room. Whenever Katie went into Hannah's room, she always found Hannah looking out the window. Katie's mother and father kept telling her that it was just a matter of time. Hannah would get used to their ways. "After all," Mama said, "we're her real family."

9. Then one night, when Katie went in to say goodnight, Hannah was gone. Her window was open wide. Katie looked around the empty room. It looked just as it had the day Hannah came, except that the wild roses on the

mantelpiece had withered and turned brown. Katie started to run down the stairs to call her mother and father, but then she stopped. The wild roses reminded Katie of the rabbit that she had caught. She would not tell. She would let her parents discover Hannah's absence in the morning. Then Hannah would have had a head start on her long journey back to her family.

1. Who is the main character in this story?
   a. Katie's mother
   b. Major Hawkins
   c. Katie

2. What does the main character most want at the beginning of the story?
   a. to have her sister back
   b. to live on the prairie
   c. to clean the spare bedroom

3. Choose the words that best describe the main character.
   a. friendly and understanding
   b. selfish and unkind
   c. shy and unhappy

4. By the end of the story, the main character
   a. has not changed in any important way.
   b. understands more than she did at the beginning of the story.
   c. understands less than she did at the beginning of the story.

5. The first important event in the story occurs when
   a. Katie was told not to walk past the fence.
   b. Major Hawkins tells Katie's family that Hannah has been found.
   c. Katie and her mother clean the spare bedroom.

6. The most important event in the middle of the story occurs when
   a. Hannah comes home.
   b. Katie puts the rosebush on the mantel piece.
   c. Katie remembers her rabbit.

7. The most exciting part of the story occurs when
   a. Katie sees that the roses have withered.
   b. Hannah sleeps in the soft bed.
   c. Katie finds Hannah's room empty.

8. The story ends when
   a. Hannah leaves the Cavanaughs' home.
   b. Katie says goodnight to Hannah.
   c. Katie gives Hannah a head start.

9. The story takes place
   a. in the present.
   b. about 150 years ago.
   c. about 1,000 years ago.

10. The setting of the story is
    a. a Sioux village.
    b. an army camp.
    c. a farm on the prairie.

11. The scene described in paragraph 6 takes place
    a. at the back door of the house.
    b. in the yard right outside the house.
    c. on the prairie.

12. Hannah's room is described in paragraph 5. What change in this setting is mentioned when the room is described again in paragraph 9?
    a. the white china pitcher was missing
    b. the rose plant had withered and turned brown
    c. the window was shut

13. Katie's experience with the rabbit that she caught helps her to believe that people
    a. belong where they are most comfortable.
    b. belong with their real family.
    c. should not run away.

14. Katie's mother believes that Hannah
    a. is free.
    b. belongs with her real family.
    c. should stay for awhile.

15. Because of this difference, there is conflict between
    a. Katie and Hannah.
    b. Katie and her mother.
    c. Katie and Major Hawkins.

16. How is the conflict resolved?
    a. Katie and Hannah become friends.
    b. Katie decides not to tell her parents that Hannah has run away.
    c. Katie understands why the rabbit has run away.

AT2

17. The title of this story best describes
    a. Hannah when she lived in the Sioux village.
    b. the rabbit when it was in the pen.
    c. Hannah when she lived at the farm.

18. By the end of the story, Katie has learned that
    a. it is wrong to interfere with other people's lives.
    b. her family is right about Hannah.
    c. it is dangerous to wander past the fence.

19. By having Hannah escape from the Cavanaughs' house, the author of the story hints that
    a. Hannah belonged with the people that brought her up.
    b. Hannah did not want a sister.
    c. Hannah made a mistake when she ran away from the farm.

20. Choose the statement that best expresses the theme of this story.
    a. It is always wrong to hate anybody.
    b. It is usually difficult to grow up on the prairie.
    c. It is sometimes more important to think of another person's happiness than one's own.

21. What can you infer about the way in which Katie feels about Hannah in paragraph 2?
    a. Katie has never seen her sister.
    b. Katie wishes her sister had never been lost.
    c. Katie thinks about the fun that she could have had with her sister.

22. What can you infer about Katie and Mama in paragraph 5?
    a. Katie and Mama want to make Hannah comfortable when she comes home.
    b. Katie and Mama clean the spare bedroom every week.
    c. Katie and Mama are afraid that Hannah will be unable to settle down easily.

23. What can you infer about Hannah in paragraph 8?
    a. Hannah is not happy at the farm.
    b. Hannah does not like Katie.
    c. Mama understands Hannah better than Katie does.

24. Choose the definition of the word *captive* that best fits the title of the story.
    a. a person who is held in prison
    b. a person held against his or her will
    c. a person who is forced to listen

25. In paragraph 1, a prairie is
    a. a fenced-in area around a farm.
    b. a broad area of grass with no trees.
    c. the name of a baby cow.

26. In paragraph 5, a mantelpiece is a
    a. rough blanket.
    b. clay pot for plants.
    c. shelf above a fireplace.

Read the following selection. Then choose the best answer for each question. Mark your answer on the answer sheet.

Ballooning

1. People fly balloons for fun and adventure. Weather forecasters use balloons to collect weather information. Scientists use balloons to study space. While hot-air balloons are used for short flights, gas balloons are used for long flights. Balloons are used for many purposes.

2. What makes a balloon go up? A balloon rises because the heated air or the gas inside the balloon is lighter than the air outside the balloon. The heated air or lighter gas rises to the top of the balloon bag. This makes the balloon look like a big, upside-down pear. The pilot has some control over the upward movement of a balloon. The pilot can drop ballast, such as sandbags. By dropping weight, the pilot makes the balloon lighter, and it rises.

3. What makes a balloon go down? The pilot can also control the downward movement of a balloon. On a gas balloon, the pilot opens a valve and lets gas out of the balloon. On a hot-air balloon, the pilot controls the burners that heat the air. Cooler air makes the balloon go down.

4. Wind determines the speed and direction of a balloon. A strong wind increases the speed of a balloon. A weak wind slows its speed. Pilots study the skies and weather reports, searching for winds that will take them in the direction in which they want to go.

5. Ballooning began in France. The first balloon flight with a pilot took place near Paris on November 21, 1783. The balloon flew for more than five miles (almost 9 kilometers). The next day, a Paris newspaper ran this headline: "Balloons are a promising invention."

6. In a short time, balloons were carrying mail. It wasn't long before armies used balloons to watch enemy troop movements. Balloons were used by armies in the American Civil War.

7. Many people have been hurt or killed in balloon accidents. Leaks were a big problem with early balloons. Many balloons exploded in flight. Because most of today's balloons are made of strong nylon, they are less likely to develop leaks. However, some balloons still explode in flight. At times, clouds block the view of the ground. When this happens, the pilot flies "blind." Sometimes storms blow balloons off course, and balloon crews have had to land in icy seas and other dangerous places.

8. The dangers of ballooning have not stopped people from trying long flights. For more than a hundred years, people tried to fly balloons across the Atlantic Ocean. But all the flights failed. Then on August 11, 1978, the *Double Eagle II* lifted off from the Presque Isle, Maine. The balloon was piloted by three

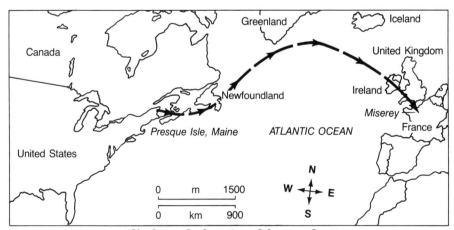

Flight of the *Double Eagle II*

Americans, Ben Abruzzo, Max Anderson, and Larry Newman. Five and a half days later, the balloon landed near the small village of Miserey in France. The *Double Eagle II* had flown 3,120 miles (4992 kilometers).

27. Because heated air inside a balloon is lighter than the air outside the balloon, the balloon becomes
    a. smaller and goes down.
    b. lighter and rises.
    c. heavier and floats.

28. Today's balloons are less likely to develop leaks because
    a. they are made of strong nylon.
    b. they are sewed tightly.
    c. they are made of steel wool.

29. When weight is removed, a balloon becomes
    a. smaller and goes down.
    b. heavier and floats.
    c. lighter and rises.

30. How are gas balloons different from hot-air balloons?
    a. Gas balloons are for long flights; hot-air balloons are for fast flights.
    b. Gas balloons are for short flights; hot-air balloons are for long flights.
    c. Gas balloons are for long flights; hot-air balloons are for short flights.

31. How are today's balloons different from earlier balloons?
    a. Today's balloons do not explode.
    b. Today's balloons are less likely to develop leaks.
    c. Today's balloons cannot be blown off course.

32. Which problem do today's balloon pilots share with past pilots?
    a. The hours are long and the pay is low.
    b. Clouds often block the view of the ground.
    c. People do not appreciate the dangers that balloon pilots face.

33. How did the flight of the *Double Eagle II* differ from earlier balloon flights across the Atlantic Ocean?
    a. During the flight, the *Double Eagle II* was lost.
    b. The flight of the *Double Eagle II* was a failure.
    c. The flight of the *Double Eagle II* was a success.

34. Another word for *ballast* in paragraph 2 is
    a. weight.
    b. sandbag.
    c. gas.

35. Which of the following statements is a fact?
    a. Balloons are shaped like upside-down pears.
    b. Ballooning is about two hundred years old.
    c. Both statements are fact.

36. Which of the following statements is an opinion?
    a. Balloons are lighter than air.
    b. Balloons have been used for watching enemy troop movements.
    c. Balloons are a beautiful sight.

37. *American balloon pilots are better than French balloon pilots.* This statement is
    a. a fact.
    b. an opinion.
    c. neither of the above.

38. *The* Double Eagle II *landed near Miserey, France.* This statement is
    a. a fact.
    b. an opinion.
    c. neither of the above.

39. Balloons were used by armies for watching enemy troop movements
    a. before the invention of airplanes.
    b. after the invention of airplanes.
    c. in recent times.

40. Balloons were invented before airplanes because
    a. balloons are more difficult to make.
    b. balloons are easier to make.
    c. people like balloons.

41. To remain on course, a pilot needs to be concerned most about
    a. wind changes.
    b. low ballast.
    c. broken valves.

42. The *Double Eagle II* took over five days to reach Europe because
    a. it made several stops.
    b. it was blown off course.
    c. its speed depended on wind speed.

43. The *Double Eagle II* was a
    a. lighter balloon.
    b. gas balloon.
    c. hot-air balloon.

44. The main idea of paragraph 1 is stated in the
    a. first sentence.
    b. second sentence.
    c. last sentence.

45. The main idea of paragraph 4 is stated in the
    a. first sentence.
    b. second sentence.
    c. last sentence.

46. The main idea of paragraph 5 is stated in the
    a. last sentence.
    b. first sentence.
    c. third sentence.

47. Which detail below supports the main idea of paragraph 1?
    a. Children like balloons.
    b. Scientists use balloons to study space.
    c. Balloons have been flown for many years.

48. Which detail below supports the main idea of paragraph 4?
    a. A strong wind increases the speed of a balloon.
    b. Wind determines what the weather will be.
    c. Wind determines how high a balloon will go.

49. Which detail below supports the main idea of paragraph 7?
    a. Many people have been hurt or killed in balloon accidents.
    b. Many balloons exploded in flight.
    c. The dangers of ballooning have not stopped people from trying long flights.

50. Choose the correct definition for the word *block* as it is used in the fifth sentence of paragraph 7.
    a. to stop movement
    b. to shape or mold
    c. to get in the way of

51. Choose the correct definition for the word *course* as it is used in the seventh sentence of paragraph 7.
    a. part of a meal
    b. direction taken
    c. line off action

52. Choose the correct definition for the word *movements* as it is used in the second sentence of paragraph 6.
    a. organized activities
    b. motions of a person
    c. changes in location

53. Which document in the selection is a primary source?
    a. speech
    b. newspaper
    c. letter

54. What is the date of this primary source?
    a. 1783
    b. 1883
    c. 1983

55. In which country was this document written?
    a. United States
    b. England
    c. France

56. What fact did you learn from this document?
    a. People had high hopes for ballooning.
    b. People thought that ballooning was dangerous.
    c. People believed ballooning was only for scientists.

Use the map to answer questions 57 through 61.

57. For the last half of its trip, the *Double Eagle II* flew
    a. southwest.
    b. southeast.
    c. northeast.

58. According to the scale of miles, how many kilometers is equal to 1,500 miles?
    a. 1,500
    b. 900
    c. 450

59. The *Double Eagle II* flew over the islands of
    a. Iceland, United Kingdom, Greenland.
    b. Iceland, Ireland, United Kingdom.
    c. Newfoundland, Ireland, United Kingdom.

60. Counting the country it left from and the country it arrived in, the *Double Eagle II* flew over
    a. three countries.
    b. four countries.
    c. six countries.

61. The *Double Eagle II* did *not* fly over which of the following countries?
    a. Iceland and Greenland
    b. Canada and the United Kingdom
    c. Greenland and Ireland

Read the following selection. Then choose the best answer for each question. Mark your answer on the answer sheet.

Winds of the World

1. Major winds blow across the world. They are called **global winds**. There are three kinds of global winds. They are called the **trade winds**, the **westerlies**, and the **easterlies**. The wind that you feel on a breezy day is part of the global winds.

2. Global winds are caused by heated air. Because of the shape of the earth, the sun's rays strike the earth at different angles. The air at the equator, the imaginary line around the middle of the earth, receives the sun's **direct rays**. It is the warmest part of the earth. Other areas of the earth receive **indirect rays**, rays that are less direct than those at the equator. The areas near the poles receive rays that are the most indirect. These areas are the coldest parts of the earth. This uneven heating of the earth causes movement of air. Air that is warm rises and air that is cold sinks.

Trade Winds

3. The **trade winds** blow north and south toward the equator. At the equator, the heated, moist air rises, forming clouds. This condition causes a great deal of rainfall. At about 30 degrees north and south of the equator, the air begins to cool and sink. Some of the sinking air travels back toward the equator. This movement of air creates winds that were once very useful to ships that crossed the ocean for trade. Thus, they were named *trade winds*.

4. Beyond the trade winds are regions of cooler air. The cooler air sinks directly down to the earth's surface so that there is very little wind. Years ago, sailing ship often stalled there because of the lack of winds. Horses on the ships died when they ran out of food and water. The regions became known as the **horse latitudes**.

5. At the equator, there is also little wind. This area is called the **doldrums**.

Westerlies

6. Beyond the horse latitudes, some of the cool, sinking air moves toward the North and South Poles. These winds are called the **westerlies** because they blow from the west. The westerlies blow away from the equator. Therefore, in the Northern Hemisphere, the westerlies blow from west to north. In the Southern Hemisphere, the westerlies blow from west to south.

Easterlies

7. The **easterlies** are quite different from the westerlies. As you can guess, the easterlies blow from the east. Unlike the westerlies, however, the easterlies blow from the North and South Poles toward the equator. Therefore, in the Northern Hemisphere, the easterlies blow to the south. In the Southern Hemisphere, the easterlies blow to the north.

8. Weather forecasters study the global winds carefully. They look for changes in the direction, speed, and temperature of these winds. This information helps them to forecast what the weather will be.

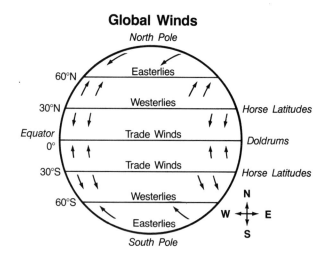

Global Winds

62. Global winds are caused by
  a. heated air.
  b. mountain ranges.
  c. oceans.

63. Sailing ship were often stalled at the horse latitudes because of
  a. the lack of winds.
  b. torn sails.
  c. running out of fuel.

64. The westerlies blow away from the equator. Therefore, in the Northern Hemisphere, the westerlies blow from
  a. west to south.
  b. west to north.
  c. west to east.

65. Which of the following is *not* a global wind?
  a. trade
  b. easterly
  c. horse latitude

66. The westerlies and the easterlies are both named for the
  a. direction from which they blow.
  b. direction toward which they blow.
  c. direction they finally take.

67. Which of the following is *not* a region of the earth?
  a. horse latitudes
  b. westerlies
  c. equator

68. The imaginary line around the middle of the earth is called the
  a. equator.
  b. horse latitudes.
  c. hemisphere.

Use the diagram to answer questions 69 through 72.

69. The horse latitudes are found around
  a. the equator.
  b. 60° north and 60° south of the equator
  c. 30° north and 30° south of the equator

70. The westerlies are found
  a. between 0° north and 30° south of the equator.
  b. between 30° north and 60° north of the equator.
  c. above 60° north and south of the equator.

71. In the Northern Hemisphere, the trade winds blow from
  a. northwest to southeast.
  b. southwest to northeast.
  c. northeast to southwest.

72. In the Southern Hemisphere, the easterlies blow from
  a. southeast to northwest.
  b. northwest to southeast.
  c. northwest to southwest.

73. The main idea of paragraph 2 is stated in the
  a. first sentence.
  b. last sentence.
  c. third sentence.

74. The main idea of paragraph 7 is stated in the
  a. third sentence.
  b. second sentence.
  c. first sentence.

75. The main idea of paragraph 8 is
  a. stated in the second sentence.
  b. stated in the first sentence.
  c. unstated.

76. The main idea of paragraph 4 is that there is an area beyond the trade wind area, called the horse latitudes, that has very little wind. What detail supports this main idea?
  a. Sailing ships often stalled in this area.
  b. Years ago, horses were carried on board ships.
  c. This area has very rough water.

77. Which detail supports the main idea of paragraph 7?
  a. The easterlies blow in a northern direction.
  b. The easterlies blow toward the equator.
  c. The easterlies are found in both the Northern and Southern Hemispheres.

78. Choose the correct definition of the word *trade* as it is used in the sixth sentence of paragraph 3.
  a. a bargain or deal
  b. a kind of work or occupation
  c. the business of buying or selling

79. Choose the correct definition of the word *stalled* as it is used in the third sentence of paragraph 4.
   a. came to a standstill
   b. were kept in a stall
   c. avoided action

Questions 80 through 83 are word problems. Use the space below each one for your calculations.

80. In one desert, daytime temperatures rise to 120°F. Nighttime temperatures drop to 30°F. What is the difference between the day and night temperatures?
   a. 40°F
   b. 90°F
   c. 150°F

81. Camel A traveled 27 kilometers in one day. Camel B traveled twice as far. How many kilometers did camel B travel?
   a. 34 k
   b. 13.5 k
   c. 54 k

82. An airplane is flying at 300 kilometers per hour. The wind behind it is blowing at 60 kilometers per hour, making it move that much faster. How fast is the plane actually moving?
   a. 360 kph
   b. 1,800 kph
   c. 240 kph

83. An airplane is flying at 325 kilometers per hour. A wind is blowing from directly ahead at 70 kilometers per hour, making it move that much slower. How fast is the plane actually moving?
   a. 2,275 kph
   b. 255 kph
   c. 395 kph

A. Study the following dictionary entry. Then answer questions 84 through 87.

---

skin (skin) *n.* **1** the tissue covering the body of persons and animals. **2** the hide or pelt of an animal [Early settlers made coats from beaver *skins*.] **3** the outer covering of some fruits and vegetables [tomato *skin*]. **4** something like skin in looks or use. ◆*v.* **1** to remove the skin from [to *skin* a rabbit; to *skin* one's elbow by falling]. **2** to cheat or swindle: *used only in everyday talk.* —**skinned, skin′ning —by the skin of one's teeth,** by the smallest possible margin; barely. —**have a thick skin,** to pay little attention to blame, insults, etc. —**have a thin skin,** to be easily hurt by blame, insults, etc. —**save one's skin,** to keep oneself from getting killed or hurt: *used only in everyday talk.* —**skin′less** *adj.*

---

84. How many verb meanings are given?
   a. two
   b. four
   c. six

85. Which of the following is the respelling of the entry word?
   a. skin
   b. save one's skin
   c. skinned

86. Which of the following is a noun meaning?
   a. by the smallest possible margins
   b. the hide or pelt of an animal
   c. to cheat or swindle

87. The expression "have a thin skin" is
   a. a definition.
   b. an idiom.
   c. used only in everyday talk.

B. Study the following encyclopedia index. Then answer questions 88 through 91.

CANADA
　　Agriculture C:50-54
　　　government and C:55-56
　　　honey B:76
　　　irrigation I:150
　　　wheat C:50, W:82 (tables)
　　Climate C:54
　　　Arctic N:147-148
　　　rainfall N:150 *with map*
　　Education
　　　agricultural education A:132
　　　colleges and universities U:260
　　　primary and secondary schools E:68-69
　　Furs and fur trade F:223-228, C:56
　　　Hudson's Bay Co. H:350
　　　seals S:78-79
　　Geological history N:152-153
　　History. *See in Index* Canadian History
　　Indians I:52, 53-54, 62
　　　art A:214-217
　　　folktales F:136-139

---

88. Where would you find information about agricultural education in Canada?
   a. C:50-54
   b. A:132
   c. I:150

89. Where would you find a map showing rainfall in Canada?
   a. N:150
   b. C:54
   c. N:147-148

90. Where would you find a table showing wheat production in Canada?
   a. C:50
   b. C:50-54
   c. W:82

91. Where else in the index would you look for references to the history of Canada?
   a. under geological history
   b. under Hudson's Bay Co.
   c. under Canadian history

92. Choose the root word in *truthfulness*.
   a. truth
   b. ful
   c. truthful

93. Choose the root word in *infielder*.
    a. in
    b. fielder
    c. field

94. Choose the suffix that will make the word *slow* mean "in a slow manner."
    a. ness
    b. ly
    c. ful

95. Choose the suffix that will make the word *preach* mean "one who preaches."
    a. er
    b. en
    c. able

96. Choose the prefix that will make the word *fair* mean "not fair."
    a. pre
    b. un
    c. re

97. Choose the prefix that will make the word *historic* mean "before history."
    a. pre
    b. re
    c. un

98. Choose the prefix that will make the word *do* mean "do again."
    a. un
    b. re
    c. pre

99. Choose the correct way to divide the word *unhappy* into syllables.
    a. un hap py
    b. un happ y
    c. un ha ppy

100. Choose the correct way to divide the word *simple* into syllables.
    a. si mple
    b. simp le
    c. sim ple

Name_____

Student Answer Sheet

Test 1	Test 2	Test 3	Test 4
a b c	a b c	a b c	a b c
1 ○ ○ ○	27 ○ ○ ○	62 ○ ○ ○	84 ○ ○ ○
2 ○ ○ ○	28 ○ ○ ○	63 ○ ○ ○	85 ○ ○ ○
3 ○ ○ ○	29 ○ ○ ○	64 ○ ○ ○	86 ○ ○ ○
4 ○ ○ ○	30 ○ ○ ○	65 ○ ○ ○	87 ○ ○ ○
5 ○ ○ ○	31 ○ ○ ○	66 ○ ○ ○	88 ○ ○ ○
6 ○ ○ ○	32 ○ ○ ○	67 ○ ○ ○	89 ○ ○ ○
7 ○ ○ ○	33 ○ ○ ○	68 ○ ○ ○	90 ○ ○ ○
8 ○ ○ ○	34 ○ ○ ○	69 ○ ○ ○	91 ○ ○ ○
9 ○ ○ ○	35 ○ ○ ○	70 ○ ○ ○	92 ○ ○ ○
10 ○ ○ ○	36 ○ ○ ○	71 ○ ○ ○	93 ○ ○ ○
11 ○ ○ ○	37 ○ ○ ○	72 ○ ○ ○	94 ○ ○ ○
12 ○ ○ ○	38 ○ ○ ○	73 ○ ○ ○	95 ○ ○ ○
13 ○ ○ ○	39 ○ ○ ○	74 ○ ○ ○	96 ○ ○ ○
14 ○ ○ ○	40 ○ ○ ○	75 ○ ○ ○	97 ○ ○ ○
15 ○ ○ ○	41 ○ ○ ○	76 ○ ○ ○	98 ○ ○ ○
16 ○ ○ ○	42 ○ ○ ○	77 ○ ○ ○	99 ○ ○ ○
17 ○ ○ ○	43 ○ ○ ○	78 ○ ○ ○	100 ○ ○ ○
18 ○ ○ ○	44 ○ ○ ○	79 ○ ○ ○	
19 ○ ○ ○	45 ○ ○ ○	80 ○ ○ ○	
20 ○ ○ ○	46 ○ ○ ○	81 ○ ○ ○	
21 ○ ○ ○	47 ○ ○ ○	82 ○ ○ ○	
22 ○ ○ ○	48 ○ ○ ○	83 ○ ○ ○	
23 ○ ○ ○	49 ○ ○ ○		
24 ○ ○ ○	50 ○ ○ ○		
25 ○ ○ ○	51 ○ ○ ○		
26 ○ ○ ○	52 ○ ○ ○		
	53 ○ ○ ○		
	54 ○ ○ ○		
	55 ○ ○ ○		
	56 ○ ○ ○		
	57 ○ ○ ○		
	58 ○ ○ ○		
	59 ○ ○ ○		
	60 ○ ○ ○		
	61 ○ ○ ○		

	Test 1	Test 2	Test 3	Test 4		
Number Possible	26	35	22	17	Total	100
Number Incorrect	___	___	___	___	Total	___
Score	___	___	___	___	Total	___

AT13

Class Record–Keeping Chart

Name

Test Item	Skill									
1–4	Understanding character									
5–8	Recognizing sequence of events									
9–12	Identifying setting									
13–16	Identifying conflict and resolution									
17–20	Inferring theme									
21–23, 39–43	Making inferences									
24	Recognizing multiple meanings of words									
25–26, 34, 68	Using context clues									
27–29, 62–64	Identifying cause and effect									
30–33	Comparing and contrasting									
35–38	Distinguishing fact from opinion									
44–46, 73–75	Identifying the main idea									
47–49, 76–77	Identifying the main idea and supporting details									
50–52, 78–79	Recognizing multiple meanings of words									
53–56	Using a primary source									
57–61	Using a map									
65–67	Classifying									
69–72	Reading text with diagrams									
80–83	Solving word problems									
84–87	Using a dictionary entry									
88–91	Using an encyclopedia									
92–100	Recognizing root words, prefixes, suffixes, and syllables									
	Total Incorrect									
	Score (subtract total incorrect from 100)									

AT14